"There are lots of books availabl~~~~~~~~~~~~~~~~~~~~~ ~~~ ~~~, but few, if any, that do a good job of presenting all the key arguments in a historical and contemporary way. Professor Beck's book *Does God Exist?* is a rare exception. It is important to realize that, setting aside a disdain for old books, a careful study of an argument as it develops in the history of philosophy is more than a mere expression of intellectual curiosity. Much can be learned from the past that is of immense contemporary importance. Beck is a well-respected philosopher and brings decades of teaching and research to this book. I highly recommend it."

J. P. Moreland, distinguished professor of philosophy at Talbot School of Theology, Biola University, and author of *Scientism and Secularism*

"Finally! A single volume that contains as a historical narrative a compendium of arguments pertaining to God's existence—pro, con, and from most religious perspectives—all under one cover. Fantastic! Highly recommended!"

Gary R. Habermas, distinguished research professor of apologetics and philosophy at Liberty University

"In this herculean effort, David Beck has written a superb guide and rich resource on the major arguments for God's existence. Not only does he astutely summarize the breadth of positions articulated by particular thinkers on the respective arguments—pro and con—but he includes much material from primary sources, which significantly enhances the value of this volume. A fine achievement!"

Paul Copan, Pledger Family Chair of Philosophy and Ethics at Palm Beach Atlantic University, coauthor of *The Gospel in the Marketplace of Ideas*

To Fortner

Does God Exist?

A History of Answers to the Question

W. DAVID BECK

W. David Beck

IVP Academic

An imprint of InterVarsity Press
Downers Grove, Illinois

InterVarsity Press
P.O. Box 1400, Downers Grove, IL 60515-1426
ivpress.com
email@ivpress.com

*InterVarsity Press® is the book-publishing division of InterVarsity Christian Fellowship/USA®, a movement
of students and faculty active on campus at hundreds of universities, colleges, and schools of nursing
in the United States of America, and a member movement of the International Fellowship of Evangelical Students.
For information about local and regional activities, visit intervarsity.org.*

*All Scripture quotations, unless otherwise indicated, are taken from The Holy Bible, New International Version®,
NIV®. Copyright © 1973, 1978, 1984, 2011 by Biblica, Inc.™ Used by permission of Zondervan. All rights reserved
worldwide. www.zondervan.com. The "NIV" and "New International Version" are trademarks registered
in the United States Patent and Trademark Office by Biblica, Inc.™*

Cover design and image composite: David Fassett
Interior design: Daniel van Loon
Images: the school of Athens: © Photos.com / Getty Images
    Maimonides portrait: © johan10 / iStock / Getty Images Plus
    beige craft paper texture: © Katsumi Murouchi / Moment Collection / Getty Images
    *Portrait images from Wikimedia Commons / United States public domain: Immanuel Kant by Johann
    Gottlieb Becker; portrait of David Hume by Allan Ramsay; portrait of John_Locke by Godfrey Kneller;
    Buddha_meditating by unknown; photo of Cornelius Van Til from The Works of Cornelius Van Til,
    1895-1987, CD-ROM (New York: Labels Army Co., 1997); Gottfried Wilhelm Leibniz by Christoph
    Bernhard Francke; Saint Thomas Aquinas by Carlo Crivelli; Blaise Pascal by unknown*

ISBN 978-0-8308-5300-7 (print)
ISBN 978-0-8308-5301-4 (digital)

Printed in the United States of America ♾

*InterVarsity Press is committed to ecological stewardship and to the conservation of natural resources
in all our operations. This book was printed using sustainably sourced paper.*

Library of Congress Cataloging-in-Publication Data
A catalog record for this book is available from the Library of Congress.

P	25	24	23	22	21	20	19	18	17	16	15	14	13	12	11	10	9	8	7	6	5	4	3	2	1
Y	37	36	35	34	33	32	31	30	29	28	27	26	25	24	23	22	21								

To my fourteen grandchildren:

May each one of you always trust in the
God who is real
and who is the source of all that is real

Contents

Detailed Contents

Preface

THIS BOOK HAS BEEN A LONG TIME COMING. In my first year of graduate school, 1969, I was a graduate assistant to Norman Geisler, who decreed that after teaching a course five times, one must write the textbook. He seems to always have adhered to that maxim. On the other hand, I myself have been teaching courses on the subject of God's existence for almost fifty years and am just now getting around to writing it down. Now I did have some good excuses. Within ten years I became entangled in administrative responsibilities at a new institution, soon to become Liberty University, which needed to develop its basic documents and administrative procedures.

I certainly enjoyed all of that work, but along with a full load of teaching, it allowed little time for anything else. Now, with those administrative duties a thing of the past, it is a joy to get around to research and writing again. I am certainly grateful to InterVarsity Press for the opportunity to take on this challenge, and especially David McNutt for his good guidance throughout the writing. And I am grateful to Liberty University, and my dean, Roger Schultz, for research release time that has made this project so much easier.

I can think of no topic that demands greater attention in this global culture than the existence and reality of God. Our world is divided and divisive. I am convinced that this is a result of the fact that our global culture has given up on finding any truth that would unite us—any truth at all. Many people even think that to be a virtue. But the relativistic skepticism that is in danger of engulfing us cannot provide a unifying factor. Without truth there is only power. I think we are headed for dark days if we continue on this course. That is certainly my overriding motivation in writing this book.

The obvious difficulty with a project like this is that my decision-making procedure for inclusion is bound to fully please no one. Many, even most, of the philosophers included in this story are obvious and necessary. But beyond that everyone has their favorites and essentials. How could I possibly have included Rob but left out Bob? Especially when Bob was the first one to get this most important point, or who wrote the ultimate refutation. Sometimes I have had to be very restrictive. After all, who has *not* weighed in on the ontological argument in the last fifty years? Or on how evil does or does not have a bearing on any one of the arguments? Or on fine-tuning? So, all I can say is that I did my best to include what I thought was most important to *my* purposes at hand. I should add that I often included more in the early stages of each argument just to make the point that little if any of the current discussion is at all new.

Another difficulty arises from presenting this as history: narrating a story that has developed and is still developing. That is, I mention many identifying facts about individuals that are subject to change. Even by the time this is published there will likely be a few changes. I apologize to those so affected, but I have tried my best to get all the facts right.

Acknowledgments

THERE ARE SO MANY TO THANK. My students in Philosophy of Religion in the spring term of 2019 and of 2020 have all played some part in research and review: Jonathan Smith, Chester Walker, Noah Perrault, Asher Thompson, Kedrick Bradley, Devonte Narde, Corey Walton, Mike Consiglio, and Scout Powell. Thank you! Thanks to my student Israel Healy for doing the contents page. Don Zeyl, Andrew Loke, David Baggett, Gary Habermas, Alexander Pruss, Jeffrey Koperski, James East, and Lad Sessions, as well as my former assistants Max Andrews and Caleb Brown, have read parts of this and given me comments. My colleagues and friends Ed Martin and Eberhard Bertsch read the whole manuscript. I'm so grateful to all of them. Whatever mistakes remain are mine.

Most of all, I'm grateful to my wife, Jean, who spent endless hours typing in longer quotes, and just putting up with a year's obsession—our fiftieth year together, actually. I might wish for fifty more like this, but we will have so many more than that together—endlessly more.

CHAPTER 1

The Beginnings of the Arguments

1.1 Introducing the Characters in This Story

It seems that human beings have been thinking about God from the very beginning. The first chapters of the Bible certainly have it so. Recent excavations of Gobekli Tepe, located right where those same chapters place the Garden of Eden, show a society centered on worship dated by many archaeologists to around 10,000 BC.[1] The late nineteenth-century sociologist of religion Andrew Lang documented how even the most isolated cultures around the world know of God, and refer to him as creator and maker, often even as father.[2] One of my favorite quotes is this one from Greenland:

> The first missionaries in Greenland supposed that there was not, there, a trace of belief in a Divine Being. But when they came to understand their language better, they found quite the reverse to be true . . . and not only so, but they could plainly gather from a free dialogue they had with some perfectly wild Greenlanders . . . that their ancestors must have believed in a Supreme Being. . . . But an [Inuit] said to a missionary, "Thou must not imagine that no Greenlander thinks about these things. Certainly there must be some Being who made all these things. He must be very good too. . . . Ah, did I but know him, how I would love and honor him."[3]

---

[1] See, for example, Andrew Curry, "Gobekli Tepe: The World's First Temple?," *Smithsonian Magazine*, November 2008, https://www.smithsonianmag.com/history/gobekli-tepe-the-worlds-first-temple-83613665/.

[2] I will settle in this book for the male pronoun for God. All of my sources do so, and so I am just being consistent with their usage.

[3] Andrew Lang, *The Making of Religion* (London: Longmans, Green, 1898), 184. On early African cultures, where many historians like to claim that *Homo sapiens* got its start, see John S. Mbiti, *Concepts of God in Africa* (New York: Praeger, 1970).

Eventually these insights and intuitions that our world is unimaginable without a creator take on the status of formal arguments: the characters of this story. This provides them a life of their own. Why this human endeavor begins in sixth-century-BC Greece has long been a matter of speculation, and I have nothing really to add to the discussion after teaching ancient philosophy for some forty years.[4] Suffice it to say, many forces came together and produced the Milesian school of Thales, and the philosophical discussion of these arguments has never ceased since then. That is the story of this book.

Initially this interaction was focused on what Aristotle called the search for the *archē*, the source and origin, the operating principle, of our universe. It took two hundred years of discussion after Thales to bring this idea to the explicit concept of God. This initial argument about the cause of existence of the universe comes to be called the cosmological argument. It stems from our everyday observations that things around us exist as parts of sequences of causal connections. Nothing we have observed, though of course we have not observed everything, simply exists by itself, but only within fields, networks, chains, trees of other things to which it is connected in cause-effect relationship. From this observation, our reasoning concludes that there must be an ultimate or final "something" that is itself uncaused.

A second type of argument is lurking behind this same reasoning. The causal connections in the universe do not exist in some random way, but in what appears to us to be lawlike, purposeful, and designed patterns. This organization itself seems to demand an explanation. Given our experience of our own artistic and technological inventions, the most likely explanation would have to be some creative and intelligent source. This argument has come to be known as the teleological argument.

---

[4]Perhaps the best account of this can be found in part 1 in vol. 1 of Frederick Copleston's masterpiece, *A History of Philosophy* (London: A&C Black, 2003).

A third type of argument emerges as a special case of this observed orderliness and lawfulness of our universe: the moral argument. One thing that is truly unique about us as human beings is our perception of moral obligation. We experience ourselves as part of a social order that expects us to act justly, lovingly, tolerantly, but also *not* to act with hatred, violence, or discrimination. And we seem intuitively to expect the same of others, society as a whole, and even ourselves. This demands a much more specialized explanation, since only a personal and intentional intelligence would appear to fit the bill here.

There is a fourth and quite different sort of argument that comes to us from the great medieval theologian and philosopher Anselm of Canterbury: the ontological argument. What is different here is that it is not based on observations of states of affairs in the real world and is thus not a posteriori but a priori—that is, it is based solely on the logic of the words or concepts involved.

A comment is in order here regarding my use of the word *argument* in this book. I mean by it simply any pattern or sequence of reasoning that implies a conclusion. Logicians distinguish three general types: deductive, inductive, and abductive. I will have more to say about these differences later as the story develops.

The word I will avoid, except where it appears in quotations, is the word *proof*. This is actually the traditional word. In more recent years, however, *proof* has come to be used for the kind of reasoning unique to mathematics. This is a sort of purely logical relationship that exists quite apart from any real or actual world considerations, and derives entirely from the particular rules of a given mathematical system.

Using the word *argument* is also meant to avoid the idea that any one of these stands by itself as a once-and-for-all clinching proof for a fully defined God. What we will see is that each argument has a very narrow focus, in terms of both the evidence used in the premises and the scope and the strength or probability of the conclusion. And so each of these arguments, along with others I will only mention in passing, functions best as part of a cumulative case.[5]

The idea here is that of a court case as presented by the attorneys. There is not simply a single argument given for guilt or innocence. Rather, there is a whole story that is woven together from many pieces of evidence, eyewitnesses, character witnesses, elimination of alternatives, and so on. The same is true here. We need to look at multiple arguments of different types, based on different sorts of evidence, with each giving us a different part of a larger conclusion. Of course, each piece of the case needs to be a sound argument in order to give us, overall, the best explanation.

I will then take a brief look at some preliminary stages in the development of arguments for the reality of a God. I will avoid trying to advance some sort of minimal definition of God. This is an issue fraught with controversy. I will simply ignore the matter and allow the arguments themselves to define their conclusions, to whatever extent they do, as we go along. None of them, not even the ontological argument, as is often alleged, actually presuppose some sort of minimal definition of God, and then argue circularly back to God so defined. They begin, rather, with certain known facts or observations, including *possible* definitions, from which explanatory conclusions may be drawn.

One more matter: What does all of this have to do with faith or belief? To answer this, we need an important distinction between believing *that* and believing *in*. When one says the Apostles' Creed beginning with "I believe in God the Father almighty," what is happening? This is clearly an affirmation of my trust, commitment, loyalty, or confidence in the person to whom I am referring. When I say that I believe in my wife, I mean that I trust her and have confidence in her.

---

[5]For a full discussion of this idea see Basil Mitchell's *The Justification of Religious Belief* (London: Macmillan, 1973), chap. 3. We will come back to this at the end of this account in 6.1.1.

These are not statements about someone's existence, though there is certainly an underlying assumption that they do in fact exist.

That is what I have in mind. The question here is whether we can, and how we can, *know* that God exists. And knowing is having a justified true belief. This is a justified true belief *that*. So knowing *that*, including believing *that* God exists, is very different from believing *in* God. On the other hand, how can I commit myself or be loyal to someone unless I first know that they really exist? So faith has to have a basis in justified true belief. You cannot have real faith in, or trust, God unless you "believe that he exists and that he rewards those who earnestly seek him" (Heb 11:6). I will come back to this at the end of my story.

That brings me to the last up-front matter. The July 2018 cover of *Time* magazine asked this critical question: "Is Truth Dead?" This is, I think, the most important question of our day. *Time* was mostly interested in the political ramifications. Crucial, no doubt! But even more destructive to our now global culture has been the loss of truth related to religion in general. It is largely considered intolerant, warmongering, hateful, and misconceived to even ask for the truth about God.

1.1.1 Blaise Pascal. We *must*, however, ask this question about the truth, because there is so much that hinges on our getting it right—or wrong! I like the way the French philosopher and mathematician Blaise Pascal (1623–1662) handled this. A child prodigy who grew up in the home of a tax collector, Pascal thought of this as assessing the outcomes of a decision process.

There are four possible outcomes to weigh, given that God either exists or does not, and given that I may choose to believe in God or not. If God does not exist, then my believing or not believing makes very little difference. Like with Santa Claus when we were kids, I might be happier if I believe, and I might have the advantage of being right if I do not. But either way, no big deal. The same is the case with God, if he does not exist. However, if God *does* exist, as Pascal puts it, "there is here an infinity of an infinitely happy life to gain."[6] And if you wager incorrectly about God, you lose everything—both right now in this life and in the future life. This is itself not an argument for God's reality, but it is an argument which demonstrates that God's reality is a critical issue that we must face squarely.

So in fact we have everything, individually and as a society, to lose or gain by getting this question of the truth about God correct. It is possible, of course, that we cannot, for whatever reason, acquire truth about God. But seek it we must. We simply cannot avoid it.

That is the point of this narrative: to see how the justification of the claim that God is a reality has developed over the years, how objections to it have been placed, and how they have been answered and often changed the narrative in important ways. Then, of course, we will need a final assessment of where things stand today and whether we do, in fact, know the truth.

1.2 Prequels to the Story

Long before thinking about God took the form of full-blown arguments for his existence and nature, it took the form of simple observations of the world around us, in which people could not miss divine activity. All of the world's religions and cultures evidence this. And at some early point, human beings began writing down their thoughts and songs. These may not have the formal structure of an argument, but the essential inferences are there. Just a few examples follow.

---

[6]This is taken from his *Pensées*, 233. There is much discussion about this wager. What most interpreters agree on is that (1) this is not an argument for God's existence; (2) it is a valid-outcomes assessment; and (3) the only substantive objection is precisely that it is meaningless just in case God does not exist, to which I assume Pascal would have agreed. For a good discussion of all this see Alan Hajak, "Pascal's Wager," *The Stanford Encyclopedia of Philosophy*, ed. Edward N. Zalta, summer 2018 ed., https://plato.stanford.edu/archives/sum2018/entries/pascal-wager/.

1.2.1 Jewish sources. The first is taken from the book of Psalms. It is attributed, at least much of it, to the second king of Israel, David, which would date it at sometime around 1000 BC.

> The heavens declare the glory of God;
>> the skies proclaim the work of his hands.
> Day after day they pour forth speech;
>> night after night they display knowledge.
> There is no speech or language
>> where their voice is not heard.
> Their voice goes out into all the earth,
>> their words to the ends of the world.
> In the heavens he has pitched a tent for the sun,
>> Which is like a bridegroom coming forth from his pavilion,
>> like a champion rejoicing to run his course.
> It rises at one end of the heavens
>> and makes its circuit to the other;
>> nothing is hidden from its heat. (Ps 19:1-6 NIV 1984)

In this poem, notice that the word "proclaim" plays the inferential role between "heavens" and "sky," which are the evidence, and the conclusion, which is "the work of his hands." We should note, too, that there are several times in this passage that we are told that this is something everyone understands, regardless of their language group.

The following is from the book of Job. We do not know with certainty who the author was, though Jewish rabbinic tradition ascribes it to Moses, whom they often date as having lived from 1391 to 1271 BC. But many current scholars place him as much as two hundred years earlier, and the book itself perhaps even earlier than that and by an earlier but unknown author.

> Then the LORD spoke to Job out of the storm. He said:

>> "Who is this that obscures my plans
>>> with words without knowledge?

Brace yourself like a man;
    I will question you,
    and you shall answer me.

"Where were you when I laid the earth's foundation?
    Tell me, if you understand.
Who marked off its dimensions? Surely you know!
    Who stretched a measuring line across it?
On what were its footings set,
    or who laid its cornerstone—
while the morning stars sang together
    and all the angels shouted for joy?

"Who shut up the sea behind doors
    when it burst forth from the womb,
when I made the clouds its garment
    and wrapped it in thick darkness,
when I fixed limits for it
    and set its doors and bars in place,
when I said, 'This far you may come and no farther;
    here is where your proud waves halt'?

"Have you ever given orders to the morning,
    or shown the dawn its place,
that it might take the earth by the edges
    and shake the wicked out of it?
The earth takes shape like clay under a seal;
    its features stand out like those of a garment.
The wicked are denied their light,
    and their upraised arm is broken.

"Have you journeyed to the springs of the sea
    or walked in the recesses of the deep?
Have the gates of death been shown to you?
    Have you seen the gates of the deepest darkness?
Have you comprehended the vast expanses of the earth?
    Tell me, if you know all this." (Job 38:1-18)

This monologue continues for two long chapters with example after example of intricate design and amazing living beings whose origin is clearly beyond human ingenuity. The logic of the argument is here reversed, coming as it does from God himself, but the conclusion is the same: We can provide no explanation for the origin of things we observe, even when we see the scientific process that brings them about, without concluding to the intelligence and creative power of God.

1.2.2 Christian sources. The New Testament has several such proto-argument passages. The most notable is this from the apostle Paul (ca. AD 5–67), who had received extensive training in the Jewish tradition but who had concluded that the man Jesus Christ was the very same God, albeit in human form, who had spoken to Moses, Job, and David so many years earlier.

> Since what may be known about God is plain to them, because God has made it plain to them. For since the creation of the world God's invisible qualities—his eternal power and divine nature—have been clearly seen, being understood from what has been made, so that people are without excuse. (Rom 1:19-20)[7]

This passage is close to a full-blown argument, and it is quite possible that the philosophically well-trained Paul knew of Aristotle's argument.[8] The evidence is "what has been made." In the original Greek, this is one word, *poiēmasin*. This word might be translated "the made-ness of the things"—that is, the quality of the things we observe that indicates that they exist only because they are caused to do so. The philosophical term for this is *contingent*.

The role of conclusion is played here by the two attributes of God, not merely his reality, which we may infer from our observations, but

---

[7]A chapter later, in Rom 2:14-16, Paul gives what can be taken as a precursor to the moral argument, when he refers to God's law as "written on their hearts."

[8]See the discussion of Aristotle below in the next chapter. Paul was from Tarsus, near the Mediterranean coast (in present-day Turkey), a center of Greek philosophical study, in which all of the major schools were well represented in his day.

omnipotence and deity. The first is an obvious reference to God as source of all things; the latter has the connotation in Greek of non-dependence, or sovereignty. That is, God is himself not caused by or dependent on anything else. As we will see these are precisely the conclusions of the cosmological argument.

Here is another line of reasoning that sounds like the kind of dual agency we will see in Aristotle and Thomas Aquinas: "Jesus has been found worthy of greater honor than Moses, just as the builder of a house has greater honor than the house itself. For every house is built by someone, but God is the builder of everything" (Heb 3:3-4). So, God is the cause of everything, including some particular event, yet some person or some thing is also the cause of that same event.

1.2.3 Islamic sources. The Qur'an, dictated by Muhammad between 609 and 632 and directed to a diverse and polytheistic Arabic culture, contains this reference to, specifically, human beings, but it is clearly intended to apply to all of creation: "Or were they created by nothing? Or were they the creators of themselves? Or did they create the heavens and Earth? Rather, they are not certain" (Qur'an 52:35-36).[9] This passage sets out the four options from which we must choose, given our observation and contemplation of ourselves. We either have no cause, are self-caused, are caused by something else that is itself caused, or, what is left? That is precisely what we are left to contemplate, and that is what forms the basis for Arabic Islamic thinking on the argument for God's existence.

1.2.4 Greek sources. 1.2.4.1 Thales to Parmenides. While a bit of an eccentric, Parmenides draws his conclusions from a sequence of thinking by the first Greek philosophers, taking us back to an earlier and polytheistic culture. Thales (624–546 BC), who had, for the first time in

---

[9]I use the Sahih International Translation, trans. Assami, Kennedy, and Bantley (Saudi Arabia: Publishing House dar Abul Qasimi, 1997).

known history, predicted an eclipse of the sun, began by also asking the first recorded philosophical question: How can we explain a universe that allows us to predict it at every level? What would it take to make such a universe? What are the conditions under which it could originate? His answer was that such a universe must just be a single thing. Now that is a good answer because clearly there must be some unifying factor to the universe if we can make these sorts of scientific claims about everything. It is not that far-fetched to think that the unifying factor is the matter from which it is made. On the other hand, the universe is obviously *not* just one physical thing, and Thales is clearly wrong about that.[10] Still, he does get to step one: There must be a unifying factor to the universe if we are going to explain it at all. No commonalities means no science. We need the physical components, of course, but that is not enough. Even if they are eternal, which is what all the Greeks thought, there is nothing here to explain their harmonious and especially their predictable order.

The next stage in the discussion comes with Heraclitus (535–475 BC). He will argue that what is unifying and permanent is not really the physical chemistry, which, after all, is eternally and constantly changing.[11] But what is constant are the physical laws that regulate its change: the cosmic logic.[12] So, to get a unified universe you need the common list of physical components (we would refer to the Periodic Table) but primarily the laws and formulas that order it.

Now this seems clearly right. The chemical elements in the periodic table do give us a unifying matrix that allows us to identify things in our world: this is hydrogen, that is oxygen, and that there is carbon. But until we know the formulas, the patterns, the laws, we have no way to explain

---

[10]Thales, of course, had thought it was water. Given his observations of water as solid, liquid, and gas this was a reasonable conclusion, but too simple to allow for a robust chemistry.

[11]Heraclitus called it flux. He thought there were actually four elements, earth, water, air, and fire, in constant combining motion driven by the fire, itself both force and element.

[12]One of his contemporaries was Pythagoras, whom we still celebrate for identifying some of those laws, especially, of course, his most famous theorem: $a^2 + b^2 = c^2$.

that this is water, or H_2O, and that is sugar, or $C_{12}H_{22}O_{11}$. So this is an important step in our argument story. Still, something is missing if we really want to explain the world we observe. What unifies the laws? How is it that all these diverse formulas work together so that we can predict complex events? For example, how is it that sugar dissolves in water and makes it taste sweet predictably? This will lead us to the next step: Anaxagoras.

In between, however, is this odd alternate conclusion reached by the previously mentioned Parmenides (born ca. 515 BC). He drew some obviously correct inferences from Thales's view that the universe is one thing and that is all there is. Here is what he argued:

> One path only is left for us to speak of, namely, that *it is*. In this path are very many tokens that what is is uncreated and indestructible; for it is complete, immovable, and without end. Nor was it ever, nor will it be; for now it is, all at once, a continuous one. For what kind of origin for it wilt thou look for? In what way and from what source could it have drawn its increase? . . . I shall not let thee say nor think that it came from what is not; for it can neither be thought nor uttered that anything is not. And, if it came from nothing, what need could have made it arise later rather than sooner? Therefore must it either be altogether or be not at all. . . . How, then, can what *is* be going to be in the future? Or how could it come into being? If it came into being, it is not; nor is it if it is going to be in the future. Thus is becoming extinguished and passing away not to be heard of.
>
> Nor is it divisible, since it is all alike, and there is no more of it in one place than in another, to hinder it from holding together, nor less of it, but everything is full of what is. Wherefore it is wholly continuous; for what is, is in contact with what is.
>
> Moreover, it is immovable in the bonds of mighty chains, without beginning and without end; since coming into being and passing away have been driven afar, and true belief has cast them away. It is the same, and it rests in the self-same place, abiding in itself. And thus it remaineth constant in its place; for hard necessity keeps it in the bonds of the limit that holds it fast on every side. Wherefore it is not permitted to what is

to be infinite; for it is in need of nothing; while, if it were infinite, it would stand in need of everything.[13]

There is something strange going on here. Obviously these conclusions cannot be applied to the finite universe as Parmenides did, but the logic of the argument itself is unassailable. If there just is the one thing that there is, then it must be unending, unchanging, indivisible, and immovable. There is nothing else it could be or become. If it changed, what would it change *to* that it is not already? It simply is what it is! Hence, he concluded, our sensory experience of change and flux must be wrong.

At the heart of his problem is that he did not grasp the true nature of infinity. To him it connoted something that has no definition at all, hence it is nothing at all, and is "in need of everything." So to Parmenides unlimited and unchanging Being was, in fact, the finite, defined, and limited circle of the universe. Hence the improper application. However, given a proper understanding of the unlimited as truly infinite, we would now have a series of arguments that correctly defines the properties of an unlimited being. So, we need to set this aside till later and resume the sequence of argument from Thales to Heraclitus and now on to Anaxagoras.

1.2.4.2 Anaxagoras. In Anaxagoras (510–428 BC), our story takes another critical step forward. We certainly cannot explain the universe without involving its unified physical chemistry. Thales was right. We also cannot explain it apart from its laws and formulas, the cosmic logic. Heraclitus was right. The explanation, however, still lacks completeness. Laws do not and cannot by themselves account for the harmonious, precise, and repeatable operation of the physical universe. They only *describe* individual events, like the sugar dissolving in the water. They clarify the operating principles of the universe, but not its initiating unifying cause. So it dawned on Anaxagoras that there must be, not just

---

[13]This is fragment 117-18 from the collection and translation of John Burnet in his *Early Greek Philosophy*, 3rd ed. (London: A&C Black, 1920).

the individual design elements, but the Mind or Reason that knows and *is* the whole design. Not just Logos but what he calls Nous.[14] We do not have a unified theory of everything unless the laws and formulas are united in a single grand design. Here is his summation:

> All other things partake in a portion of everything, while Nous is infinite and self-ruled, and is mixed with nothing, but is alone itself by itself. For if it were not by itself, but were mixed with anything else, it would partake in all things if it were mixed with any; for in everything there is a portion of everything, as has been said by me in what goes before, and the things mixed with it would hinder it, so that it would have power over nothing in the same way that it has now being alone by itself. For it is the thinnest of all things and the purest, and it has all knowledge about everything and the greatest strength; and Nous has power over all things, both greater and smaller, that have life. And Nous had power over the whole revolution, so that it began to revolve in the beginning. And it began to revolve first from a small beginning; but the revolution now extends over a larger space, and will extend over a larger still. And all the things that are mingled together and separated off and distinguished are all known by Nous. And Nous set in order all things that were to be, and all things that were and are not now and that are. . . . And there are many portions in many things. But no thing is altogether separated off nor distinguished from anything else except Nous. And all Nous is alike, both the greater and the smaller; while nothing else is like anything else, but each single thing is and was most manifestly those things of which it has most in it.[15]

Granted, Anaxagoras was not consistent about this Nous, and interpretations of him vary greatly. Both Plato and Aristotle already recognized this. Aristotle complained that Anaxagoras got it right about Mind but

---

[14]This is a notoriously difficult term to translate, so sometimes it is left untranslated. It does not refer to some entity separate from the universe, like "the Mind," nor to a property of the universe, like "rationality," but to something like a condition. So a good translation might be more like "reasonableness" or "mindedness." Nevertheless, "Mind" has stuck as the standard translation. For a good discussion of this matter, see Stephen Menn, *Plato on God as Nous* (Carbondale: Southern Illinois University Press, 1995).

[15]Fragment 155 in Burnet, *Early Greek Philosophy*.

then never used it in his actual science of the universe's origin. Be that as it may, our only interest is his basic advance toward an argument. Anaxagoras did not think of Mind as an actual Creator, a causal agent beyond the physical universe and its actual source: God. The story of the argument is not there yet.

Nevertheless, this step is critical. Bits and pieces of knowledge cannot exist, they make no sense, without a larger theory. All those formulas in the front of my high school geometry text only make sense if there is a Euclidian geometry as a whole. The laws of physics only make sense in the context of physics. In fact, to make a larger sense of, for example, the law of gravity, there must be a specific physics, say Newtonian or Einsteinian physics. Current physicists say this same thing. Stephen Hawking says that universes, the "grand design," are initiated by quantum physics.[16] Max Tegmark's claim is even more basic: it is mathematics itself that creates them.[17]

This seems clearly right. Individual laws explain how the world works only in the context of a complete theory: a physics of everything. This is what Anaxagoras appears to mean by Nous: the Mind or, perhaps better, the Reason of the universe. We are closer but still a ways off of the concept of a single unifying cause of the universe. But it is building. If Anaxagoras himself was still something of a pantheist, so be it. Aristotle calls him the first sober philosopher, even if he got no further. Now there is one more step in this pre-argument stage in Greek thinking, and that comes with Plato.

1.2.4.3 Plato. In his dialogue *Timaeus*, Plato (427–347 BC) presents his physics: his larger account of how we have a universe and how it operates. Early in the book we get this now famous passage. I should note that it is likely that *Timaeus* was the only text out of Plato's many works, and even that was not complete, available to patristic and early

---

[16]See Stephen Hawking with Leonard Mlodinow, *The Grand Design* (New York: Bantam, 2010).
[17]See Max Tegmark, *Our Mathematical Universe* (New York: Random House, 2014).

medieval Christian scholars, and only in Latin.[18] This passage in particular is why they and many since then have thought that Plato had arrived at the truth about the Judeo-Christian Creator God. In fact, this passage was sometimes referred to as Genesis. The Latin and most subsequent English translations used creator/Creator for the Greek *demiourgos*, which actually refers simply to a craftsman or artisan, and the word translated "create" simply means "to make." What follows is the more literal translation by Donald Zeyl.

> Now as to the whole heaven [*ouranos*], or world order [*kosmos*]—let's just call it by whatever name is most acceptable in a given context—there is a question we need to consider first. This is the sort of question one should begin with in inquiring into any subject. Has it always been? Was there no origin [*archē*] from which it came to be? Or did it come to be and take its start from some origin? It has come to be. For it is both visible and tangible and it has a body—and all things of that kind are perceptible. And, as we have shown, perceptible things are grasped by opinion, which involves sense perception. As such, they are things that come to be, things that are begotten. Further, we maintain that, necessarily, that which comes to be must come to be by the agency of some cause. Now to find the maker and father of this universe [*to pan*] is hard enough, and even if I succeeded, to declare him to everyone is impossible. And so we must go back and raise this question about the universe: Which of the two models did the maker use when he fashioned it? Was it the one that does not change and stays the same, or the one that has come to be? Well, if this world of ours is beautiful and its craftsman good, then clearly he looked at the eternal model. But if what it's blasphemous to even say is the case, then he looked at one that has come to be. Now surely it's clear to all that it was the eternal model he looked at, for, of all the things that have come to be, our world is the most beautiful, and of causes the craftsman is the most excellent. This, then, is how it has come to be: it is a work of craft, modeled after that which is changeless and is grasped by a rational account, that is, by wisdom.

---

[18]Translated by Calcidius in the fourth century, but it is not complete. Cicero's translation was also known, but it has even less.

> Since these things are so, it follows by unquestionable necessity that
> this world is an image of something.[19]

An important new insight in this creation narrative is Plato's
somewhat expanded understanding of Nous, which goes something
like this: Physics is only a small part of a total theory of everything.
There is so much more! There is biology, psychology, economics,
sociology, history, and on and on. That is to say that beyond all, but
encompassing all of the individual sciences, there is the grand totality
of truth: the model of models, the pattern of patterns.[20] Truth itself. The
Form of forms. Nous for Plato is this all-encompassing, coherent formula
that places everything in a big-picture context and gives it meaning. The
grand design is total design. So if I want to explain my world, I will need
to envision and understand *the* model. Nothing less will do. This is one
of Plato's great achievements in the history of human thought.

So far, this is a more complete version of Anaxagoras. But Plato
takes another critical, new step when he tells us that it takes an actual
cause, an *agent*, to create something. That is clearly right, and crucially
so! And, again, Anaxagoras does not quite get us there. So far, so good.
But we are still not quite there. Here is where Plato's creation narrative
has a serious flaw. This is evident when he says that the craftsman
fashions the world by "looking at" the unchangeable and eternal model.
What that tells us is that the craftsman is not really the ultimate originator. The model or pattern itself is: the craftsman only follows the
(preexisting) blueprint.

What is missing here? Hawking's notion that quantum physics
makes universes may sound initially right, but ultimately it will simply
not work. When my phone falls to the floor and cracks, it is not because of the *law* of gravity, but because of gravity itself: the force of

---

[19]Plato, *Timaeus* 27c-29b, trans. Donald Zeyl (Indianapolis: Hackett, 2000). The Greek is
the translator's.

[20]Some translations, like Jowett's for example, use this word *pattern* instead of *model*. I will
occasionally use it too. Plato's word is *forma* in Latin.

gravity. Quantum physics does not *cause* anything. Likewise, Tegmark's idea of mathematics as creator fails. Plato understood this and he was surely right: what is missing is an agent. But how the pattern actually causes the craftsman—who *is* the actual efficient cause—to build the universe, and what their relationship is, is still an unknown for Plato. And until it is known, we do not have a complete explanation. Somehow the craftsman and the pattern, Plato's two great ideas, must come together to be the one ultimate cause: the Creator. We are close, but not quite there. And until we are, we do not have a fully formed argument.

This was an important part of the story, but really just the preface. It was Plato's prize pupil, Aristotle, who first spelled out the initial form of the argument for a real God. Why does a harmonious and predictable contingent universe make sense *only* if there is a God? What is the real and ultimate cause of it all, and why call that God? Only when we answer these questions can we put together a clear and full argument.

Further Reading

On the pre-Socratics see John Burnet's *Early Greek Philosophy* (London: A&C Black, 1892). There are many later editions and reprints, including online. This is still the best collection and commentary on the pre-Socratic fragments.

For an in-depth treatment of Plato's *Timaeus* and his argument see, *Plato: Timaeus*, trans. and intro. Donald Zeyl (Indianapolis: Hackett, 2000), xx-lxxxix. See also the relevant entries in the *Encyclopedia of Classical Philosophy*, ed. Donald Zeyl (Westport CT: Greenwood, 1997), and Barbara Sattler and Donald Zeyl, "Plato's *Timaeus*," in the *Stanford Encyclopedia of Philosophy*, ed. Edward N. Zalta, summer 2019 ed., https://plato.stanford.edu/entries/plato-timaeus/.

Plato has a different argument in the *Laws* 894-99. The argument there is about the priority of soul over body: soul always initiates the action of the body. There must, therefore, be a World Soul that initiates the motion of the physical world. On this see Richard Mohr, *God and Forms in Plato* (Las Vegas: Parmenides, 2006), chaps. 8 and 11.

A good discussion of Nous in the pre-Socratics and Plato is Stephen Menn, *Plato on God as* Nous (Carbondale: Southern Illinois University Press, 1995).

On the matter of the insufficiency of Plato's forms (including the Good) in creating reality see John Rist, *Real Ethics: Rethinking the Foundations of Morality* (Cambridge: Cambridge University Press, 2002).

On the early translations of Plato available to the patristics and medievals, see Barbara Sattler's helpful essay, "Plato's *Timaeus*: Translations and Commentaries in the West," https://open.conted.ox.ac.uk/resources/link/platos -timaeus-translations-and-commentaries.

CHAPTER 2

Cosmological Arguments

2.1 Contingency Arguments

2.1.1 Aristotle. The pre-argument stage as we have considered it is still rather unsophisticated and undeveloped. It simply observes the existence of a lawful and logical universe and concludes that there must be a rational cosmic source. For the first time, in Aristotle (384–322 BC), this became a highly technical argument, in particular an argument about the cause of the very existence of things as we observe them in the universe. This will come to be called the cosmological argument. How much of this he received from his teacher, Plato, is impossible to know, but no doubt a good bit. We know Plato only by way of dialogues written in colloquial language unencumbered by technical philosophical jargon, with just a few exceptions, and even they are fairly easy concepts. In Aristotle, we arrive at a completely new level, not only in technical semantics, but also in precision argumentation.

This argument is about causality and, specifically, the cause of *existence*. On this topic, Aristotle prides himself to be the culmination of two hundred years of philosophical development (and he was right about that!). To understand the argument we will have to first briefly explore his famous fourfold analysis of cause. Think of building a house. There is, Aristotle argues, first, the material cause—that is, all of the lumber, nails, bricks, windows, and so forth. Without them no house could exist. Second, there is the efficient cause—that is, the work and activity of all those who build it. Third, there is the formal cause—that is, the architect's blueprint used by the builders to organize the material in such a way that what comes to be is that specific house. Fourth, there is the final cause. This house will be the result of the intentions of the homeowners to build precisely this house, to serve exactly the purposes they had in mind. Without this intention driving the whole process (causing it, in other words) this particular house is never built.

It is this concept of final cause that Aristotle considers his great achievement in philosophy. Everything we observe in our world has what Aristotle called *telos*. This is to say that its properties are such that it is good for various ends and, of course, not good for others. A rock is thus good for building a wall or breaking a window, but not good for feeding cattle or growing roses, and we, as intentional beings, purposely use rocks in certain ways because they have certain properties. Now we can watch how Aristotle applies this concept to the existence of the universe we live in and observe as scientists. There could be no such universe of causal connectedness unless there is an uncaused cause that is separate from it but directs its operations.

Toward the end of his retelling of the history of previous philosophical thought in books one and two of his great work the *Metaphysics*, Aristotle previews the argument he will deal with at greater length much later, in book 12. So here is the short and simpler form; he has already noted that what we observe in the world is the existing of contingently caused things or events.

> Moreover, it is obvious that there is some first principle, and that the causes of things are not infinitely many either in a direct sequence or in kind. For the material generation of one thing from another cannot go on in an infinite progression (e.g. flesh from earth, earth from air, air from fire, and so on without a stop); nor can the source of motion (e.g. man be moved by air, air by the sun, the sun by Strife, with no limit to the series). In the same way neither can the Final Cause recede to infinity—walking having health for its object, and health happiness, and happiness something else: one thing always being done for the sake of

another. And it is just the same with the Formal Cause. For in the case of all intermediate terms of a series, which are contained between a first and last term, the prior term is necessarily the cause of those which follow it; because if we had to say which of the three is the cause, we should say "the first." At any rate it is not the last term, because what comes at the end is not the cause of anything. Neither, again, is the intermediate term, which is only the cause of one (and it makes no difference whether there is one intermediate term or several, nor whether they are infinite or limited in number). But of series, which are infinite in this way, and in general, of the infinite, all the parts are equally intermediate, down to the present moment. Thus if there is no first term, there is no cause at all.[1]

In book 12, after the much more extensive and developed form of this argument, he adds the following to clarify some of the properties of the conclusion:

Thus it is evident from the foregoing account that there is some substance which is eternal and immovable and separate from sensible things; and it has also been shown that this substance can have no magnitude, but is impartible and indivisible (for it causes motion for infinite time, and nothing finite has an infinite potentiality; and therefore since every magnitude is either finite or infinite, it cannot have finite magnitude, and it cannot have infinite magnitude because there is no such thing at all); and moreover that it is impassive and unalterable; for all the other kinds of motion are posterior to spatial motion. Thus, it is clear why this substance has these attributes.

It is evident that there is only one heaven. For if there is to be a plurality of heavens (as there is of men), the principle of each must be one in kind but many in number. But all things which are many in number have matter. . . . Therefore the prime mover, which is immovable, is one both in formula and in number; and therefore so also is that which is eternally and continuously in motion. Therefore, there is only one heaven.[2]

---

[1]Aristotle, *Metaphysics* 2.994a, in *Aristotle in 23 Volumes*, trans. Hugh Tredennick (Cambridge, MA, Harvard University Press, 1933), vols. 17-18.
[2]Aristotle, *Metaphysics* 12.1073a. "Heaven" here refers to sky or space.

First, we need to recall an important presupposition to this argument. Aristotle, like all of the Greek philosophers, assumes that the material universe is eternal. It has no beginning. There is no question about the origin—in particular, the cause of the origin of matter. It simply always is. The philosophical concept of creation is unique to Jewish, then Christian, and later also Islamic, thinkers. This is critical because it means that Aristotle is not looking for a beginning of time, and so he is not concerned with a sequence of causality going back in time. Even when he talks here about material causation, he is not referring to a temporal succession from some temporal starting point.

We need, then, another distinction in causes. We can talk about causal chains as they occur over time—that is, they are about the *becoming*, the sequential coming-to-be, of things, as in relations of parent to child and parent to child and so on. It is a quite different discussion to provide the causes of *being*. How is it that this something exists, as it does right now at this point in time, rather than not? This type of causality is exemplified more as conditions, fields, trees, or networks of causes. The illustration often used here is that of moving train cars pulled all at the same time by the single locomotive.

This also means that he is talking about final, not efficient, causality. The efficient cause, Aristotle says, is always internal to the process, which consists of eternal material objects/events.[3] This argument is about the final cause of a substance, that which makes it be what it is and therefore what it *can* be—what it is "good for."

Second, Aristotle's task in the *Metaphysics* is nothing less than a theory of everything, but at the highest level of abstraction: a theory of *being* itself, of what it means to be. Not surprisingly, this argument also appears at the end of his *Physics*, in books seven and eight. Here it

---

[3]As we will see, Thomas Aquinas thought he was wrong about this since matter is not eternal. So God is also the efficient cause. But this is not critical to the argument at this point. Aristotle is still right about God as final cause.

occurs with much more scientific evidence and illustration. In both cases, he argues that any explanation of the real world must conclude to a single First Unmoved Mover.

A frequent objection to Aristotle is that many of his scientific examples and illustrations are wrong. For example, the section above incudes this supposed causal sequence: "flesh from earth, earth from air, air from fire." Now, while this is dated, nothing in the argument itself depends on it. As long as what we observe are cause-effect sequences, illustrations and examples are irrelevant. In the end, what is crucial in this argument, and is the major advance over Plato, is that this is an argument from *real* things in the actual world to another *real* thing. If the effect is real, then the cause must be real.

Let me try to state Aristotle's argument in simple and succinct logical form:

(1) We observe things to exist in causally connected sequences.

(2) There cannot be an infinite regress of such a sequence.

(3) Therefore, the sequences of causes of existence must be finite.

(4) Therefore, there is a first cause.

(5) Any first cause must be uncaused, eternal, spatially and temporally unlimited, and singular.

There are here some significant advances in the argument. Premise (1) is a simple observation of conditions in the real world. It is not some general claim about everything, nor does it state some general principle of causality. It is just what we observe or experience around us.

The subargument for (2) is new and critical. Aristotle represents a causal sequence like this.

initial cause > intermediate causes and effects > final effect

The number of intermediate causes here is philosophically irrelevant, though of course important to the scientist doing research. Looking for the cause of a certain cancer, I need to know every link back only to the respective initial cause. What is relevant to the metaphysics is that, if the sequence of intermediates is allowed to regress to infinity, then there is no *initial* cause, thus no causal force in the intermediates, and therefore no final effect.

Take the train example. If John asks what is pulling the caboose he sees going by, Mary will say it is the boxcar coupled to it. If he asks what is pulling that, since it evidently has no source of its own motion, Mary will say it is the boxcar in front of that. This can go on as often as needed, but we will still not have answered why the caboose is moving. And if at some point Mary were to say there are infinite boxcars, we are still left puzzled: boxcars being boxcars, none of them can initially pull anything, and even if there is an infinity of them, we cannot hope for an answer at all. We have not *fully* explained even the caboose's motion, unless and until we talk about something that does not need to be pulled itself in order to pull the boxcars and, of course, the caboose—namely, a locomotive. So this is why there can be no infinite regress of causes of *contingently* dependent things or events. There would be nothing that actually originates the causal action, regardless of how many there are or how they are arranged.

Premise (3) simply follows from (2), and (4) from (3). Premise (5), however, needs several subarguments if it is to follow from (4). Parmenides, though, had already supplied the subarguments. Aristotle simply has to apply them to "first cause." This anticipates what will be perhaps the most frequent objection to the argument— namely, that there is a disconnect between a first cause and God. Aristotle shows, however, that a strictly first cause would be without limits—that is, infinite—and therefore eternal, unchanging, singular, and perfect in all it is. This is certainly a minimal definition of the theistic God.

Another frequent objection to Aristotle's cosmological argument is to ask what caused the first cause. A notorious example is this from Richard Dawkins:

> These arguments rely upon the idea of a regress and invoke God to terminate it. They make the entirely unwarranted assumption that God himself is immune to the regress. Even if we allow the dubious luxury of arbitrarily conjuring up a terminator to an infinite regress and giving it a name, simply because we need one, there is absolutely no reason to endow that terminator with any of the properties normally ascribed to God: omnipotence, omniscience, goodness, creativity of design, to say nothing of such human attributes as listening to prayers, forgiving sins and reading innermost thoughts.[4]

This simply misses the logic of the argument. If X is truly the *first* cause, then it is by definition *un*caused and so cannot have a cause in any respect. First is first!

Again, the cosmological argument's conclusion demands an uncaused being, and to be uncaused is to be without cause, limit, or parameter. Now granted, (5) does not appear to require any truly personal qualities, though perfection as final cause implies omniscience, which, in turn, does mean that the first uncaused cause knows what I am praying as well as my "innermost thoughts." Nevertheless, Aristotle's God does not have nor does he seek relationships, including worship. In his *Nicomachean Ethics*, Aristotle does say that in seeking a life of contemplation in order to acquire virtues we are to imitate God. So clearly, God does have some personal moral qualities.

> Therefore the activity of God, which surpasses all others in blessedness, must be contemplative; and of human activities, therefore, that which is most akin to this must be most of the nature of happiness.
>
> This is indicated, too, by the fact that the other animals have no share in happiness, being completely deprived of such activity. For while the

---

[4]Richard Dawkins, *The God Delusion* (Oxford: Oxford University Press, 2006), 77.

whole life of the gods is blessed, and that of men too in so far as some likeness of such activity belongs to them, none of the other animals is happy, since they in no way share in contemplation.[5]

This is Aristotle's grand argument. Subsequent history will take it in two directions. First, the texts and knowledge of Aristotle were retained in the Arabic portion of Alexander's empire and became a key part of Islamic philosophy. This will come to be called the kalam argument. Second, these texts were brought into Europe through the Islamic conquest of Spain, were translated into Latin, and were known in the European universities by the twelfth century. It is in Paris that Thomas Aquinas finds Aristotle and transforms Christian philosophy and theology.

Further Reading

For more on Aristotle's argument specifically, see Leo Elders, *Aristotle's Theology: A Commentary on Book* Lambda *of the Metaphysics* (Assen: Van Gorcum, 1972); and a number of chapters in Michael Frede and David Charles, eds., *Aristotle's Metaphysics* Lambda (Oxford: Oxford University Press, 2000).

For general background and overview of the argument, I recommend starting with volume one of Frederick Copleston's *A History of Philosophy* (London: A&C Black, 2003). It is available in several editions and formats, including online.

2.1.2 Thomas Aquinas. Most would agree that Thomas Aquinas (1225–1274) is the key figure in the development of the cosmological argument, certainly in terms of the Christian tradition. So many factors come together here: the emergence of the European university as a forum for debate, the reinsertion of Aristotelian metaphysics in the Christian conversation, the influence of Arabic Aristotelian theism from Andalusian Spain—all of this finds a synthesis in the genius of Thomas.

---

[5]Aristotle, *Nicomachean Ethics*, trans. William David Ross (London: Oxford University Press, 1942), 10.8.

The *Summa theologiae* is his culminating systematic treatise. The cosmological argument appears here right at the beginning as the initial and defining statement. It anchors a complex understanding of God and his actions in a simple rational exercise that demonstrates that the reality of God's existence is the only way to make sense of our world at all. It is fifteen centuries after Aristotle when Thomas picks up his argument again. Here is what has come to be known as "the Five Ways."

The existence of God can be proved in five ways.

The first and more manifest way is the argument from motion. It is certain, and evident to our senses, that in the world some things are in motion. Now whatever is in motion is put in motion by another, for nothing can be in motion except it is in potentiality to that towards which it is in motion; whereas a thing moves inasmuch as it is in act. For motion is nothing else than the reduction of something from potentiality to actuality. But nothing can be reduced from potentiality to actuality, except by something in a state of actuality. Thus that which is actually hot, as fire, makes wood, which is potentially hot, to be actually hot, and thereby moves and changes it. Now it is not possible that the same thing should be at once in actuality and potentiality in the same respect, but only in different respects. For what is actually hot cannot simultaneously be potentially hot; but it is simultaneously potentially cold. It is therefore impossible that in the same respect and in the same way a thing should be both mover and moved, i.e. that it should move itself. Therefore, whatever is in motion must be put in motion by another. If that by which it is put in motion be itself put in motion, then this also must needs be put in motion by another, and that by another again. But this cannot go on to infinity, because then there would be no first mover, and, consequently, no other mover; seeing that subsequent movers move only inasmuch as they are put in motion by the first mover; as the staff moves only because it is put in motion by the hand. Therefore it is necessary to arrive at a first mover, put in motion by no other; and this everyone understands to be God.

The second way is from the nature of the efficient cause. In the world of sense we find there is an order of efficient causes. There is no case known (neither is it, indeed, possible) in which a thing is found to be the efficient cause of itself; for so it would be prior to itself, which is impossible. Now in efficient causes it is not possible to go on to infinity, because in all efficient causes following in order, the first is the cause of the intermediate cause, and the intermediate is the cause of the ultimate cause, whether the intermediate cause be several, or only one. Now to take away the cause is to take away the effect. Therefore, if there be no first cause among efficient causes, there will be no ultimate, nor any intermediate cause. But if in efficient causes it is possible to go on to infinity, there will be no first efficient cause, neither will there be an ultimate effect, nor any intermediate efficient causes; all of which is plainly false. Therefore it is necessary to admit a first efficient cause, to which everyone gives the name of God.

The third way is taken from possibility and necessity, and runs thus. We find in nature things that are possible to be and not to be, since they are found to be generated, and to corrupt, and consequently, they are possible to be and not to be. But it is impossible for these always to exist, for that which is possible not to be at some time is not. Therefore, if everything is possible not to be, then at one time there could have been nothing in existence. Now if this were true, even now there would be nothing in existence, because that which does not exist only begins to exist by something already existing. Therefore, if at one time nothing was in existence, it would have been impossible for anything to have begun to exist; and thus even now nothing would be in existence—which is absurd. Therefore, not all beings are merely possible, but there must exist something the existence of which is necessary. But every necessary thing either has its necessity caused by another, or not. Now it is impossible to go on to infinity in necessary things which have their necessity caused by another, as has been already proved in regard to efficient causes. Therefore we cannot but postulate the existence of some being having of itself its own necessity, and not receiving it from another, but rather causing in others their necessity. This all men speak of as God.

The fourth way is taken from the gradation to be found in things. Among beings there are some more and some less good, true, noble and the like. But *more* and *less* are predicated of different things, according as they resemble in their different ways something which is the maximum, as a thing is said to be hotter according as it more nearly resembles that which is hottest; so that there is something which is truest, something best, something noblest and, consequently, something which is uttermost being; for those things that are greatest in truth are greatest in being, as it is written in *Metaph*. ii. Now the maximum in any genus is the cause of all in that genus; as fire, which is the maximum heat, is the cause of all hot things. Therefore there must also be something which is to all beings the cause of their being, goodness, and every other perfection; and this we call God.

The fifth way is taken from the governance of the world. We see that things which lack intelligence, such as natural bodies, act for an end, and this is evident from their acting always, or nearly always, in the same way, so as to obtain the best result. Hence it is plain that not fortuitously, but designedly, do they achieve their end. Now whatever lacks intelligence cannot move towards an end, unless it be directed by some being endowed with knowledge and intelligence; as the arrow is shot to its mark by the archer. Therefore some intelligent being exists by whom all natural things are directed to their end; and this being we call God.[6]

These "Five Ways" are each different ways in which contingency evidences itself to us. Motion is only possible because things take up a finite amount of space and have to be caused to move to another position. Things change because they are limited and have to be caused to change. Things come to exist only when caused to exist. Something is more than something else only because it is finite to begin with and has to be caused to be more. Finally, things come to play some role or "end," or have some use—that is, they are good for something only because they have been caused to have a certain design structure.

As I look around my office right now, there are hundreds of examples of these different forms of contingency; each of them exists as it does

---

[6]Thomas Aquinas, *Summa theologiae* I, q. 2, art. 3, trans. Fathers of the English Dominican Province (New York: Benziger Brothers, 1911, 1947). Available online at www.sacred-texts.com/chr/aquinas/summa/index.htm. I use this translation of the *Summa theologiae* throughout the book.

as the result of cause-and-effect connections, some, of course, involving me. Nevertheless, in every case there is a chain of causal dependencies without which they would not be what they are, and not "be" at all. This chain cannot be infinite or else there is no source at all that would explain their existence. Therefore, there must be a finite sequence, and therefore a first cause: Not infinite equals finite; finite implies a first.

In the *Summa contra Gentiles*, Thomas puts the argument in this simple generic form.[7]

> We find in the world, furthermore, certain beings, those namely that are subject to generation and corruption, which can be and not-be. But what can be has a cause because, since it is equally related to two contraries, namely, being and non-being, it must be owing to some cause that being accrues to it. Now . . . one cannot proceed to infinity among causes. We must therefore posit something that is a necessary being.

For Thomas this is not just some cute and convenient philosophical head game, but simple human observation and thinking. However, it is also divine revelation coming into play. This is what God allows us to see when we open our eyes.[8] Aristotle was right that our ordinary perceptions of causal connections demand there be an uncaused first cause. He was even willing to call this God.

As to the denial of an infinite regress, Thomas is content to use Aristotle's argument.

> In *Metaphysics* II Aristotle also uses another argument to show that there is no infinite regress in efficient causes and that we must reach one first cause—God. This way is as follows. In all ordered efficient causes, the first is the cause of the intermediate cause, whether one or many, and this is the cause of the last cause. But, when you suppress a cause, you

---

[7]Thomas Aquinas, *Summa contra Gentiles* 1.15.5, trans. Anton Pegis (New York: Hanover House, 1955–1957). I use this translation of *Summa contra Gentiles* throughout the book. This is close to the third way, of course. "Possible to be and not to be" is Thomas's definition of "contingent." That is, it exists, but only because some cause makes it exist.

[8]See Paul's discussion in Rom 1:18-20. Note Paul's insistence that this so obvious everyone can see it and is without excuse.

suppress its effect. Therefore, if you suppress the first cause, the intermediate cause cannot be a cause. Now, if there were an infinite regress
among efficient causes, no cause would be first. Therefore, all the other
causes, which are intermediate, will be suppressed. But this is manifestly
false. We must, therefore, posit that there exists a first efficient cause.
This is God.[9]

As far as the format of the argument itself is concerned, Thomas does
not add much of anything new, except to give the argument in five
variations of ways in which contingency demonstrates itself to us.[10]
Even these are not entirely original to Thomas, however. Most had been
developed by earlier medieval philosophers, including Augustine. The
fourth way even has some roots in Plato.[11]

What is unique to Thomas is that he sees how a whole metaphysics
of God unfolds out of this simple argument and from that the entire
theology of the *Summa theologiae*. The insight that enables this was
already evident in Parmenides, as we saw earlier.

It was Parmenides who, inadvertently perhaps, concluded to the
conditions of unlimited being. Thomas can now extend his argument
to conclude to infinity, simplicity, eternality, and immutability. If a
being is uncaused, unlimited, and without boundaries, then it cannot
have finite parts, it cannot be restricted by space or time, and it cannot
change into something different.

This is important in responding to the most frequent objection to
this argument: that this first uncaused cause is not God. Christians and
atheists alike have argued that the cosmological argument yields at best
an abstract impersonal and nonrelational cause, but not the God of love,
mercy, and grace, not the God of Abraham, Isaac, and Jacob. Perhaps it
is just the laws of physics, or the force of evolution, or the universe itself.

---

[9]Aquinas, *Summa contra Gentiles* 1.13.33.
[10]There are actually more than five. See his parallel discussion in the *Summa contra Gentiles*.
[11]See my discussion of the fourth way in "A Fourth Way to Prove God's Existence," in *Revisiting Aquinas' Proofs for the Existence of God*, ed. Robert Arp (Leiden: Brill, 2016), 147-72.

However, Thomas argues that the extensions of the argument take care of the real weight of these objections. Aristotle had already begun this process, based on Parmenides's argument, but Thomas extends it in much more detail. Here is the list of properties that follow from "first uncaused cause" as listed in the *Summa contra Gentiles* following the brief form of the argument at the beginning of section 15.[12]

15.121 no beginning or ending

15.122 not temporal

15.124 not dependent

16.128 no passive potential

17.134 not material

17.137 not a material cause

18.141 not composite, therefore simple

19.142 not subject to coercion

20.154 not corporeal

21.197 no property other than its nature

22.203 not a being other than its nature

23.214 no accidents

24.224 no differentiations or parts

25.228 no genus therefore only one

25.233 not defined or limited by its properties

25.234 no a priori argument possible

26.238 not a universal formal cause

27.251 not the form of an object

28.259 not imperfect

---

[12] Aquinas, *Summa contra Gentiles* 1.15-28.

First, to Christian objectors Thomas concludes that the uncaused cause is infinitely relational, omniscient, and involved, precisely as the ultimate cause of every event. As the artist is to every dab of paint on the canvas, so is the first cause to every flap of butterfly wing, and every neuron firing in my brain, regardless of how many intermediate causes there might be. There could be no greater intimacy.

This is possible because Thomas understands this argument to be about efficient causality. God's relationship to the world is not just as planner, coordinator, mastermind even, but as ultimate agent. Nothing happens that he does not originate. All agency is his, as Thomas sees it in this argument.

Second, the atheist is here also countered. The relationship of first cause to all other causes is made radically different by the fact that this first cause is not a finite, contingent being, hence cannot be the universe itself nor any event or part of it. Yet it is a real cause, and so not an abstract law or principle: it must be an actual infinite entity. This argument is about existence, pure and simple. If something exists, then its cause exists.

Another objection atheists often bring forward, specifically to the third way, but often to all attempts at cosmological arguing, is that it commits the fallacy of composition. This has been effectively countered by Rem Edwards in his *Reason and Religion*.[13] He notes that fallacies are defined as logical strategies that are unreliable. That is, there is at least one possible circumstance in which the conclusion is unwarranted. That is certainly the case when we try to argue that the whole has a property on the basis that each part has that same property.

For example, if each piece of a picture puzzle is triangular, what is the shape of the whole puzzle? While triangular is an option, it is not the only one, and hence this strategy fails, and hence we have the fallacy of composition. The curiosity, however, is that for some other properties composition works just fine. If all the pieces are red, then

---

[13]Rem Edwards, *Reason and Religion* (New York: Harcourt, Brace, Jovanovich, 1972).

clearly the whole puzzle is red. The problem is that after much wrangling, logicians have never come up with a decision procedure to tell us when composition works and when it does not. We simply have to take it on a case-by-case basis. In this case, contingency seems clearly to be a composing property. If each of the parts of X needs to be caused to exist, how could the set of those parts escape contingency? In this case the whole is not greater than the parts; it just *is* all of the parts.[14]

We should, of course, also note that Thomas's other arguments are not whole-universe arguments anyway, and likely the third way is not either, so the fallacy-of-composition objection carries no weight here anyway. We will encounter it later, however, in cases when we definitely do have whole-universe reasoning. His point in the third way is merely that if everything is only possible—that is, contingent—there would still be nothing, since a possible entity or entities cannot cause anything at all.

Thomas himself discusses two larger objections to the argument. They are remarkably current.

> Objection 1: It seems that God does not exist; because if one of two contraries be infinite, the other would be altogether destroyed. But the word "God" means that He is infinite goodness. If, therefore, God existed, there would be no evil discoverable; but there is evil in the world. Therefore God does not exist.
>
> Objection 2: Further, it is superfluous to suppose that what can be accounted for by a few principles has been produced by many. But it seems that everything we see in the world can be accounted for by other principles, supposing God did not exist. For all natural things can be reduced to one principle which is nature; and all voluntary things can be reduced to one principle which is human reason, or will. Therefore there is no need to suppose God's existence.[15]

---

[14]See Edwards, *Reason and Religion*, 266-70, on this. Edwards uses different examples, but this is his point.

[15]Aquinas, *Summa theologiae* I, q. 2, art. 3.

The first objection is simply that the presence of evil in a world created by an infinitely good God seems contradictory; the second is the claim that science and its "laws of nature" account, or, in today's version, evolution, makes God's activity superfluous. Here are Thomas's responses:

> Reply to Objection 1: As Augustine says (Enchiridion xi): "Since God is the highest good, He would not allow any evil to exist in His works, unless His omnipotence and goodness were such as to bring good even out of evil." This is part of the infinite goodness of God, that He should allow evil to exist, and out of it produce good.
>
> Reply to Objection 2: Since nature works for a determinate end under the direction of a higher agent, whatever is done by nature must needs be traced back to God, as to its first cause. So also whatever is done voluntarily must also be traced back to some higher cause other than human reason or will, since these can change or fail; for all things that are changeable and capable of defect must be traced back to an immovable and self-necessary first principle, as was shown in the body of the Article.[16]

This is essentially Alvin Plantinga's answer to the logical problem of evil in his *God, Freedom, and Evil*.[17] The point is that as long as God has some good reason for allowing evil, there is no contradiction between his infinite goodness and evil's presence. One such good reason, Thomas says elsewhere, once again agreeing with Plantinga, would be free will. That is, that the value of creating persons with the capacity to deliberate their behavior and thus behave deliberately outweighs the evil they will perpetuate with their freedom.[18]

The second reply remains the standard response that the actual operation of natural law, for example in the form of gravity, quantum

---

[16]Aquinas, *Summa theologiae* I, q. 2, art. 3.

[17]Alvin Plantinga, *God, Freedom, and Evil* (Grand Rapids, MI: Eerdmans, 1989).

[18]This is, of course, a huge issue all its own on which the current literature has much to say. My only point here is to note that the problem of evil as an objection to the arguments for God's existence has been around for a long time and has been shown to be irrelevant to them, though remaining a formidable issue. More on this below in section 2.3.6.

mechanics, or just the process of evolution, is itself contingent and in need of a cause. Hence, while it describes the process, it explains nothing: it is simply another link in the causal chain.

In summary, the argument remains the simple Aristotelian move from transitive contingency relations to the requirement of a non-contingent first cause.[19] Then it becomes a distinctly theistic argument by showing the extensions of noncontingency to the major attributes of God as recognized by Judaism, Christianity, Islam, and most other religious traditions, including even some forms of Hinduism and even Buddhism.

We should note that while Thomas has answered the larger objection, there are some elements of this objection left unanswered, especially the apparent absence of distinctly subjective personal qualities associated with the primarily Christian concept of God as loving, caring Father. This will remain something of a deficiency for any form of the cosmological argument. It seems unavoidable for an argument based on purely real-world causal considerations. Philosophical argument, or any form of human reasoning, has no way of introspecting God's inner life. For that, we would need revelation from God.

This is not, however, an objection to the actual logic of the argument, but rather points to the inevitable limitations of the conclusion. The cosmological argument by itself simply does not yield a full conception of the traditional God. However, if God is infinite then clearly no single and simple argument ever could somehow handle such an assignment. We will find further attempts to expand the cosmological argument to deal with some of this deficit, but to do so proponents will have to sacrifice much of the simplicity of Aristotle and Thomas's version.

---

[19] I take the word *transitive* from a very important discussion of the infinite-regress problem by Paterson Brown, "Infinite Causal Regression," *Philosophical Review* 75, no. 4 (1966): 510-25.

Further Reading

There is so much to read on Thomas's arguments it is hard to know where to start. A good bibliography of recent literature (through 2000), along with a catalog of objections, is my article "The Cosmological Argument: A Current Bibliographical Appraisal," *Philosophia Christi* 2, no. 2 (2000): 283-304.

For a critical discussion see Anthony Kenny, *The Five Ways: Saint Thomas Aquinas' Proofs of God's Existence,* 2nd ed. (Notre Dame, IN: University of Notre Dame Press, 1980). For pro and con see Robert Arp, ed., *Revisiting Aquinas' Proofs for the Existence of God* (Leiden: Brill, 2016).

For an excellent, though advanced, discussion of the objection to the third way— that is, that there could be an actual infinity of causes—see Robert Geis, "*Possibilia non Esse* and Number in Aquinas' Third Way," *Science et Esprit* 71, no. 1 (2019): 1-10.

Perhaps the best discussion of why there cannot be an infinite series of contingent causes for Thomas is Paterson Brown, "Infinite Causal Regression," *Philosophical Review* 75, no. 4 (1966): 510-25.

For some general introductions to Thomas for beginners that include the Five Ways see Frederick Copleston, *Aquinas* (Baltimore: Penguin, 1961); Brian Davies, *The Thought of Thomas Aquinas* (Oxford: Oxford University Press, 1992); and Edward Feser, *Aquinas: A Beginner's Guide* (London: Oneworld, 2009).

The best advanced discussion of the Five Ways, along with good bibliographic detail, is Leo Elders, *The Philosophical Theology of St. Thomas Aquinas* (Leiden: Brill, 1990). See as well Paul Weingartner, *God's Existence: Can It Be Proven? A Logical Commentary on the Five Ways of Thomas Aquinas* (Frankfurt: Ontos, 2010); John Wippel, *The Metaphysical Thought of Thomas Aquinas* (Washington, DC: Catholic University of America Press, 2000); Gavin Kerr, *Aquinas's Way to God: The Proof in* De Ente et Essentia (Oxford: Oxford University Press, 2015).

2.1.3 Duns Scotus and John Locke. Thomas Aquinas represents an important synthesis in medieval philosophy. Following him, we begin the transition to Renaissance and modern philosophy. Duns Scotus (1266–1308) is the beginning of this transition, and John Locke (1632–1704) is at the end. At the same time, Locke is also the beginning of the empiricist moderns.

Scotus's argument is much like Thomas's, but Scotus is more concerned to bring out the modal elements in its logic. That is, he formulates the argument in terms of what is possible and what is necessary given our observations of our world. It is also more intricate and detailed, so we will look at it more fully. Scotus was not referred to as the Subtle Doctor without good reason. This is pretty dense argumentation.

Section three of Scotus's *A Treatise on God as First Principle*, which follows below, is preceded by two sections of definitions and extensive metaphysical groundwork. Despite all that, we still see here the basic argument of Aristotle and Thomas based on our simple observations of causes producing effects in the real world.

> (First conclusion) Some nature among beings can produce an effect.
>
> This is shown to be so because something can be produced and therefore something can be productive. . . .
>
> (Second conclusion) Something able to produce an effect is simply first, that is to say, it neither can be produced by an efficient cause nor does it exercise its efficient causality in virtue of anything other than itself.
>
> It is proved from the first conclusion that something can produce an effect. Call this producer A. If A is first in the way explained, we have immediately what we seek to prove. If it is not such, then it is a posterior agent either because it can be produced by something else or because it is able to produce its effect only in virtue of some agent other than itself. . . . However, an infinity in the ascending order is impossible; hence a primacy is necessary because whatever has nothing prior is not posterior to anything posterior to itself, for the second conclusion of chapter two does away with a circle in causes.
>
> An objection is raised here on the grounds that those who philosophize admit that an infinity is possible in an ascending order. . . . I declare that the philosophers did not postulate the possibility of an infinity in causes essentially ordered, but only in causes accidentally ordered. . . .
>
> What we intend to show from this is that an infinity of essentially ordered causes is impossible, and that an infinity of accidentally ordered causes is also impossible unless we admit a terminus in an essentially

ordered series. Therefore there is no way in which an infinity in essentially ordered causes is possible. . . . Here three propositions are assumed. For the sake of brevity, call the first A, the second B and the third C.

The proof of these: first, A is proved. (1) If the totality of essentially ordered causes were caused, it would have to be by a cause which does not belong to the group, otherwise it would be its own cause. The whole series of dependents then is dependent upon something which is not one of the group. (2) [If this were not so], an infinity of essentially ordered causes would be acting at the same time (a consequence of the third difference mentioned above). Now no philosopher assumes this. . . .

Proof of B: If we assume an infinity of accidentally ordered causes, it is clear that these are not concurrent, but one succeeds another so that the second, though it is in some way from the preceding, does not depend upon it for the exercise of its causality. For it is equally effective whether the preceding cause exists or not. A son in turn may beget a child just as well whether his father be dead or alive. But an infinite succession of such causes is impossible unless it exists in virtue of some nature of infinite duration from which the whole succession and every part thereof depends.

Proof of C: From the first conclusion, some nature is able to produce an effect. But if an essential order of agents be denied, then this nature capable of causing does not cause in virtue of some other cause, and even if we assume that in one individual it is caused, nevertheless in some other it will not be caused, and this is what we propose to prove to be true of the first nature.

(Third conclusion) If what is able to cause effectively is simply first, then it is itself incapable of being caused, since it cannot be produced and is independently able to produce its effects.

This is clear from the second conclusion, for if such a being could cause only in virtue of something else or if it could be produced, then either a process ad infinitum or a circle in causes would result, or else the series would terminate in some being which cannot be produced and yet independently is able to produce an effect. . . .

(Fourth conclusion) A being able to exercise efficient causality which is simply first actually exists, and some nature actually existing is capable of exercising such causality.

Proof of this: Anything to whose nature it is repugnant to receive existence from something else, exists of itself if it is able to exist at all. . . .

(Fifth conclusion) A being unable to be caused is of itself necessarily existent.

Proof: By excluding every cause of existence other than itself, whether it be intrinsic or extrinsic, we make it impossible for it not to be. . . .

(Sixth conclusion) It is the characteristic of but one nature to have necessary being of itself. . . .

Besides, two natures included under a common class are unequal. Proof of this is to be found among the different kinds of things into which a genus is divided. But if the two such natures are unequal, one will be of a more perfect being than the other. Nothing however is more perfect than a being having necessary existence of itself.

Moreover, if there were two natures having necessary being of themselves, neither would depend upon the other for existence and consequently no essential order would exist between them.[20]

Scotus's argument concludes that this first principle or cause is actual, uncaused, necessary, and singular. In the following section four he further argues that it is simple or without parts, infinite and omnipotent, and intelligent. Therefore, Scotus does not hesitate to conclude that this is God.

The bulk of this argument involves the closure argument for an infinite regress. He here provides three proofs, the first of which we are already familiar with from Aristotle and Thomas, but he does note that the denial of infinite regress only holds for accidentally ordered causes. That is, as he notes again, any necessary being could not be part of an ordered causal series of contingent things.

This emphasizes the point already evident in Thomas, that it is simply the noncontingency of the conclusion of this argument that does all the heavy lifting. Why does the argument stop here? Why can we not ask

---

[20]Duns Scotus, *A Treatise on God as First Principle*, trans. Allan B. Wolter (1966; repr., Irondale, AL: Aeterna Press, 2015), 13-19. This is sections 3.4–26, with several sections of lesser significance left out.

what caused God? Why should we think we have arrived at God? All of this is answered simply by noting that the argument concludes to a "not contingent" being.

John Locke's argument, as produced in his *Essay Concerning Human Understanding*, betrays its modern empiricist origins. Nevertheless, it remains an argument about causality in the medieval tradition, including the implications for the nature of God:

> We are capable of knowing certainly that there is a God. Though God has given us no innate ideas of himself; though he has stamped no original characters on our minds, wherein we may read his being; yet having furnished us with those faculties our minds are endowed with, he hath not left himself without witness: since we have sense, perception, and reason, and cannot want a clear proof of him, as long as we carry ourselves about us. Nor can we justly complain of our ignorance in this great point; since he has so plentifully provided us with the means to discover and know him; so far as is necessary to the end of our being, and the great concernment of our happiness. But, though this be the most obvious truth that reason discovers, and though its evidence be (if I mistake not) equal to mathematical certainty: yet it requires thought and attention. . . .
>
> For man knows that he himself exists. I think it is beyond question, that man has a clear idea of his own being; he knows certainly he exists, and that he is something. He that can doubt whether he be anything or no, I speak not to; no more than I would argue with pure nothing, or endeavour to convince nonentity that it were something. If any one pretends to be so sceptical as to deny his own existence, (for really to doubt of it is manifestly impossible,) let him for me enjoy his beloved happiness of being nothing, until hunger or some other pain convince him of the contrary. This, then, I think I may take for a truth, which every one's certain knowledge assures him of, beyond the liberty of doubting, viz. that he is something that actually exists.
>
> He knows also that nothing cannot produce a being; therefore something must have existed from eternity. In the next place, man knows, by an intuitive certainty, that bare nothing can no more produce any real

being, than it can be equal to two right angles. If a man knows not that nonentity, or the absence of all being, cannot be equal to two right angles, it is impossible he should know any demonstration in Euclid. If, therefore, we know there is some real being, and that nonentity cannot produce any real being, it is an evident demonstration, that from eternity there has been something; since what was not from eternity had a beginning; and what had a beginning must be produced by something else.

And that eternal Being must be most powerful. Next, it is evident, that what had its being and beginning from another, must also have all that which is in and belongs to its being from another too. All the powers it has must be owing to and received from the same source. This eternal source, then, of all being must also be the source and original of all power; and so this eternal Being must be also the most powerful.

And most knowing. Again, a man finds in himself perception and knowledge. We have then got one step further; and we are certain now that there is not only some being, but some knowing, intelligent being in the world.

And therefore God. Thus, from the consideration of ourselves, and what we infallibly find in our own constitutions, our reason leads us to the knowledge of this certain and evident truth—that there is an eternal, most powerful, and most knowing Being; which whether any one will please to call God, it matters not. The thing is evident; and from this idea duly considered, will easily be deduced all those other attributes, which we ought to ascribe to this eternal Being.[21]

Locke's argument is certainly the standard argument, though turned inward in typically empiricist fashion. Given what we know about ourselves, we must be caused to exist, and this sequence cannot be infinite. From this it follows that there is a being that actually exists and is most powerful, knowing, and eternal.

Following Locke, the attention of philosophy and common discussion largely shifted to the teleological argument. It was far more in tune with

---

[21]John Locke, *An Essay Concerning Humane Understanding* (London: Thomas Basset, 1690), 4.10.1-6. 'Humane' was Locke's original spelling. This is available in many editions and anthologies, including online.

the scientific and empirical mood of the times. There were, however, a few notable exceptions. One, of course, was the continued discussion of Thomas within Catholic circles and universities. Most of this, however, is interpretive, and there was little real progress until the late nineteenth century. In 1879, Pope Leo XIII's encyclical *Aeterni Patris* ordered a renewed discussion of Thomas in the universities as an attempt to halt the incursion of liberalism in Catholic theology. This brought about a movement known as neo-Thomism, which included renewed attention to the cosmological argument, but, again, this attention went little beyond Catholic circles, and was primarily restricted to Europe, especially France, though it did spread to the United States as well.

Further Reading

For good discussions of Duns Scotus's version of the argument see the following: Bernardino Bonansea, *God and Atheism* (Washington, DC: Catholic University of America Press, 1979), chap. 5; Peter van Inwagen, *Metaphysics* (Boulder, CO: Westview Press, 2002); James F. Ross, *Philosophical Theology* (Indianapolis: Hackett, 1980), chaps. 4-5.

A briefer discussion is Thomas Williams, "John Duns Scotus," in *Stanford Encyclopedia of Philosophy*, ed. Edward N. Zalta, winter 2019 ed., sec. 2.2, https://plato .stanford.edu/archives/win2019/entries/duns-scotus/#ProExiGod. This includes a helpful summary of Scotus's cosmological argument.

For a collection of more general articles see Marilyn McCord Adams, ed., *The Philosophical Theology of John Duns Scotus* (Ithaca, NY: Cornell University Press, 1990); Thomas Williams, ed., *The Cambridge Companion to Duns Scotus* (New York: Cambridge University Press, 2002).

On John Locke's natural theology see Matthew Stuart, *Locke's Metaphysics* (Oxford: Oxford University Press, 2013).

You can find good discussions of the Thomistic argument after *Aeterni Patris* in Catholic philosophers such as Jacques Maritain and Étienne Gilson.

2.1.4 Buddhist and Hindu Arguments. This section represents something of a direction change in this story. We leave the European milieu and look at another culture entirely, where, curiously enough, the very same conversation was going on. That is exactly why I insert it here. The terminology and the religious framework may be much different, but the logic of human thinking about the source and cause of our universe is still much the same. I should add that in this section I am only looking at one particular interaction. Hindu and especially Buddhist cultures are widely diverse across much of Asia, and they are often quite unique to specific geographies, especially when it comes to their conceptions of Brahman, as well as the use of human reasoning in relation to it, which some reject entirely.

Hinduism is first given philosophical reflection in the *Upanishads*, written between 800 and 200 BC.[22] Here we find the early development of Brahman as the supreme creator God, above all gods, who possesses infinite-like qualities. Here is a descriptive passage from the *Mundaka Upanishad*:

> He said to him: "Two kinds of knowledge must be known, this is what all who know Brahman tell us, the higher and the lower knowledge.
>
> "The lower knowledge is the Rig-veda, Yagur-veda, Sama-veda, Atharva-veda, Siksha (phonetics), Kalpa (ceremonial), Vyakarana (grammar), Nirukta (etymology), Khandas (metre), Gyotisha (astronomy); but the higher knowledge is that by which the Indestructible (Brahman) is apprehended.
>
> "That which cannot be seen, nor seized, which has no family and no caste, no eyes nor ears, no hands nor feet, the eternal, the omnipresent (all-pervading), infinitesimal, that which is imperishable, that it is which the wise regard as the source of all beings."[23]

There is here no explicit argument, either for these qualities, or even for the existence of Brahman. Nor are any real conclusions drawn. Nevertheless, this is certainly a philosophical and monotheistic conception.

---

[22] I should note here that all of the dates in this section are approximate at best. In addition, our textual evidence is not very good either. Most of our copies of these texts are more than a thousand years after the original.

[23] *Mundaka Upanishad*, trans. F. Max Muller (Mineola, NY: Dover Publications, 1962), 1.1.4-6.

What is most important, however, is that by being infinite, Brahman escapes the confines of the cause-effect world and yet acts on it.

2.1.4.1 Gautama Buddha. Gautama Buddha (ca. 600 and 400 BC) rejected any concept of an omnipotent and omniscient God, Brahman, on several grounds. One such counterargument is that of dependent origination, or *pratîtyasamutpâda.* This is the principle of universal causation shared by both Hindus and Buddhists—that is, that everything is caught in the cause-effect nexus and so any god must be also. Therefore, there cannot be a God. So there are *devas,* meaning shining or radiant beings, but no transcendent and uncaused creator God.

The more important counterargument is just the problem of evil. The universal prevalence of suffering (*dukkha*) is clear evidence that the supreme God, *Maya Brahman,* of the Hindu and Brahmanic literature is simply an illusion in the *deva* Brahman's mind. Here is a statement of this argument from the *Bhuridatta Jataka*:

> He who has eyes can see the sickening sight;
> Why does not Brahma set his creatures right?
>
> If his wide power no limits can restrain,
> Why is his hand so rarely spread to bless?
>
> Why are his creatures all condemned to pain?
> Why does he not to all give happiness?
>
> Why do fraud, lies, and ignorance prevail?
> Why triumphs falsehood,—truth and justice fail?
>
> I count your Brahma one th' injust among,
> Who made a world in which to shelter wrong.[24]

As noted, the Buddha is here explicitly countering much of Hindu tradition, which goes back at least two millennia BC, and took written form in the *Vedas* as early as the twelfth to tenth centuries BC, well

---

[24]*The Jataka,* vol. 4, no. 543, sec. 208, trans. E. B. Cowell and W. H. D. Rouse. Available at www .sacred-texts.com/bud/j4/index.htm. This translation was originally published in 1901 by Cambridge University Press.

before even the *Upanishads*. His objections to a standard monotheism are intriguing since they are the same two that are repeatedly advanced in the West against Jewish, Christian, and Islamic conceptions and arguments right down to the present.

2.1.4.2 Udayana. Hindu philosophers seem to have made little response to the Buddha's objections until the tenth-century-AD logician Udayana. In his *Nyayakusumanjali*, or *A Handful of Flowers of Logic*, he briefly gives eight arguments for the real existence of Maya Brahman, of which the first four relate to the cosmological argument.

> From effects, combination, support, &c., traditional arts, authoritativeness, *hud* (revealed scriptures), the sentences thereof, and particular numbers, an everlasting omniscient Being is to be established.
>
> The earth must have had a maker because they have the nature of "effects" like a jar; by a thing's having a maker we mean that it is produced by some agent who possesses the wish to make, and has also a perceptive knowledge of the material cause out of which it is to be made.
>
> "Combination" is an action, and therefore the action which produced the conjunction of two atoms, initiating the binary compound, at the beginning of a creation, must have been accompanied by the volition of an intelligent being, because it has the nature of an action, like the actions of bodies such as ours.
>
> "Support": The world depends upon some being who possesses a volition which hinders it from falling, because it has the nature of being supported, like a stick supported by a bird in the air; by being supported we mean the absence of falling in the case of bodies possessing weight. By the {?} we include destruction. Thus the world can be destroyed by a being possessed of volition, because it is destructible, like cloth which is rent.
>
> "From traditional arts": The traditional arts now current, as that of making cloth, must have been originated by an independent being, from the very fact that they are traditional usages like the tradition of modern modes of writing.[25]

---

[25]Udayana, *Nyayakusumanjali*, Stabaka 1.5.1., trans. Sarvepalli Radhakrishnan and Charles A. Moore (Princeton, NJ: Princeton University Press, 1957), 383-84.

These are all versions of the cosmological argument, each arguing from a different aspect of contingency relations. While not spelled out in any great detail, there is enough here to answer the Buddha's objections. Since Brahman is outside of dependent origination as cause, he is clearly not subject to it. Furthermore, the evidence of evil cannot destroy the logic of this argument. At best, it can demand refinement in the conclusion, and since Udayana advocates a level of free will, Brahman's responsibility is either removed or at least diminished.

Further Reading

This is a big topic, of course, but a good place to start is Richard King, *Indian Philosophy: An Introduction to Hindu and Buddhist Thought* (Washington, DC: Georgetown University Press, 2007).

For an outline discussion see Shyam Ranganathan, "Hindu Philosophy," in *Internet Encyclopedia of Philosophy*, https://www.iep.utm.edu/hindu-ph/; and Abraham Velez, "Buddha," https://www.iep.utm.edu/buddha/. Both have good bibliographies.

2.1.5 The current scene. We now pick up the story of the cosmological argument in the more recent past. In most philosophical circles, except, as I noted, for Catholic ones in the early twentieth century, the argument was largely dormant for more than a century and a half. What discussion there was tended to be commentary on Thomas's arguments. This was largely the result of Immanuel Kant's seemingly devastating critique in his 1781 *Critique of Pure Reason*. He argued there that the ontological argument fails and that the cosmological argument depends on it and so fails as well. In the eighteenth and nineteenth centuries, the teleological argument received much attention as a culture of science developed, and especially so after Darwin seemed to place a roadblock in its path. The late nineteenth and early twentieth centuries also witnesses the return of another character in our narrative: the moral argument. On that, more later.

In the middle decades of the twentieth century it seemed to most of academia that evolution had finally displaced any rational talk about God. Textbooks and anthologies in philosophy of religion omit discussion of the arguments or include just a few selections only as a historical curiosity.[26] An exception that proves the point was the January 28, 1948, debate between the great Catholic historian of philosophy Frederick Copleston and British atheistic philosopher Bertrand Russell broadcast by the BBC.

The debate had little influence at the time. In fact, Russell was so convinced that he had made his point that he included a transcript in subsequent editions of his *Why I Am Not a Christian*.[27] What is interesting is that Copleston here uses a different form of the argument—namely, one based on a principle of sufficient reason that goes back to Leibniz. We will look at this form in a separate section to follow. It plays an important role in our narrative because it is this sufficient-reason argument in which the cosmological argument begins to regain its status in the 1960s.

First, I want to look at an example that crystalizes everything that has happened in the 150 years before it, and that sets the stage for what will begin a few years afterward. It was 1959 when Paul Edwards published his now classic paper critiquing Thomas's cosmological argument.

2.1.5.1 Paul Edwards. Paul Edwards (1923–2004) was the editor of *The Encyclopedia of Philosophy*, author of many books and articles, and no doubt one of the eminent American philosophers of the twentieth century. He was professor at New York University, Brooklyn College,

---

[26]For example, as late as 1982 Steven Kahn and David Shatz, both well-established philosophers of religion, published their textbook, *Contemporary Philosophy of Religion*, with Oxford University Press, without a single discussion of any of the arguments for God's existence.

[27]Originally published as a pamphlet by the National Secular Society: Bertrand Russell, *Why I Am Not a Christian* (London: Watts, 1927). Russell, *Why I Am Not a Christian and Other Essays on Religion and Related Subjects*, ed. Paul Edwards, was published in 1957 by George Allen & Unwin in London, and included the debate transcript. The debate itself can be readily found on YouTube and has been transcribed and reprinted in many anthologies. I will discuss it later in the section on the sufficient-reason form of the argument at 2.3.2.

and the New School for Social Research into the 1990s. His essay "A Critique of the Cosmological Argument" quickly became the standard on the topic and has been reprinted in many anthologies. What follows are the critical excerpts in which Edwards progressively hones in on the essential problems with Thomas's argument.

He begins by noting that, in any case, Thomas does not give us something worthy of the title "God," lacking as it does some key traits. But he thinks that supporters of the argument would readily concede this point and argue that there is still sufficient depth to the conclusion. Does Thomas, primarily in the second way, even succeed in eliminating an infinite series of causes? He supports this premise by maintaining that the opposite belief involves a plain absurdity. To suppose that there is an infinite series of causes logically implies that nothing exists now; but we know that plenty of things do exist now; and hence any theory which implies that nothing exists now must be wrong.[28] Edwards then continues,

> This argument fails to do justice to the supporter of the infinite series of causes. Aquinas has failed to distinguish between the two statements:
>
> > (1) A did not exist, and
> > (2) A is not uncaused.
>
> To say that the series is infinite implies (2), but it does not imply (1). The believer in the infinite series is not "taking A away." He is taking away the privileged status of A; he is taking away its "first causiness." He does not deny the existence of A or of any particular member of the series. He denies that A or anything else is the first member of the series. Since he is not taking A away, he is not taking B away, and thus he is also not taking X, Y, or Z away. . . . He is merely committed to denying that such a being, if it exists, is uncaused. He is committed to holding that whatever other impressive attributes a supernatural being might possess, the attribute of being a first cause is not among them.

---

[28]Paul Edwards, "A Critique of the Cosmological Argument," in *The Rationalist Annual for the Year 1959* (London: Pemburton, 1959), sec. 2.

Even if otherwise valid, the argument would not prove a *single* first cause. For there does not seem to be any good ground for supposing that the various causal series in the universe ultimately merge. Hence even if it is granted that no series of causes can be infinite the possibility of a plurality of first members has not been ruled out. Nor does the argument establish the present existence of the first cause.

Many defenders of the causal argument would contend that at least some of these criticisms rest on a misunderstanding. . . . They would in this connection distinguish between two types of causes—what they call "causes *in fieri*" and what they call "causes *in esse*." A cause *in fieri* is a factor which brought or helped to bring an effect into existence. A cause *in esse* is a factor which "sustains" or helps to sustain the effect "in being."

Using this distinction, the defender of the argument now reasons in the following way. To say that there is an infinite series of causes *in fieri* does not lead to any absurd conclusions. But Aquinas is concerned only with causes *in esse* and an infinite series of such causes is impossible.

But waiving this and all similar objections, the restatement of the argument in terms of causes *in esse* in no way avoids the main difficulty which was previously mentioned. A believer in the infinite series would insist that his position was just as much misrepresented now as before. He is no more removing the member of the series which is supposed to be the first cause *in esse* than he was removing the member which had been declared to be the first cause *in fieri*. He is again merely denying a privileged status to it. . . . He is again merely taking away its "first causiness."

No staunch defender of the cosmological argument would give up at this stage. Even if there were an infinite series of causes *in fieri* or *in esse*, he would contend, this still would not do away with the need for an ultimate, a first cause. . . . The demand to find the cause of the series as a whole rests on the erroneous assumption that the series is something over and above the members of which it is composed. . . . Supposing I see a group of five [Inuit] standing on the corner of Sixth Avenue and 50th Street and I wish to explain why the group came to New York. Investigation reveals the following stories:

> [Inuit] No. 1 did not enjoy the extreme cold in the polar region and decided to move to a warmer climate.

No. 2 is the husband of [Inuit] No. 1. He loves her dearly and did not wish to live without her.

No. 3 is the son of [Inuit] 1 and 2. He is too small and too weak to oppose his parents.

No. 4 saw an advertisement in the *New York Times* for an [Inuit] to appear on television.

No. 5 is a private detective engaged by the Pinkerton Agency to keep an eye on [Inuit] No. 4.

Let us assume that we have now explained in the case of each of the five [Inuit] why he or she is in New York. Somebody then asks: "All right, but what about the group as a whole; why is *it* in New York?" This would plainly be an absurd question. . . . It is just as absurd to ask for the cause of the series as a whole as distinct from asking for the causes of individual members.[29]

Now it is intriguing that Edwards begins the next section by, again, noting that the defender of Thomas's argument would not likely give up yet. He is certainly right. So far, Edwards has alleged nothing that Thomas himself did not answer or that, in fact, is actually true about his form of the argument. Aristotle, as we have seen, had already provided a defense against an infinite regress of contingent causes *in esse*. What Edwards misses is that mathematical possibilities do not settle questions of metaphysical possibility. Mathematically I can, of course, always think of there being one more cardinal number in any series. For every n there is an $n+$. But it does not follow that that is true for a sequence of causally dependent contingents. And Aristotle already demonstrated that there must be a first cause or there is no effect, and that cannot occur with infinite intermediate causes. So the first cause in a series of contingent causes *must* have first-causiness.

Edwards's five-Inuit story is also suspicious. To begin with, it just does not ring true. If there really are five Inuit, in full dress, on a New

---

[29]Edwards, "A Critique of the Cosmological Argument," secs. 2, 3, 4, excerpts.

York City street corner, Edwards's five individual explanations, while superficially perhaps correct, clearly demand a deeper explanation that covers them all. This is just *too* big a coincidence. The same holds for the universe. There are clearly deep connections in this ecosphere that will demand unifying explanations. The Inuit story is just a bad illustration. But Edwards is also wrong to think that this is a category mistake. Demanding an explanation for the whole series of contingents does not mean I am thinking of the series itself as something above and beyond its members. The problem is that no contingent explains itself by itself. And the only way to account for each and every one of them individually as causes is by concluding to a first and noncontingent cause. Think about the train!

That brings us to the final objection that is meant to clinch the refutation. This needs a quick advance warning, however. Edwards suddenly shifts here to a different form of the argument, namely Samuel Clarke's as put forward by Copleston in his famous debate with Russell.[30] Since, however, he thinks that this is the form of argument Thomas uses in the third way, we can consider it here.

As I said, Edwards begins section five by noting that it is "most unlikely that a determined defender of the cosmological line of reasoning would surrender even here."[31] He notes that this argument runs afoul of Kant's criticism that existence is not a predicate. We will take this up in the discussion of Kant in the chapter on the ontological argument,[32] but in any case Edwards assumes that this too can be surmounted here. In the end, the objection he thinks carries "great weight" is the one Russell brings up that we have already discussed—that is, that the notion that an explanation has to be "entire" to do the trick just misunderstands what an explanation is. Edwards concludes that to "assume

---

[30]Actually Copleston uses Leibniz's version of the sufficient-reason argument. I will discuss this form of the cosmological argument in detail in section 2.3.

[31]Edwards, "A Critique of the Cosmological Argument," sec. 5.

[32]See section 5.2.4.

without further ado that phenomena have explanations or an explanation in this sense is to beg the very point at issue. . . . But this is *a gross non sequitur.*"[33]

We will look at this objection when we discuss the Russell-Copleston debate later. Suffice it to say for now, Edwards's objection is a perfectly appropriate point in reference to practical life, as well as normal scientific research. If you are looking for a missing sock, or for a cure for cancer, you only need to pay attention to a few immediate causal links in order to succeed. But if I am looking for a *full* explanation of anything, if I am doing philosophy, and especially if what I really want is to say something about the larger meaning of my life, then I will need to track down every link: the *entire* chain right down to the first cause. So, Edwards's and Russell's objection misfires.

Given his admission that the other objections ultimately fail, I have to conclude that Edwards was simply not successful in advancing any telling objections to Thomas's argument.

In the next several sections, we will look at the new discussion of the contingency form of the argument as it occurred primarily in the 1980s and later. In most Western universities at that point, philosophy faculties were still largely inhospitable to theism and its arguments. There had been some winds of change blowing: the Society of Christian Philosophers started in 1978 as part of the American Philosophical Association. The year before saw the birth of the Evangelical Philosophical Society. One of the founders of the Evangelical Philosophical Society was Norman Geisler (1932–2019). His 1974 *Philosophy of Religion*,[34] which became a popular textbook, defended a version of the Thomistic argument and began to make it accessible in Christian circles again, especially to students at evangelical Protestant, not just Catholic Christian colleges and universities.

---

[33]Edwards, "A Critique of the Cosmological Argument," sec. 5.
[34]Norman Geisler, *Philosophy of Religion* (Grand Rapids, MI: Zondervan, 1974).

It would take a few decades for this movement to really gather steam, but both are today having an increasingly powerful voice, certainly in American universities, but in Europe and Australia as well. As a result, there were many philosophers who discovered Thomas and his argument and have advanced it to a new generation.[35]

2.1.5.2 Mortimer Adler. A book-length statement of the argument came in 1980 from Mortimer Adler (1902–2001). He was born into a Jewish family but early on found Thomas Aquinas intellectually attractive. *How to Think About God: A Guide for the Twentieth-Century Pagan* came after a long search for the reality of God.[36] "Pagan" here refers to the author himself at the time, but he was baptized an Episcopalian four years later. Adler was also one of the founders of the Great Books Foundation and was on the editorial board of the *Encyclopaedia Britannica*.

Here is his own summarized argument in chapter 14 toward the end of the book:

1. THE EXISTENCE OF AN EFFECT REQUIRING THE CONCURRENT EXISTENCE AND ACTION OF AN EFFICIENT CAUSE IMPLIES THE EXISTENCE AND ACTION OF THAT CAUSE. The causal principle, thus stated, is self-evidently true. . . .

2. THE COSMOS AS A WHOLE EXISTS. Here we have the existential assertion that is indispensable as a premise in any existential inference. While it does not have the same certitude possessed by my assertion of yours, it can certainly be affirmed beyond a reasonable doubt.

3. THE EXISTENCE OF THE COSMOS AS A WHOLE IS RADICALLY CONTINGENT, WHICH IS TO SAY THAT, WHILE NOT NEEDING AN EFFICIENT CAUSE OF ITS COMING TO BE, SINCE IT IS EVERLASTING, IT NEVERTHELESS DOES NEED AN EFFICIENT CAUSE OF ITS CONTINUING EXISTENCE, TO PRESERVE IT

---

[35]See the discussion in Stephen Davis, "Recent Christian Philosophy," *Philosophia Christi* 21, no. 1 (2019): 17-20.
[36]Mortimer Adler, *How to Think About God: A Guide for the Twentieth-Century Pagan* (New York: Macmillan, 1980).

IN BEING AND PREVENT IT FROM BEING REPLACED BY NOTHINGNESS. In the light of all that has gone before, there should be no difficulty in understanding what this proposition says. The only question is whether it is true. . . .

4. *If* THE COSMOS NEEDS AN EFFICIENT CAUSE OF ITS CONTINUING EXISTENCE TO PREVENT ITS ANNIHILATION, *Then* THAT CAUSE MUST BE A SUPERNATURAL BEING, SUPER-NATURAL IN ITS ACTION, AND ONE THE EXISTENCE OF WHICH IS UNCAUSED; IN OTHER WORDS, THE SUPREME BEING, OR GOD. We have understood that no natural cause can be an exnihilating cause, and that no natural cause is uncaused in its existence or action. In the light of this understanding, we are in a position to affirm the truth of the hypothetical proposition—this IF-THEN premise. Since natural and supernatural represent an ex-haustive set of alternatives, the cause being sought must be super-natural if it cannot be natural.[37]

As Adler noted, the remaining question has to do with the truth of the third premise. To this he devotes the entire next chapter. The ar-gument for it is essentially as follows. First, assertions about the *whole* cosmos need to avoid the fallacy of composition. You cannot draw conclusions about a property of the whole based on a property of its parts. Now, the problem is that there are times when such inferences *are* legitimate, but for that to be the case, two conditions must be met. First, the property must be present in all of the parts. That is evidently true here. Second, the property must be identical in the parts and in the whole. And that, he argues, is not the case here. The kind of "superficial" contingency found in individual things is quite different from the "radical" contingency of the cosmos, radical in the sense not that it could have been otherwise but in the sense that the only other alternative is nothingness.[38] So this option to prove the contingency of the whole fails.

---

[37] Adler, *How to Think About God*, 136-37. The capitalization and italicization are Adler's.
[38] Adler, *How to Think About God*, 141. We discussed this objection earlier in the section on Thomas Aquinas.

That, however, brings Adler to the second option. It is precisely the radical contingency of the universe that implies that it "would not exist at all were its existence not caused."[39] Thus he can conclude:

> A merely possible cosmos cannot be an uncaused cosmos. A cosmos that is radically contingent in its existence, and needs a cause of that existence, needs a supernatural cause—one that exists and acts to exnihilate the merely possible cosmos, thus preventing the realization of what is always possible for a merely possible cosmos; namely, its absolute nonexistence or reduction to nothingness.[40]

This argument is unique in trying to say something about the entire universe. Further, it does so without the step of a justified composition argument. While this all seems unnecessary—neither Aristotle nor Thomas bother with it—it would be helpful in yielding a fuller conclusion, that is, a more complete definition of God. It does, however, invite the criticism that we simply do not know enough about the whole universe to make such a claim of radical contingency. Nevertheless, contemporary physicists certainly agree: if the universe, or multiverse, emerges from a big bang out of nothing, then it is a radically contingent event, and we can legitimately say something about the whole universe.[41]

2.1.5.3 Robert Koons. There have been many restatements or modified, updated versions of the contingency argument in recent years. I will select one from one of the best philosophers to enter the discussion. Robert Koons (b. 1957) is a professor at the University of Texas. In 1997 he published his "A New Look at the Cosmological Argument" in one of the leading journals, the *American*

---

[39] Adler, *How to Think About God*, 144.

[40] Adler, *How to Think About God*, 144.

[41] There is an important difference between "the whole universe"—that is, the set of all events or things that make up the universe—and "the universe-as-a-whole"—that is, the universe itself taken as a single event or thing. Aristotle, Thomas, and Adler clearly mean this to refer to the former. Whether we can say something about the latter is a difficult question, but one we do not need to answer here.

Philosophical Quarterly.[42] Here is the argument itself, where C refers to the cosmos:

1. All the parts of a necessary fact are themselves necessary.

2. Every contingent fact has a wholly contingent part.

3. If there are any contingent facts, C is a wholly contingent fact.

4. If there are any contingent facts, C has a cause.

5. Every contingent fact overlaps C.

6. Therefore: If there are any contingent facts, then C has a cause that is a necessary fact.[43]

This argument bypasses several traditional objections. It treats the universe, or cosmos, as itself a contingent fact among others and so is not susceptible to composition issues. The argument itself does not provide any reasons for identifying God as the conclusion, but Koons handles this in further discussion, just as Thomas does. So he shows that God cannot be in space and time, be physical or constituted by physical parts, and must have only immeasurable attributes.[44] It also makes use of, and Koons provides an introduction to, modal logic, especially in premises (1) and (2). Finally, as stated, it has no need of an infinite regress defeater.[45]

There are, of course, possible objections, but Koons spends the bulk of the article deflating them. The obvious one is his use of a principle of universal causality in premise (4). He notes that this is justified by the fact that every "success of common sense and science for reconstructing the causal antecedents of particular events and classes of events provides confirmation."[46] And further, any attempt to deny it

---

[42]Robert Koons, "A New Look at the Cosmological Argument," *American Philosophical Quarterly* 34, no. 2 (1997): 191-211.

[43]Koons, "A New Look," 198-99. I have changed the premise numbering to fit my context here.

[44]See Koons, "A New Look," 200.

[45]This and issues of composition and of necessary existence are discussed in Koons, "A New Look," 204.

[46]Koons, "A New Look," 196.

would entail radical skepticism.[47] In any case, the argument in the Aristotelian/Thomistic tradition really does not need this, except as a way of making the argument speak to the whole universe.

Further Reading

For more on the recent history of the Society of Christian Philosophers and the Evangelical Philosophical Society see the lead articles in *Philosophia Christi* 21, no. 1 (2019).

There are many more current restatements of the Thomistic form of the argument. Here are a few you might consider: Michael Almeida, *Cosmological Arguments* (Cambridge: Cambridge University Press, 2018); Brian Davies, *The Reality of God and the Problem of Evil* (London: Continuum, 2006), chap. 2; Stephen T. Davis, *God, Reason and Theistic Proofs* (Grand Rapids, MI: Eerdmans, 1997), chap. 4; Edward Feser, *Five Proofs of the Existence of God* (San Francisco: Ignatius, 2017), chap. 1 (on Aristotle's argument), chap. 4 (on Thomas's); Bernard Katz and Elmar Kremer, "The Cosmological Argument Without the Principle of Sufficient Reason," *Faith and Philosophy* 14, no. 1 (1997): 62-70; Robert Koons, "A New Look at the Cosmological Argument," *American Philosophical Quarterly* 34, no. 2 (1997): 191-211; Norman Kretzmann, *The Metaphysics of Theism* (Oxford: Clarendon, 1997); H. G. Hubbeling, "A Modern Reconstruction of the Cosmological Argument," *Communication and Cognition* 15, no. 2 (1982): 165-71; Brian Leftow, *God and Necessity* (Oxford: Oxford University Press, 2012); Barry Miller, *From Existence to God: A Contemporary Philosophical Argument* (London: Routledge, 1992); Timothy O'Connor, *Theism and Ultimate Explanation: The Necessary Shape of Contingency* (London: Wiley-Blackwell, 2008); Alexander Pruss, *Infinity, Causation, and Paradox* (Oxford: Oxford University Press, 2018); Michael Rota, *Taking Pascal's Wager: Faith, Evidence and the Abundant Life* (Downers Grove, IL: IVP Academic, 2016), chap. 5; John Shepherd, *Experience, Inference and God* (London: Macmillan, 1975).

On Koons's argument, see also his "Epistemological Foundations for the Cosmological Argument," in *Oxford Studies in the Philosophy of Religion*, ed. Jonathan L. Kvanvig (Oxford: Oxford University Press, 2008), 105-33.

For much more on the history of philosophy of religion and the arguments in the twentieth century see Alan Sell, *The Philosophy of Religion 1875-1980* (Bristol, England: Thoemmes Press, 1996).

---

[47]Koons, "A New Look," 197.

2.1.5.4 Michael Martin. Michael Martin (1932–2015) held a PhD from Harvard and taught for many years at Boston University. He was certainly one of the most thoughtful and careful advocates of atheism in the past fifty years. His 1990 book, *Atheism*, is a detailed study of each of the theistic arguments, but it also advances a strong positive argument for atheism, which, it turns out, is an argument about the problem of evil. It is virtually encyclopedic in its coverage of objections to the arguments, and hence it is a very valuable resource in general, as well as to us.

His discussion of the cosmological argument comes in three sections. The first includes general objections to the simple Aristotelian/Thomistic argument. He then discusses some specific issues that pertain only to Thomas's second and third way and concludes with other specific problems in a few current versions.

Martin claims that his objections to the simple form defeat virtually all of the versions of the argument. I will therefore be content to look only at them, since he appears to allow (twice in this short section below!) that aside from these objections the argument may just be successful.

> Perhaps the major problem with this version of the argument is that even if it is successful in demonstrating a first cause, this first cause is not necessarily God. A first cause need not have the properties usually associated with God. For example, a first cause need not have great, let alone infinite, knowledge or goodness. A first cause could be an evil being or the universe itself. In itself this problem makes the argument quite useless as support for the view that God exists. However, it has at least one other equally serious problem.
>
> The argument assumes that there cannot be an infinite sequence of causes, but it is unclear why this should be so. Experience does not reveal causal sequences that have a first cause, a cause that is not caused. So the idea that there can be no infinite sequences and that there must be a first cause, a cause without a cause, finds no support in experience.

Further, we have no experience of infinite causal sequences, but we do know that there are infinite series, such as natural numbers. One wonders why, if there can be infinite sequences in mathematics, there could not be one in causality. No doubt there are crucial differences between causal and mathematical series; but without further arguments showing precisely what these are, there is no reason to think that there could not be an infinite regression of causes. Some recent defenders of the cosmological argument have offered just such arguments, and I examine these arguments later. But even if they are successful, in themselves they do not show that the first cause is God.[48]

We have seen these two objections before. The primary one, that a first cause is not God, has seen answers ever since Aristotle, and extensively in Thomas. The second, that infinite regresses are not only possible but actually occur, also is answered in Aristotle. In fact, it really just is the main point of the cosmological argument itself. Of course there are infinite regresses,[49] but an infinite sequence of actual causal contingents could not provide an effect. As Aristotle argues, there would only be intermediate causes, even if an infinity of them, but no initial and originating cause to produce any final effect.

Further Reading

For other critiques of the argument see Peter Angeles, *The Problem of God* (Columbus, OH: Charles, 1974); Robin Le Poidevin, *Arguing for Atheism* (New York: Routledge, 1996); Graham Oppy, *Arguing About Gods* (Cambridge: Cambridge University Press, 2006).

---

[48]Michael Martin, *Atheism: A Philosophical Justification* (Philadelphia: Temple University Press, 1990), 97.

[49]What is notable here, and Martin himself notes it, is that the known infinite regresses occur only in mathematics. As he admits, we have no experience of actual-world infinite regresses. However, the point here is that the argument does not refer simply to infinite regresses but to infinite regresses of causal contingents. We will look at this point more extensively in the discussion of the kalam form of this argument.

2.2 Kalam Arguments

2.2.1 Islamic versions—plus a few others. Aristotle's cosmological argument, as previously noted, presumes the eternality of matter. Hence, there is no need to talk about beginnings, or how, in general, the causality and motion that is the universe got its start. However, as the argument entered Jewish and Christian and, later, Islamic contexts, this appears to have needed modification. The doctrine of *creatio ex nihilo*, precious to all three theologies, demands it.

Following the death of Alexander the Great in 323 BC, the city he founded in Egypt, Alexandria, became the capital of the Arabian portion of his empire, and was soon second only to Rome in importance and population, and it was certainly the primary center of learning and science. It was an amazing confluence of cultures, boasting Hellenistic Greek, Egyptian, Jewish, and Christian schools and population centers.

2.2.1.1 John Philoponus. Within this context, we encounter John Philoponus (AD 490–570), a Christian theologian and scientist.[50] Though he was part of the Alexandrian Peripatetics or Aristotelians, he did not shy away from correcting his master on a few points. In particular he wrote a treatise titled *Against Aristotle on the Eternity of the World*. Here and in other treatises, he provided several arguments against an actual infinite that became standard and were adopted by Islamic philosophers a few hundred years later. They also wished to defend a creationist view of God's causal relation to the universe, as did the Jewish philosopher Maimonides (1135–1204), as well as the Seraphic Doctor, the Christian philosopher and theologian Bonaventure (1221–1274), who was a contemporary of both Thomas Aquinas and Roger Bacon.

2.2.1.2 Simplicius. The relevant section of *Against Aristotle*, identified as fragment 132, we know only from Philoponus's great

---

[50]As a scientist, Philoponus is best known for developing, again contrary to Aristotle, the contemporary theory of impetus.

Alexandrian antagonist Simplicius (490–560).[51] Simplicius himself was a Hellenistic Greek from Cilicia, who became one of the very last members of Plato's Academy in Athens.[52] What follows is actually Simplicius's reproduction of the Philoponus passage (which he refers to as "rotten chatter"), in the context of commenting on, and defending, Aristotle on the eternity of the world.[53] We should note that 132 is merely Philoponus's summary. He spends the entire book refuting Aristotle's arguments for, and elaborating his own arguments against eternality, but here is the summary:

> For this proof [Philoponus] assumes three axioms beforehand: one axiom is that if in order to be generated, each of the things generated necessarily needs something which pre-exists . . . then it will not be generated if those things have not been generated before. The second axiom is that it is impossible for an infinite number to exist in actuality, or for anyone to traverse the infinite in counting, and that it is also impossible that anything should be greater than the infinite, or that the infinite should be increased. The third one is: If it were necessary for the generation of something that an infinite set of things should pre-exist, one generated out of another, then it would be impossible for that thing to be generated.[54]

We can summarize these three axioms—the second is itself really three—as two arguments against an eternal past: First, there cannot be an actual (that is real-world) infinite. Second, an actual infinite cannot be generated by finite increments: it cannot be reached or exceeded by incremental addition. These became the standard arguments used by Christian, Jewish, and Islamic philosophers to defeat

---

[51]This is true of many ancient and early medieval philosophers' writings. We are greatly indebted to Simplicius for much of our knowledge of these texts. While he is an opponent of Philoponus, his reporting of positions and quotations is generally regarded as accurate.

[52]Emperor Justinian closed it in 529, forcing him to move to Persia.

[53]In his *On Aristotle Physics*.

[54]Philoponus, *Against Aristotle on the Eternity of the World*, trans. Christian Wildberg (Ithaca, NY: Cornell University Press, 1987), 144. The actual text of Philoponus' work is lost. This is a reconstruction based on quotes and references in other authors, principally Simplicius, and others, including al-Farabi, who wrote a treatise titled *Against Philoponus*.

the proposition that the world's past is eternal, and hence that it must have been created in a finite past by some actual existent and that, therefore, there must be an uncaused cause, and that this has the characteristics entitling us to identify it as God. That is the kalam cosmological argument.

One point we should clarify right from the start, and it will apply repeatedly throughout this whole discussion of the kalam. It is this: Would not a denial of an actual infinite also have reference to God? Is he not an actual infinite? The difference is that God is an actual *infinite being*. As we saw in the discussion of Thomas, God, as concluded from the cosmological argument, cannot have parts. He is not an infinite composition of anything. The universe, however, if it were infinite, would be an infinity of finites. That is, it would be an actual *infinite compound* of finite contingent things or events, not a simple actual infinite. So it is an entirely different question being asked in the kalam as to whether there can be an actual infinite.

2.2.1.3 Al-Kindi. The earliest example of the full kalam argument appears to come from Abu Yūsuf Yaʿqūb ibn 'Isḥāq aṣ-ṣabbāḥ al-Kindī, commonly known simply as al-Kindi (801–873). The debates in early Islam—al-Kindi lived, after all, only two hundred years after Muhammad—were quite similar to those among the church fathers within the first several hundred years of Christianity. Whenever there is a claimed revelation from God, one has to ask how its content should relate to the conclusions of human reason. It is not surprising that philosophical argument, especially in relation to the existence of God, has hard going in both contexts, not only to begin with, but continuing right up to the present.

Al-Kindi taught in Baghdad, which, under caliphs friendly to science and philosophy, had become the center of Islamic learning and was a lively academic community that also involved Christians, Jews, and Hellenistic Greeks. Al-Kindi was responsible for the translation of many Greek scientific and philosophical works into Arabic, including much of Aristotle.

His great work is *On First Philosophy*. What we get here is a largely Aristotelian metaphysics, modified by Philoponus's arguments against an actual infinity of motion, which produces a temporal cosmological argument. He begins with the argument against an actual infinite, much like what had been handed down from Philoponus. He provides several such arguments, the final and most succinct of which follows.

> Let us now explain in another way that it is not possible for time to have infinity in actuality, either in the past or future. We say:
>
> Before every temporal segment there is another segment, until we reach a temporal segment before which there is no segment, i.e., a segmented duration before which there is no segmented duration. It cannot be otherwise—if it were possible, and after every segment of time there was a segment, infinitely, then we would never reach a given time—for the duration from past infinity to this given time would be equal to the duration from this given time regressing in times to infinity; and if the duration from infinity to a definite time was known, then the duration from this known time to temporal infinity would be known, and then the infinite is finite, and this is an impossible contradiction.[55]

Now he can proceed with the main argument.

> As it has now been explained that the association is caused, the cause must be either from itself, or the association will have another cause other than itself, outside of and separate from it. If the cause of its association were from itself, then it would be part of it, and that part would be prior to the rest.
>
> Nothing remains, therefore, other than their association have another cause, other than themselves, more illustrious, more noble and prior to them, since in essence the cause precedes the effect, as we have mentioned previously in the writings in which we have spoken of the separation (of cause and effect). This cause is not associated with them, for,

---

[55] Alfred Ivry, trans., *Al-Kindī's Metaphysics: A Translation of Ya'qub ibn Isḥāq al-Kindī's Treatise "On First Philosophy" (fī al-Falsafah al-Ūlā)* (Albany: State University of New York Press, 1974), 74.

as we have stated previously, being associated requires, in the associated things, a cause outside of the associated things. If this were the case, however, causes would go on indefinitely, and an infinity of causes is impossible, as we stated previously, since it is not possible for there to be an actual thing having infinity.

It has thus been explained that all things have a first cause, which does not have their genus, and has no resemblance nor likeness nor association with them. It is, rather, superior, more noble and prior to them, being the cause of their generation and perdurance.[56]

From this argument we can then draw certain conclusions as to the identity of this first cause.

As the cause of coming to be is the True One, the First, so the cause of creation is the True One, the First; and it is the cause from which there is a beginning of motion, i.e., that which sets in motion the beginning of motion; meaning that "that which sets in motion" is the agent. As the True One, the First, is the cause of the beginning of the motion of coming to be, i.e., of the affection, it is the creator of all that comes to be. As there is no being except through the unity in things, and their unification is their coming to be, the maintenance of all being due to its unity, if (things which come to be) departed from the unity, they would revert and perish, together with the departure (of the unity), in no time. The True One is therefore the First, the Creator who holds everything He has created, and whatever is freed from His hold and power reverts and perishes.[57]

This now completes the transformation of Aristotle's contingency argument, which presumes the eternality of matter, into a temporal creation argument suitable to Muslims, Christians, and Jews. The primary difference is that the closure argument against an infinite regress has become a demonstration that there cannot be an actual infinite. This is based on the conclusion that a process of cause-effect

---

[56]Al-Kindi, *On First Philosophy*, 93-95.
[57]Al-Kindi, *On First Philosophy*, 114.

that traverses infinite time would amount to an actually infinite substance, or, as we might now say, it would have to encompass an infinite space-time universe.

2.2.1.4 Al-Farabi and Saadia Ben Joseph. The kalam argument became the standard for Islamic and Jewish thinkers. We find it in Al-Farabi (872–951)[58] and in the great Jewish scholar Saadia Ben Joseph (882–942),[59] both of whom were also part of the Baghdad circle. Rabbi Sa'adiah ben Yosef Gaon—his proper full name—was an important part of this scholarly community. He translated the Jewish Scriptures into Arabic and, in 933, completed the first systematic philosophical theology of Judaism, titled *Book of the Articles of Faith and Doctrines of Dogma.*

His version of the kalam begins with an adaptation of Zeno's paradoxes and argues that one cannot traverse an infinite time and so we could never have arrived at the present. This is, of course, absurd, and therefore time must be finite, and must have a beginning. Then, he concludes, since existence cannot come from nothing, there must be a creator: God.[60]

2.2.1.5 Al-Ghazali. Among the Islamic philosophers, it is the Persian Sunni scholar Abu Hamid Muhammad al-Ghazali (1058–1111) who will oppose al-Kindi's whole project of metaphysics. In general, he is an opponent of philosophy, and of Aristotle in particular, since he does not think that human reason can attain the full truth, or a complete metaphysics. There are, however, some things our logic can grasp on its own, and among them is the simple argument against the eternality of the world that leads to its Creator. Here is his brief summation of the kalam argument from his *Incoherence of the Philosophers:*

---

[58]The argument can be found in several places but most accessibly in Al-Farabi, *Philosophy of Plato and Aristotle.*

[59]See Saadia Gaon, *The Book of Beliefs and Opinions*, trans. Samuel Rosenblatt (New Haven, CT: Yale University Press, 1948).

[60]Gaon, *The Book of Beliefs and Opinions*, 44-47.

You reject as impossible the procession of a temporal from an eternal being. But you will have to admit its possibility. For there are temporal phenomena in the world. And some other phenomena are the causes of those phenomena. Now it is impossible that one set of temporal phenomena should be caused by another, and that the series should go on *ad infinitum*. No intelligent person can believe such a thing. If it had been possible, you would not have considered it obligatory on your part to introduce the Creator [into your theories], or affirm the Necessary Being in whom all the possible things have their Ground.

So if there is a limit at which the series of temporal phenomena stops, let this limit be called the Eternal.

And this proves how the possibility of the procession of a temporal from an eternal being can be deduced from their fundamental principles.[61]

2.2.1.6 Avicenna and Averroes. There are, however, two important Islamic philosophers who continue the study of Aristotle's original argument. We find it in the notable Persian mathematician, scientist, and philosopher Avicenna (980–1037), or Ibn Sina, often regarded as the father of modern medicine. He, curiously, sees no need to bother with the rejection of an infinite regress, but argues in his *The Proof of the Truthful* that the entire set of contingent things would, in any case, still be contingent, and thus would need a necessary being that exists outside of it as its cause.[62] He does, however, think that the necessary being must cause necessarily, and so he rejects the doctrine of a temporal creation *ex nihilo* on logical grounds but also does not think that it is taught by the Qur'an. Thus he adopts a neo-Platonic emanation view.

The Islamic culmination of Aristotle studies comes with Ibn Rushd, whose name is usually Latinized as Averroes (1126–1198). He was an Andalusian thinker who wrote on philosophy, including extensive commentaries on Aristotle, theology, medicine, astronomy, physics, Islamic jurisprudence and law, and linguistics. He was part of another

---

[61]Al-Ghazali, *Tahafut al-Falasifah* (original 1095), trans. Sabih Ahmad Kamali (Lahore: Pakistan Philosophical Congress, 1958), 32.

[62]This is an influence especially on Duns Scotus.

cultural melting pot, this time in Moorish Spain. It included Jewish, Christian, and Islamic thinkers from many fields. Its strategic location meant that many of the Arabic texts and commentaries were now translated into Latin and became part of the European university discussion.

Averroes solved the consistency problem with the Qur'an by positing a two-truth theory. Philosophy gives us the literal metaphysical truth, whereas theology, the language of the Qur'an, is allegory for common people, and the two cannot contradict. So Aristotle's view of eternal matter is not a problem, even though Averroes himself rejected the metaphysical premises of the cosmological argument in favor of two simple observations of order: one is a basic design argument, and the other an argument based on the fine-tuning of the universe. Nevertheless, he was very important in transmitting the argument to the medieval philosophers at Paris. He is also the last of the great Islamic philosophers.

2.2.1.7 Maimonides, Bonaventure, and Thomas Aquinas. Crucially, however, Averroes transmits the Aristotelian argument to the Jewish philosopher Maimonides (1135–1204), who gives the argument in book 2 of his *Guide for the Perplexed.* He also influences the Christian theologian Bonaventure (1221–1274), who gives the argument in his *Commentary on the Sentences.*[63] It is from him that Thomas Aquinas at Paris acquires his knowledge of the cosmological argument. He accepts much from Avicenna, but is also heavily dependent on Averroes's commentaries.

Thomas here proves himself also to be a loyal student of Aristotle and rejects the argument against the possibility of an eternal world. He argues that we know of creation-in-time only on the basis of Scripture, not just Genesis 1, but especially Hebrews 11:3: "By faith we understand that the universe was formed at God's command, so that what is seen was not made out of what was visible." He takes this to confirm his position that there are no logical or philosophical arguments to be

---

[63]See Bonaventure, *Sentences* II, D.1, 1, 1, 2.

made against an actual infinite; we know it only on the basis of an authenticated revelation from the Creator.

His specific counterargument can be found in several places, but most extensively in the *Summa contra Gentiles*. His argument is that neither eternality nor noneternality of contingent things can be proved by philosophical argument.

Article 1

I answer that, Nothing except God can be eternal. . . .

Objection 5. Further, it is certain that nothing can be equal to God. But if the world had always been, it would be equal to God in duration. Therefore it is certain that the world did not always exist.

Reply to Objection 5. Even supposing that the world always was, it would not be equal to God in eternity . . . because the divine Being is all being simultaneously without succession; but with the world it is otherwise.

Article 2

I answer that, By faith alone do we hold, and by no demonstration can it be proved, that the world did not always exist. . . . But the divine will can be manifested by revelation, on which faith rests. Hence that the world began to exist is an object of faith, but not of demonstration or science. . . .

Objection 2. Further, if it is necessary to say that the world was made by God, it must therefore have been made from nothing or from something. But it was not made from something; otherwise the matter of the world would have preceded the world. . . .

Objection 6. Further, if the world always was, the consequence is that infinite days preceded this present day. But it is impossible to pass through an infinite medium. Therefore we should never have arrived at this present day; which is manifestly false.

Reply to Objection 2. Those who would say that the world was eternal, would say that the world was made by God from nothing, not that it was made after nothing. . . .

Reply to Objection 6. Passage is always understood as being from term to term. Whatever bygone day we choose, from it to the present day there is a finite number of days which can be passed through. The objection is founded on the idea that, given two extremes, there is an infinite number of mean terms.[64]

The essential point of Thomas's argument is that only God is eternal in the sense that his existence is infinite and thus its duration is not segmented in temporal sequences. The world, on the other hand, is a finite collection of finites, so if there were an infinite succession of them, their existence would always be contingent on God. Hence the world by itself could not be eternal in the strict sense, but it could be without beginning or end. That it is not without beginning we know only from Scripture. The discussion of this point continues into the present, and we will revisit it later.

2.2.1.8 Hamza Tzortzis. Islamic philosophers today continue to use the kalam argument. One current example is Hamza Tzortzis in his *The Divine Reality*.[65] While he refers to it as the Qur'an's argument, since it is based on the options given at 52:35-36, he is clear that this is an argument available to human reasoning quite apart from the Qur'an:

(1) The universe is finite.

(2) Finite things could have come from nothing, created themselves, been ultimately created by something created, or been created by something uncreated.

(3) They could not have come from nothing, created themselves, or have been ultimately created by something created.

(4) Therefore, they were created by something uncreated.[66]

---

[64] Aquinas, *Summa contra Gentiles* 1.46.1-2. Note his point in art. 2 that knowing by faith is knowing from Scripture. Further, there is an apologetic to be given for the divine revelation in Scripture. This is the standard meaning of "knowing by faith" up to recent times, when it has taken on the meaning of blind acceptance.

[65] Hamza Tzortzis, *The Divine Reality: God, Islam and the Mirage of Atheism* (San Clemente: FB Publishing, 2016).

[66] Tzortzis, *The Divine Reality*, 78.

Now this argument retains the standard tradition stemming from al-Kindi of eliminating options to the conclusion of an uncaused cause. It is a temporal argument directed to prove creation *ex nihilo*, and so it depends on a premise that denies the possibility of an actual infinite universe. The subargument for (1) is one of the standard ones we have seen ever since Philoponus: "The universe is real. It is made up of discrete physical things. Since the differentiated infinite cannot exist in the real world, it follows that the universe cannot be infinite. This implies that the universe is finite, and since it is finite it must have had a beginning."[67] The real weight of the argument, then, is to eliminate the first three possible explanations, leaving the fourth as the best explanation. So could it come from nothing?

> For something to arise from nothing it must have at least some type of potential or causal conditions. Since nothing is the absence of all things, including any type of causal condition, then something could not arise from nothing. . . .
>
> A common contention to this argument is that the universe could come from nothing because in the quantum vacuum particles pop into existence. This contention assumes that the quantum vacuum is nothing. However, this is not true. The quantum vacuum is *something*; it is not an absolute void and it obeys the laws of physics. The quantum vacuum is a state of fleeting energy. So it is not nothing, it is something physical.[68]

Could it have caused its own existence? This of course is contradictory: it would have to exist and not exist at the same point in time. Was it created by something itself caused? That just continues the argument's regress and leaves the initial question unanswered. Therefore, we have to conclude, Tzortzis argues, that the universe was ultimately created, in time and *ex nihilo*, by an uncreated. He continues this argument to show, along standard lines, that if uncreated, the cause of the

---

[67]Tzortzis, *The Divine Reality*, 80.
[68]Tzortzis, *The Divine Reality*, 81.

universe must be eternal, transcendent, knowing, powerful, and possessing of will.

Further Reading

For starters I recommend Frederick Copleston's overview of Islamic and Jewish philosophy in part four in volume two of his *A History of Philosophy* (London: A&C Black, 2003). This is especially valuable on the interaction of Islamic, Jewish, and Christian philosophers.

A bit more in depth, but more limited in scope, is part 1 of William Lane Craig's *The Kalam Cosmological Argument* (New York: Macmillan, 1979). He focuses on al-Kindi, Saadia (the Jewish philosopher), and al-Ghazali.

A thorough treatment of Islamic philosophy is Peter Adamson, *Philosophy in the Islamic World: A History of Philosophy Without Any Gaps* (Oxford: Oxford University Press, 2016).

You can also check the relevant articles in Brill's online *Encyclopedia of Islam*, ed. P. Bearman, Th. Bianquis, C. E. Bosworth, E. van Donzel, and W. P. Heinrichs, 2nd ed. (Leiden: Brill, 2012), https://referenceworks.brillonline.com /browse/encyclopaedia-of-islam-2.

An extensive bibliography on the kalam can be found in William Lane Craig and James Sinclair, "The Kalam Cosmological Argument," in *The Blackwell Companion to Natural Theology*, ed. William Lane Craig and J. P. Moreland (Chichester, UK: Wiley-Blackwell, 2009).

For more advanced discussions of Philoponus, see the excellent volume edited by Richard Sorabji, *Philoponus and the Rejection of Aristotelian Science* (Ithaca, NY: Cornell University Press, 1987). I suggest especially his own chapter, "Infinity and the Creation."

For Simplicius's response to Philoponus see Simplicius, *On Aristotle Physics* 8.1-5, trans. Istvan Bodnar, Michael Chase, and Michael Share (London: Bloomsbury Academic, 2012).

For the full text and extensive commentary of al-Kindi's *On First Philosophy*, see Alfred Ivry, *Al-Kindī's Metaphysics: A Translation of Ya'qub ibn Isḥāq al-Kindī's Treatise "On First Philosophy" (fīal-Falsafah al-Ūlā)* (Albany: State University of New York Press, 1974).

For more on al-Farabi see *Alfarabi's Philosophy of Plato and Aristotle*, trans. with an introduction by Muhsin Mahdi (Ithaca, NY: Cornell University Press, 2001).

On Saadia see Gyongyi Hegedeus, *Saadya Gaon: The Double Path of the Mystic and Rationalist* (Leiden: Brill, 2013). A good overview of Saadia is William Bacher, "Saadia B. Joseph (Saʿid al-Fayyumi)," *Jewish Encyclopedia*, http://www.jewishencyclopedia.com/articles/12953-saadia-b-joseph-sa-id-al-fayyumi.

For more on Avicenna and his argument see Peter Adamson, "From the Necessary Existent to God," in *Interpreting Avicenna: Critical Essays*, ed. Peter Adamson (Cambridge: Cambridge University Press, 2013), 170-89.

2.2.2 William Lane Craig. Certainly, no one has been more influential in reviving the kalam argument in recent days than William Lane Craig (b. 1949). It has been his repeated concern in numerous publications ever since his dissertation at the University of Birmingham in 1977 under John Hick, which was published as *The Kalam Cosmological Argument* in 1979.[69] His interest in the argument was sparked by Stuart Hackett's seminal use of the kalam in his 1957 book *The Resurrection of Theism*.[70]

Craig's concise statement of the argument is simply this:

1. Everything that begins to exist has a cause of its existence.

2. The universe began to exist.

3. Therefore the universe has a cause of its existence.[71]

The argument for the first premise takes up only a few pages. It requires little defense because he thinks it to be intuitively obvious that something cannot begin to exist from nothing, which seems to be the only other alternative. Nothing comes from nothing!

He does, however, briefly defend it in two ways: First is the argument from empirical facts. "Constantly verified and never falsified, the causal proposition may be taken as an empirical generalization, enjoying the

[69]William Lane Craig, *The Kalam Cosmological Argument* (New York: Macmillan, 1979).
[70]Stuart Hackett, *The Resurrection of Theism* (Chicago: Moody Press, 1957). This book has been reprinted several times, including by Wipf & Stock in 2009.
[71]Hackett, *Resurrection of Theism*, 63.

strongest support experience affords."[72] Second, he formulates an argument based on the a priori nature of the category of causality—that is, that "we do possess speculative knowledge of the categories; therefore they cannot be restricted to the realm of sense experience."[73] Our intentional self-conscious thought about the world could not occur without them.

The second premise is a different matter. Its defense takes up more than a third of the book. It consists, however, of two philosophical arguments we have seen before: the argument for the impossibility of an actual infinite and the argument for the impossibility of forming an actual infinite by successive addition. Both of these arguments depend on the critical distinction between mathematical or potential infinites (especially as defined by the great German mathematician Georg Cantor) that have conceptual existence, and real-world or actual infinites that (if they did exist) really exist in this actual world.[74]

The first philosophical argument rests on the absurdity of an actual infinite: "What I shall argue is that while the actual infinite may be a fruitful and consistent concept in the mathematical realm, it cannot be translated from the mathematical world into the real world, for this would involve counter-intuitive absurdities."[75] Craig uses a number of traditional illustrations here, but the most frequent in his publications has been "Hilbert's Hotel," first used by David Hilbert, the great German mathematician of the late nineteenth and early twentieth centuries. Imagine, he says, a hotel with infinite rooms, all of them occupied. When a new prospective guest arrives the proprietor gladly welcomes him and places him in room one, which is now vacant since he has moved the guest in room one to room two, then the one in room one to room three, and so on, till all infinite guests are moved. Next, suppose

---

[72]Hackett, *Resurrection of Theism*, 145.
[73]Hackett, *Resurrection of Theism*, 146.
[74]See here Craig's discussion on *Kalam Cosmological Argument*, 65-69.
[75]Craig, *Kalam Cosmological Argument*, 69.

an infinite number of new guests arrive. The proprietor now moves the guest in room one to room two, that in room two to room four, that in room three to room six, and so on, so that the infinite present guests are now occupying the infinity of even-numbered rooms. He can now move the infinite new arrivals into the infinity of now vacant odd-numbered rooms, and all is well.[76]

Now the real problem seems to be that this situation violates a cardinal rule of arithmetic. That is, that the same calculation carried out with the same numbers must always yield the same result. But here it does not work out right. In the first scenario, infinity minus infinity equals 1. However, in the second, infinity minus infinity equals infinity.

This is mind-bendingly counterintuitive. In the real world, if all the rooms are occupied, no moving around of guests will open up a room. But mathematically all of the movements in the story are perfectly sensible, given the properties of infinity. From this and other similar illustrations, Craig concludes, as did Hilbert, that an actual infinite cannot exist in reality.[77] We can conceptualize a hotel with infinite rooms, but we cannot build one.

The second philosophical argument shows that an actual infinite could not be formed by successive addition. Why is this?

> The reason is that for every element one adds one can always add one more. Therefore, one can never arrive at infinity. What one constructs is a potential infinite only, an indefinite collection that grows and grows as each new element is added. Another way of seeing the point is by recalling that $\aleph_0$ [the number of elements in the infinite natural number series] has no immediate predecessor. Therefore one can never reach $\aleph_0$ by successive addition or counting, since this would involve passing through an immediate predecessor to $\aleph_0$. *Notice that the argument has nothing to do with any time factor.* Sometimes it is wrongly

---

[76]See Craig, *Kalam Cosmological Argument*, 84. The illustration was first introduced by Hilbert in a 1924 lecture "Über das Unendliche" (On the infinite), and was popularized in George Gamow's 1947 book *One Two Three . . . Infinity* (London: Macmillan, 1946).

[77]Craig, *Kalam Cosmological Argument*, 87.

alleged that the reason an actual infinite cannot be formed by successive addition is because there is not enough time. But this is wholly beside the point. Regardless of the time involved, an actual infinite cannot be completed by successive addition due to the very nature of the actual infinite itself. No many how many elements one has added, one can always add one more. A potential infinite cannot be turned into an actual infinite by any amount of successive addition; they are conceptually distinct.[78]

Craig adds to this two empirical scientific confirmations. The first is the expansion of the universe as measured by Hubble in 1929, and the resulting big bang models beginning in 1965. The second is the laws of thermodynamics. Both are scientific evidence, he argues, that there is an absolute beginning of the universe—that is, that it has had a finite duration in time.[79]

Rejoinders to Craig's argument, almost without exception, have been assertions regarding mathematical possibilities and/or impossibilities. Almost invariably there has been the same response: mathematical, conceptual, or potentiality arguments are meaningless here in relation to actual real-world metaphysics. We will look at one recent example.

2.2.3 James East. There are, of course, many current objections brought against this argument from all sides.[80] Most have to do with the argument against an actual infinite, the roots of which go all the way back to Philoponus and Simplicius. James East (b. 1980), a mathematician presently at Western Sydney University, has argued that Craig's reasoning holds for finite numbers but has no application to transfinite and infinite numbers. Here is his argument, starting with the conclusion.

---

[78]Craig, *Kalam Cosmological Argument*, 104.

[79]See Craig's conclusions in *Kalam Cosmological Argument*, 137-40, for more detail.

[80]A thorough discussion of both sides of the debate can be found in William Lane Craig and Quentin Smith, *Theism, Atheism, and Big Bang Cosmology* (Oxford: Clarendon, 1993).

If actual infinite collections were to exist, then they would naturally have properties that were not shared by finite collections. For one obvious example if one attempted to count through an actual infinite collection at a constant pace, then one would never finish (and this is also the case with potential infinite collections, such as a future eternity of discrete days). The story of Hilbert's Hotel simply highlights another such property that distinguishes actual infinite collections from finite ones: just knowing that an infinite subcollection has been removed from an infinite collection of objects does not allow one to determine how many objects remain. But this property itself does not entail that actual infinite collections are impossible.[81]

East's point is that in finite collections the normal rules or theorems of addition and subtraction are obeyed. But in Craig's Hilbert's Hotel example, two identical subtraction operations yield two different results. From this anomaly Craig concludes that actual infinites are absurd. But what he should have concluded, East argues, is simply that the theorems only apply to finite numbers and have no application to transfinites. So, Craig is not entitled to any conclusion at all about actual infinites based on examples like Hilbert's Hotel.

2.2.4 Andrew Loke. Among current defenders of the kalam argument is Andrew Ter Ern Loke (b. 1975), presently at Hong Kong Baptist University. In his *God and Ultimate Origins*, he argues for a novel cosmological argument, but still in the kalam tradition, and responds to several critics, including James East.[82] He proposes an argument that has all the advantages of both the Thomistic argument and the kalam, but one that avoids the possible pitfalls of both. First, his "novel" argument:

(1) There exist entities that: (i) are members of a temporal causal series; and (ii) begin to exist.

---

[81]James East, "Infinity Minus Infinity," *Faith and Philosophy* 30, no. 4 (2013): 433.
[82]Andrew Loke, *God and Ultimate Origins: A Novel Cosmological Argument* (Cham, Switzerland: Springer Nature, 2017).

(2) Everything that begins to exist has a cause.

(3) If there is an entity that: (i) is a member of a temporal causal series; and (ii) begins to exist, then there is an uncaused entity X.

(4) There exists an X which is uncaused and beginningless (From 1, 2, and 3).

(5) If X is uncaused and beginningless, nothing exists prior to it, and therefore it is a First Cause.

(6) X is a First Cause (From 4 and 5).[83]

This argument is intended to be a kalam argument in the sense that it is about tracing events back in time in order to conclude to a cause of the first-in-time. It is Thomistic in that its closure depends on denying an infinite regress, though a temporal one, rather than an actual infinite. Now he does agree with Craig's two-pronged denial of actual infinites and in fact defends this approach against recent objections. In the process, he takes up East's argument and responds to it. This is our primary concern here.

> To begin, the sort of reply East offers by no means proves that concrete actual infinities are possible. It should be noted that what is mathematically possible is not always metaphysically possible. For example, the quadratic equation $x^2 - 4 = 0$ can have two mathematically consistent results for "x": 2 or -2, but if the question is "how many people carried the computer home," the answer cannot be "-2," for in the concrete world it is metaphysically impossible that "-2 people" carried a computer home. Thus the conclusion of "2 people" rather than "-2 people" is not derived from mathematical equations alone, but also from metaphysical considerations: "-2 people" lack the causal powers to carry a computer home. This shows that metaphysical considerations are more fundamental than mathematical considerations.[84]

---

[83]Loke, *God and Ultimate Origins*, 93-94.
[84]Loke, *God and Ultimate Origins*, 55-56. Loke continues this argument giving specific metaphysical considerations against East.

This discussion will, no doubt, continue. Specifically in reference to Loke's argument, can premise (3) above be further defended?[85] Nevertheless, two matters seem clear: First, mathematical or conceptual possibilities have to yield to metaphysical possibilities when it comes to real-world issues. This is not to say that there is no connection between logic and reality. It only implies that the human intellect can conceptualize possibilities, including mathematical ones, that cannot actually exist in the real world—that is, they have no causal efficacy.

Second, nothing in this conversation shows that actual infinites *are* possible. Both East and Loke make that clear. East, in response, says this:

> I broadly agree with everything Loke says here; in particular, my article did not attempt to argue that concrete actual infinities are possible, but rather that one particular argument (of Craig) against their possibility was flawed. I perhaps would say that "-2 people" makes no sense, rather than that "'-2 people' lack the causal powers to carry a computer home." I'd also add that while metaphysical considerations can sometimes help rule out certain mathematical possibilities, this is not always the case; for example, if the number of people who carried the computer home satisfies $x^2 - 3x + 2 = 0$, then both mathematical possibilities ($x = 1$ and $x = 2$) are metaphysically possible. But nothing that Loke says here refutes my position that Craig's argument is flawed, and I'm not even sure if Loke is claiming to refute my position. As I explain in my article, Craig's argument rests on an incorrect assumption: that if infinite collections were possible, then the statement "infinitely many objects have been removed from an infinite collection" ought to be enough information to calculate the number of remaining objects.[86]

Loke responded by reemphasizing his main point.

> In reply, the reason why $x = 1$ and $x = 2$ are possible is because these answers are not only mathematically possible but also metaphysically possible; i.e. they do not violate any metaphysically necessary truths,

---

[85]Beyond what Loke does in section 3.4 in *God and Ultimate Origins*.
[86]By permission of the author, personal email correspondence, July 30, 2019.

unlike "-2 people carrying a computer home." My point is that if the answers are metaphysically impossible then that trumps mathematical possibility, and the metaphysical considerations I gave on pages 55-61 show that concrete infinities would violate metaphysically necessary truth and therefore are metaphysically impossible.[87]

I conclude that there are still sufficient grounds to hold that there cannot be an actual infinite, and so the kalam argument, which goes all the way back to Philoponus, seems to stand as a philosophical argument that demands that the universe began with time, and therefore must have a Creator.

2.2.5 Paul Draper. Another important objection to Craig's argument comes from Paul Draper (b. 1957), professor at Purdue University. Draper's objection has it that Craig's argument equivocates on the meaning of "to begin to exist." This can mean, in what Draper calls the narrow sense, that something begins to exist in time, such that at some prior point in time it did not exist. But it can also have the broader meaning of beginning to exist that does not presume a prior time, and may indicate a beginning of time.[88]

Draper then argues that Craig's first premise—"everything that begins to exist has a cause"—uses the former, while his second premise—"the universe began to exist"—uses the latter, broader meaning. Thus the argument suffers from equivocation.[89]

Worse yet, it is just unclear how we could support the first premise. Craig, Draper says, considers it an empirical generalization.[90]

> Experience only supports the claim that anything that begins to exist within time has a cause of its existence. For we have no experience

---

[87]By permission of the author, personal email correspondence, October 15, 2019.
[88]Paul Draper, "A Critique of the Kalam Cosmological Argument," in *Philosophy of Religion*, ed. Louis Pojman and Michael Rea, 5th ed. (Belmont, CA: Thompson Wadsworth, 2008), 49. This article was originally published in 1997.
[89]Draper, "A Critique," 49.
[90]Draper, "A Critique," 50.

whatsoever of things beginning to exist with time. Such things would require timeless causes. And even if it is conceptually possible for a temporal event to have a timeless cause, we certainly have no experience of this. Of course, Craig also claims that premise (1) is intuitively obvious—that it needs no defense at all. But it is far from obvious that a universe that begins to exist with time needs a cause of its existence. Like an infinitely old universe that begins to exist with time has always existed—for any time t, the universe existed at t. And once again, it's far from obvious that something that has always existed requires a cause for its existence. It's not even clear that such a thing *could* have a cause of its existence.[91]

So Draper concludes that Craig has not shown that the argument should be dismissed. Perhaps someone could show that a universe that begins with time needs a cause. "It is just that it has not yet been adequately defended. I still wonder whether the argument is a good one."[92]

Craig has responded to this objection in his debate book with Quentin Smith, *Theism, Atheism, and Big Bang Cosmology*. His point is that what comes into existence *with* the beginning of time, is the contingent t1 of the universe, which is just like the contingent t2 and every other contingent event in the universe, and so the only alternative is that something came from nothing. But that something cannot come from nothing is surely a solid metaphysical intuition that is supported by everything we know in science.[93] He adds that only an aversion to theism "would lead the empiricist to think that the denial of the principle is more plausible than the principle itself."[94]

Draper responded that Craig's defense was unconvincing. Clearly "metaphysical intuitions about contingent matters are notoriously

---

[91]Draper, "A Critique," 50.

[92]Draper, "A Critique," 50.

[93]William Lane Craig, "The Caused Beginning of the Universe," in Smith and Craig, *Theism, Atheism, and Big Bang Cosmology*, 147n12. See also Craig's discussion in *Kalam Cosmological Argument*, 141-48.

[94]Craig, "Caused Beginning of the Universe," 147n13.

unreliable—that's why so many contemporary philosophers are, quite justifiably, 'hard-headed empiricists.'"[95]

This is, of course, a largely inductive argument. But it simply does not make metaphysical sense, nor have we ever observed something to come into existence without cause, whether from nothing or from something else. No doubt this is not a mathematical proof, but it is, absent such proofs, as good an argument as we can expect to have.

Further Reading

For a listing of Craig's work on the kalam, both popular and scholarly, see the listings on his website Reasonable Faith, www.reasonablefaith.org/writings, where you can access his full-text responses to many objectors.

Especially valuable in working through objections as well as his responses to objections, you can consult his two books that record debates with atheists: William Lane Craig and Quentin Smith, *Theism, Atheism and Big Bang Cosmology* (Oxford: Clarendon, 1993); and Craig and Walter Sinnott-Armstrong, *God? A Debate Between a Christian and an Atheist* (Oxford: Oxford University Press, 2004). See also Craig and James Sinclair, "The Kalam Cosmological Argument," in *The Blackwell Companion to Natural Theology*, ed. William Lane Craig and J. P. Moreland (Chichester: Wiley-Blackwell, 2009), 101-201. This includes an extensive bibliography on objections and rejoinders, of which there continue to be many.

For an exchange on beginnings see Craig, "Must the Beginning of the Universe Have a Personal Cause? A Rejoinder," *Faith and Philosophy* 19, no. 1 (2002): 94-105, itself a response to Wes Morriston, whose redirect comes then in "Causes and Beginnings in the Kalam Argument: Reply to Craig," *Faith and Philosophy* 19, no. 2 (2002): 233-44.

For a restatement of the kalam argument and a response to the actual-infinites objection see J. P. Moreland, "A Response to a Platonistic and to a Set-Theoretic Objection to the Kalam Cosmological Argument," *Religious Studies* 39 (2003): 373-90.

An interesting comment on the infinite-regress issue is Paul Kabay, "An Infinite Temporal Regress Is Compatible with the Doctrine of *Creatio Originans*," *International Journal for Philosophy of Religion* 57 (2005): 123-38.

---

[95]Draper, "A Critique," 51.

For a discussion of Craig's view of time and his kalam argument see Christopher
   Bobier, "God, Time and the Kalam Cosmological Argument," *Sophia* 52
   (2013): 593-600.

On the matter of uncaused beginnings see G. E. M. Anscombe, "'Whatever Has
   a Beginning of Existence Must Have a Cause': Hume's Argument Exposed,"
   Analysis 34 (1973–1974): 145-51.

For a recent anthology on the kalam argument see Paul Copan and William
   Lane Craig, eds., *The Kalam Cosmological Argument*, vol. 1, *Philosophical
   Arguments for the Finitude of the Past*, and vol. 2, *Scientific Evidence of the
   Beginning of the Universe* (New York: Bloomsbury, 2017).

For more on Andrew Loke see his bibliography at the University of Hong
   Kong site: https://www.researchgate.net/scientific-contributions/2121294932
   _Andrew_Ter_Ern_Loke.

For James East's many publications see his Western Sydney University site: https://
   www.westernsydney.edu.au/staff_profiles/uws_profiles/doctor_james_east.

2.3 Sufficient-Reason Arguments

2.3.1 Samuel Clarke and Gottfried Wilhelm Leibniz. In 1704, Samuel
Clarke (1675–1729) delivered the annual Boyle Lectures in the
Cathedral Church of St. Paul. They were published in 1714 as *The Being
and Attributes of God*, along with the 1705 lectures. These lectures were
intended as a defense of Isaac Newton and in opposition to Thomas
Hobbes and Baruch Spinoza.

In that same year Gottfried Wilhelm von Leibniz (1646–1716) published his *Monadology*, which was a summary version, in brief num-
bered paragraphs, of his overall metaphysics. The argument for God's
existence, much expanded, first appeared in his 1710 *Theodicy*. Following the publication, Clarke and Leibniz engaged in correspondence
during 1715 and until the latter's death in 1716.

Both were attempting to formulate a systematic metaphysics that
would provide a framework for science and a complete understanding
of the universe. In the process they both wanted to demonstrate the
existence of God as the underlying grounding of all science. There

has been much argument as to whose ideas came first, but it is quite likely that both emerged out of the larger discussion about the foundations of science that involved many, maybe most, of Europe's eminent scientists, mathematicians, philosophers, and theologians of the day.

The argument they both produce is certainly recognizable as the cosmological argument, but modified in several ways. First, since they are the basis of a full-blown metaphysics underlying, in turn, a complete physics, they must be arguments about everything. So, unlike the Aristotelian/Thomistic version, they do not begin with specific observations of particular items in the universe, but rather with general propositions about the whole.

Second, they form a deductive system and thus need to proceed by means of a general principle that will allow the argument to move from this first premise to a universal cause that is God. This is the principle of sufficient reason, hereafter simply PSR, hence the designation as sufficient-reason arguments.

Third, this universality in the premises allows for a more expansive conclusion. We no longer need the Parmenidean subarguments to derive a single, all-powerful, all-knowing, and infinite creator. The PSR seems to directly imply it.

This appears to be a great advantage. We move from a simple, generally recognized principle to a moderately, but still well-defined God. Thomas's argument, without a general causal principle like PSR, moves from a series of simple observations to a mere thinly defined "first uncaused cause" by way of a denial of infinite regress. So, while both are effect-to-cause—that is, *cosmological* arguments—they are also very different.

So, first, here is Clarke's version from the 1704 Boyle Lectures: *A Demonstration of the Being and Attributes of God*:

Nothing is, without a sufficient reason why it is, rather than not; and why it is thus, rather than otherwise.[96]

To suppose an infinite succession of changeable and dependent beings produced one from another in an endless progression, without any original cause at all, is only a driving back from one step to another, and (as it were) removing out of sight, the question concerning the ground or reason of the existence of things. It is in reality, and in point of argument, the very same supposition, as it would be to suppose one continued being, of beginningless and endless duration, neither self-existent and necessary in itself, nor having its existence founded in any self-existent cause; which is directly absurd and contradictory.[97]

Now this argument is by itself very basic and the conclusion quite thin. However, it is followed by a lengthy discussion of the necessary properties of such a self-existent being. It includes necessary, incomprehensible, infinite, omnipresent, single, intelligent, free, omnipotent, and infinitely wise, good, just, and true.[98]

Here is Leibniz's argument from the 1714 *Monadology*:

A sufficient reason, however, must also exist for contingent truths or truths of fact, that is, for the series of things comprehended in the universe of creatures. Here the resolution into particular reasons could be continued without limit: for the variety of natural things is immense, and bodies are infinitely divided. There is an infinity of figures and movements, past and present, which contribute to the efficient cause of my presently writing this. And there is an infinity of minute inclinations and dispositions of my soul, which contribute to the final cause of my writing.

Now, all of this detail again implies previous or more particular contingents, each of which again stands in need of a similar analysis to be accounted for, so that nothing is gained by such an analysis. The

---

[96]Samuel Clarke, *A Demonstration of the Being and Attributes of God: And Other Writings*, ed. Ezio Vailati, Cambridge Texts in the History of Philosophy (Cambridge: Cambridge University Press, 1998), sec. 1.

[97]Clarke, *A Demonstration*, sec. 2.

[98]Clarke, *A Demonstration*, secs. 3-10.

sufficient or ultimate reason must therefore exist outside the succession or series of contingent particulars, infinite though this series may be.

Consequently, the ultimate reason of all things must subsist in an infinite substance, in which all particular changes may exist only virtually as in its source: this substance is what we call *God*.

Now, this substance is the sufficient reason for all this particular existence which is, moreover interconnected throughout. Hence there is but one God, and this God suffices.[99]

No doubt these two thinkers had a somewhat differing basis for their PSR. Clarke is more the British empiricist, and Leibniz the German rationalist. That will have some bearing on the critique of PSR, but in the end they both intended it as a universal principle that governs all of physics. It is precisely this universality of PSR that will play an important role in contemporary objections to the argument.

2.3.2 Bertrand Russell and Frederick Copleston. Perhaps the most famous philosophical debate in recent history took place on January 28, 1948, live on the BBC.[100] Bertrand Russell (1872–1970), Third Earl Russell, aristocrat (his grandfather was prime minister under Queen Victoria), social liberal and activist, Nobel laureate to be (1950), Cambridge graduate and don, was a well-known progressive and atheist. His widely used introductory textbook in philosophy, *The Problems of Philosophy*,[101] did not even mention God. Frederick Copleston (1907–1994) was a Jesuit priest, graduate of Oxford, and professor at Heythrop College. Young, but already well established in his philosophical career, he would go on to be most acclaimed for his monumental nine-volume *A History of Philosophy* (1946–1974).

Britain at this point was barely beginning to recover from World War II; its economy was shattered, and all essential goods were still

---

[99]G. W. F. Leibniz, *The Monadology* 36-39, trans. Paul and Anne Schrecker (New York: Bobbs-Merrill, 1965).

[100]A quick Google search will yield numerous recordings of the debate, including on YouTube.

[101]First published in 1912 and reprinted many times through 1956 by Oxford University Press.

rationed. The British people, however, were triumphant and optimistic: a new age was dawning. To the average listener, Russell, the debonair bon vivant (married four times) must have sounded contemporary and in touch. Copleston, the priest, came across as hopelessly antiquated both in his arguments and his language, even though he was actually much younger, and even though most listeners at the time agreed with his conclusions. Russell was so confident that he had won that the debate was later included in his *Why I Am Not a Christian* (originally published in 1927) after 1957.[102]

Copleston began with a standard presentation of Leibniz's argument, and then defended it quite ably. Since I am primarily interested in Russell's objections, that is what follows, leaving out Copleston's remarks in between:

> The best point with which to begin is the question of a Necessary Being. The word "necessary" I should maintain, can only be applied significantly to propositions. And, in fact, only to such as are analytic—that is to say—such as it is self-contradictory to deny. I could only admit a Necessary Being if there were a being whose existence it is self-contradictory to deny.
>
> . . . I don't admit the idea of a Necessary Being and I don't admit that there is any particular meaning in calling other beings "contingent." These phrases don't for me have a significance except within a logic that I reject.

Copleston here supplied a standard definition of contingent being as that "which has not in itself the complete reason for its existence." Russell replied, "'Does the cause of the world exist?' is a question that has meaning. But if you say 'Yes, God is the cause of the world' you're using God as a proper name; then 'God exists' will not be a statement that has meaning; that is the position that I am maintaining." The debate now turned to the issue of how to define "sufficient reason."

---

[102]Bertrand Russell, *Why I Am Not a Christian* (London: George Allen & Unwin, 1957).

So it all turns on this question of sufficient reason, and I must say you haven't defined "sufficient reason" in a way that I can understand—what do you mean by sufficient reason? You don't mean cause?

But when is an explanation adequate? Suppose I am about to make a flame with a match. You may say that the adequate explanation of that is that I rub it on the box.

Then I can only say you're looking for something which can't be got, and which one ought not to expect to get.

Because I see no reason to think there is any. The whole concept of cause is one we derive from our observation of particular things; I see no reason whatsoever to suppose that the total has any cause whatsoever.

I can illustrate what seems to me your fallacy. Every man who exists has a mother, and it seems to me your argument is that therefore the human race must have a mother, but obviously the human race hasn't a mother—that's a different logical sphere.

I think—there seems to me a certain unwarrantable extension here; the physicist looks for causes; that does not necessarily imply that there are causes everywhere. A man may look for gold without assuming that there is gold everywhere; if he finds gold, well and good, if he doesn't he's had bad luck. The same is true when the physicists look for causes. As for Sartre, I don't profess to know what he means, and I shouldn't like to be thought to interpret him, but for my part, I do think the notion of the world having an explanation is a mistake. I don't see why one should expect it to have.

Copleston then concluded the matter by asking if Russell claimed that one cannot even ask the question about the cause of the world. "Yes, that's my position."[103]

Russell had three objections in this part of the debate. There is, first, the matter that the term "necessary" can be applied only to propositions. Therefore, to use it in the metaphysical context of a being is meaningless. Second, Russell can make no sense of the idea of

---

[103]The debate was published in several places including *Bertrand Russell: On God and Religion*, ed. Al Seckel (Amherst, NY: Prometheus, 1986). The text can also be found in many places online, and the broadcast itself is available on YouTube.

"sufficient reason," at least apart from the simple notion of cause. And third, he thinks it is a straightforward fallacy to speak of the universe as a single entity. One cannot, then, ask about the cause of the universe itself, only of particulars.

Now all of these objections had already been answered, including by Aristotle and Thomas, but they were then answered again by John Hick and others.

2.3.3 John Hick. As we have seen, Russell's primary objection to Leibniz, Thomas, and Copleston has to do with the concept of "necessary being." This was a frequent objection, created by the logical positivist view of language in the first half of the twentieth century. It held that there were only two kinds of statements: analytic, that is, statements about the logic of language, and sense-data reports, that is, statements about the facts of my experience or observation. Since, by definition it seems, statements about or referring to God cannot be sense-data reports, they must be logical claims, empty of any reference to the real world. Therefore, claims about God's necessary being must refer to some sort of *logical* necessity. Hence Russell's claim that he simply sees no meaningful claim here.

John Hick (1922–2012), who held the DPhil from Oxford University, argued that there is an obvious way in which necessary being is meant to be factual. In a groundbreaking—well, re-groundbreaking—article in the *Journal of Philosophy*, "God as Necessary Being,"[104] he begins with this distinction:

> Two importantly different concepts may be, and have been, expressed by the phrase "necessary being." "Necessary" usually has the force of "logically necessary," and gives rise in theology to the concept of a being such that it is logically impossible that this being should not exist. But, less

---

[104]John Hick, "God as Necessary Being," *Journal of Philosophy* 57 (1960): 22-23. This paper was read that year at the December meetings of the American Philosophical Association, Eastern Division.

commonly, "necessary" signifies what we may distinguish as "factually necessary"—"empirical," "material," and "causal" necessity being kinds of factual necessity.[105]

Hick continues by developing the concept of logical necessity as seen in a number of philosophers in the 1950s. He shows how this has been held to be the meaning of "necessary being" in Thomas's third way. We have just seen that this is also Russell's understanding of Leibniz's PSR argumentation, and hence his refutation of Copleston's version of Leibniz. But this, he argues, is to misunderstand their use of "necessary" in relation to God's being. They all clearly meant to say, not that God's nonexistence is or would be contradictory, but rather that his being is to be distinguished from contingent being. It is an existence that does not merely happen to exist nor might it cease to exist.

> Eternity is one of the ingredients of the concept of the adequate object of man's worship, but it is not by itself sufficient. For it is possible to conceive of something existing eternally, not because it is such that there is and could be no power capable of abolishing it, but only because, although there are powers capable of abolishing it, they always refrain from doing so. Such a being would be eternal by courtesy of the fact that it is never destroyed, but not by the positive virtue or power of being indestructible. And it is surely integral to the monotheistic concept of God that God, as the ultimate Lord of all, is not capable of being destroyed.
>
> We must add at this point that, as the ultimate Lord of all, God is also incorruptible, in the sense of being incapable of ceasing either to exist or to possess his divine characteristics by reason of a decay or a discerption not due to external factors. God, then, can neither be destroyed from without nor suffer dissolution from within.
>
> Indestructibility and incorruptibility, however, even taken together, cannot replace but must supplement the notion of eternal being. For it is possible to conceive of something being both indestructible and incorruptible and yet not eternal, in the sense of being without beginning or

---

[105]Hick, "God as Necessary Being," 726.

end. Such a being would exist only if created, but once created would be indissoluble and indestructible.

We have arrived thus far, then, at an identification of the necessary being of the Godhead with incorruptible and indestructible being without beginning or end. These properties, however, can be regarded as different aspects of the more fundamental characteristic which the Scholastics termed aseity, or being *a se*. . . .

What may properly be meant, then, by the statement that God is, or has, necessary as distinguished from contingent being is that God is, without beginning or end, and without origin, cause, or ground of any kind whatsoever. He *is*, as the ultimate, unconditioned, absolute, unlimited being.[106]

This is an important clarification that bypasses Russell's objection. He was quite right that the concept of a *logically* necessary being creates difficulties in an argument about the *real* world. And it is true that the medievals often use the term "necessary being." But they mean by it that God is noncontingent—that is, that his real existence has to be described by a different logic from ours—but this is a real metaphysical logic not a conceptual logic. And this is precisely what Hick here clarifies by using the term "factual."

This distinction actually goes back to Kant's *Critique of Pure Reason*.[107] He refers there to factual necessity as material or causal necessity. It is also important to remember this distinction in other contexts of discussion of God. The inappropriateness of logical necessity is often brought as an objection to all forms of the cosmological argument. But Hick's corrective applies.

2.3.4 Bruce Reichenbach. The sufficient-reason argument became the standard form of the cosmological argument in modern philosophy. Both the contingency and the kalam arguments faded from view, at

---

[106]Hick, "God as Necessary Being," 732-34.
[107]Immanuel Kant, *Critique of Pure Reason*, B 184 and 279-80.

least in the general discussion of Western philosophy.[108] However, even the PSR argument received little attention by the early twentieth century. Atheistic and naturalistic philosophy dominated academic circles, and there was simply no room for such metaphysical arguments. Even philosophy of religion textbooks covered the traditional arguments, if at all, merely as a historical oddity that disappeared after Kant's *Critique of Pure Reason* in 1781.

In the 1960s, however, some courageous voices began to resume the discussion. Foremost perhaps was Bruce Reichenbach (b. 1943) of Augsburg College with his 1972 publication of *The Cosmological Argument: A Reassessment*.[109]

Important to the current restatement of the argument is Reichenbach's understanding of PSR itself:

> First of all, it is possible to distinguish two varieties of the principle of sufficient reason. The first form, which is the strong form of the principle . . . namely, that there is a sufficient reason for *all* beings and events. However, we may also note a weaker form of this same principle, namely, a form which states that there is a sufficient reason for all *contingent* beings. This weaker form leaves open the question whether or not there is a sufficient reason for non-contingent beings as well; it simply states that there must be a sufficient reason for all *contingent* beings.[110]

PSR is no longer necessary in the sense of being a universal and a priori principle. It is thus not necessary as a result of the principles of logic. It is, rather, necessary only in virtue of the way things actually are in the world.[111] This is arrived at inductively from our experience of just how the world is for us. So, if Leibniz held to a *strong* form of PSR,

---

[108]Though, of course, Thomas's argument remained alive in some Catholic contexts, and even saw a revived interest in philosophers like Jacques Maritain, Étienne Gilson, and others. And the kalam version was still discussed in some Islamic circles.

[109]Bruce Reichenbach, *The Cosmological Argument: A Reassessment* (Springfield, IL: Charles Thomas, 1972).

[110]Reichenbach, *Cosmological Argument*, 68.

[111]Reichenbach, *Cosmological Argument*, 87-88.

Reichenbach holds to a *weak* form. He argues that it is only this form of PSR that is needed for the cosmological argument. On the one hand, the argument itself has changed very little. On the other hand, this new understanding of PSR makes for a rather different argument.

We may summarize the detailed argument as follows:

(S_1) A contingent being exists.

a. This contingent being is caused either (1) by itself, or (2) by another.

b. If it were caused by itself, it would have to precede itself in existence, which is impossible.

(S_2) Therefore, this contingent being (2) is caused by another, i.e. depends on something else for its existence.

(S_3) That which causes (provides the sufficient reason for) the existence of any contingent being must be either (3) another contingent being, or (4) a non-contingent (necessary) being.

c. If 3, then this contingent cause must itself be caused by another, and so on to infinity.

(S_4) Therefore, that which causes (provides the sufficient reason for) the existence of any contingent being must be either (5) an infinite series of contingent beings, or (4) a necessary being.

(S_5) An infinite series of contingent beings (5) is incapable of yielding a sufficient reason for the existence of any being.

(S_6) Therefore, a necessary being (4) exists.

We have here what appears, at least initially, to be a true and valid cosmological argument. From what appear to be true premises we have argued to a valid conclusion.[112]

Reichenbach spends considerable space responding to objections. I will note two in particular here that have application to all forms of the

---

[112]Reichenbach, *Cosmological Argument*, 19–20. This is the end of chap. 1, after a detailed discussion of each of his premises (S_1) to (S_6).

cosmological argument. The first is the response that this is merely talk about metaphysical principles and says nothing about the real causes of the real world. To this Reichenbach notes that "the cosmological argument argues for a real being, not a regulative principle. And the causal principle which the cosmological argument wants to uphold is one which is informative in that it tells us about the real world, not merely about our experience of such."[113]

Another objection to versions of the argument, including most PSR arguments, that refer to the whole universe is that they commit the fallacy of composition. They conclude the contingency of the whole from the contingency of the parts. The problem with this fallacy, Reichenbach notes, is that there are instances when such a conclusion is justified and some when it clearly is not. We have encountered this point before: If I have a picture puzzle in which all of the pieces are triangles, can I conclude that the completed puzzle will be a triangle? No! But what if each piece is red? Now, obviously the puzzle itself is red. What is curious is that logicians have never found a workable decision procedure for composition arguments.

So here the question is whether the contingency of the whole universe follows from the contingency of each of its parts. Reichenbach argues as follows:

> The totality of contingent beings is nothing more than the sum total of individual contingent beings; it is nothing over and above these beings. Each individual being, then, if it exists could conceivably not be. But what would occur if all these beings cease to exist at the next moment, something which is a distinct possibility since each is contingent? Obviously, if such were the case, the totality itself would cease to exist. For if the totality is the sum total of all its parts, and if there were no parts, then it would be impossible for the totality to exist. But if this is the case, it is perfectly conceivable that the totality could not exist. And if the totality

---

[113]Reichenbach, *Cosmological Argument*, 87. Metaphysics is just that: our generalization of our generalizations in science. Thus it is about the real world.

could conceivably not exist, then it too must be contingent. Therefore, if all the parts of something are contingent, the totality likewise *must* be contingent; it could conceivably not exist.[114]

So the fallacy of composition remains a fallacy in logic textbooks. But clearly "contingency" is a property that allows, at least under certain circumstances, a valid argument to go through.[115]

This is essentially the form the PSR argument has taken in recent years. Defeaters to it have focused on the principle itself. The most prominent objecting voice over the years has been that of William Rowe, to whom we turn next.

2.3.5 William Rowe. William Rowe (1931–2015), who considered himself a "friendly atheist," spent virtually his entire career at Purdue University. He departed from evangelical Christianity over a period of years, beginning in the final years of his doctoral program. While he accepted much of the cosmological argument, he objected to the PSR. The full treatment appeared in his 1975 *The Cosmological Argument*,[116] three years after Reichenbach's book. He certainly remained at the center of the dispute on this matter for the next forty years, until his death.

Rowe's discussion focuses on Samuel Clarke's formulation of the PSR, which he regarded as "perhaps the most complete, forceful, and cogent presentation of the Cosmological Argument we possess."[117] He begins with a distinction between a strong form and a weak form of the PSR, and we need to carefully note that this strong-weak distinction is a somewhat different one than Reichenbach's.

---

[114]Reichenbach, *Cosmological Argument*, 102.

[115]This solution is also important for Thomas's third way, but actually for any argument that reasons to a whole-universe conclusion. We discussed it more thoroughly in the section on Thomas Aquinas.

[116]William Rowe, *The Cosmological Argument* (Princeton, NJ: Princeton University Press, 1975; rev. ed., New York: Fordham University Press, 1998).

[117]William Rowe, *Philosophy of Religion: An Introduction*, 4th ed. (Belmont, CA: Thompson Wadsworth, 2007), 21.

The strong form, on which, Rowe claims, both Clarke and Leibniz depend, states that "whatever *exists* must have an explanation of its existence—either in the necessity of its own nature or in the causal efficacy of some other being."[118] The weak version requires this only of whatever *comes into existence*. The strong PSR, however, has a fatal flaw that can be expressed in the following argument:

1. PSR implies that every state of affairs has a reason either within itself or in some other state of affairs.
2. There are contingent states of affairs.
3. If there are contingent states of affairs then there is some state of affairs for which there is no reason.

Therefore:

4. PSR is false.[119]

Now clearly it is premise (3) that needs defending. The problem here is that PSR cannot be true of itself. Rowe argues as follows.

> Consider the state of affairs S expressed by the proposition "There are contingent states of affairs." Clearly it is a contingent matter that there are states of affairs. Hence, S itself is a contingent state of affairs. There must, then, according to PSR, be some state of affairs that is the reason for S, which accounts for the fact that there are contingent states of affairs rather than not. Suppose someone says that the state of affairs constituted by the existence of God is what accounts for S, giving as his reason that God caused there to be contingent states of affairs. We then ask whether the existence of God is a contingent or a necessary state of affairs. If the existence of God is a contingent state of affairs, it cannot account for S; it cannot explain why there are contingent states of affairs rather than not—no more than citing the existence of Adam and his act of generating children can explain why there are any men rather than none. Hence, the defender of PSR must say that the state of affairs

---

[118]William Rowe, *The Cosmological Argument*, rev. ed. (New York: Fordham University Press, 1998), 73.

[119]Rowe, *Cosmological Argument*, 99-100.

constituted by the existence of God is a *necessary* state of affairs. We then ask whether the state of affairs recorded by the proposition "God caused there to be contingent states of affairs" is a contingent or a necessary state of affairs. If *God's causing there to be contingent states of affairs* is itself a contingent state of affairs then it cannot account for S; it cannot explain why there are contingent states of affairs rather than not. That is, if the question to be answered is "Why are there any contingent states of affairs rather than none?" we cannot answer it by appealing to some contingent state of affairs. Consequently, the defender of PSR must say that *God's causing there to be contingent states of affairs* is itself a necessary state of affairs. But if the existence of God is necessary and God's causing there to be contingent states of affairs is also necessary, it follows that it is *necessary* that there are contingent states of affairs. But as we noted at the outset, it is contingent, not necessary, that there are contingent states of affairs. Hence, there can be no explanation of S; there can be no explanation of the fact that there are contingent states of affairs. Consequently, since PSR implies that there is a reason for S, implies that there is an explanation of the fact that there are contingent states of affairs, PSR is false.[120]

Why, then, have so many come to think that PSR is true?

Most of the theologians and philosophers who accept PSR have tried to defend it in either of two ways. Some have held that PSR is (or can be) known *intuitively* to be true. By this they mean that if we fully understand and reflect on what is said by PSR we can see that it must be true. . . . The difficulty with the claim that PSR is known intuitively to be true, however, is that a number of very able philosophers fail on careful reflection to apprehend its truth, and some have developed serious arguments for the conclusion that the principle is in fact false. It is clear, therefore, that not everyone who has reflected on PSR has been persuaded that it is true, and some are persuaded that there are good reasons to think it is false. . . .

The second way philosophers and theologians who accept PSR have sought to defend it is by claiming that although it may not be known to

---

[120]Rowe, *Cosmological Argument*, 100-101.

be true, it is, nevertheless, a presupposition of reason, a basic assumption that rational people make, whether or not they reflect sufficiently to become aware of the assumption. It is probably true that there are some assumptions we all make about our world, assumptions which are so basic that most of us are unaware of them. And, I suppose, it might be true that PSR is such an assumption. What bearing would this view of PSR have on the Cosmological Argument? Perhaps the main point to note is that even if PSR is a presupposition we all share, the premises of the Cosmological Argument could still be false. For PSR itself could still be false. The fact, if it is a fact, that all of us *presuppose* that every existing being and every positive fact has an explanation does not imply that no being exists, and no positive fact obtains, without an explanation.[121]

Two other properties of the Leibniz-Clarke PSR must also be brought up here, since they are important, both to Rowe's objections and to much of the ensuing debate. First, this form of PSR is to be understood as a *necessary* principle.[122] It is not entirely clear how to take this, but it must at least mean that it has a kind of logical status. That it is true a priori. And so it is not an inductively arrived at, scientifically observable fact about the universe. It must just be true *about* and *in* any possible universe.

Second, its necessity implies that it is true for every, and every possible, state of affairs. So it must be true of the set of states of affairs, as Rowe argues. And by extension, it would be true of the set of all sets of sets, and so on. It is this point that enables the apparent self-referring paradoxes of any complete and necessary PSR.

Now the debate over the strong form of PSR continues. I am inclined to conclude that Rowe is right, that given this strong PSR, impossible states of affairs would follow. So could there be another form of PSR that is more likely to be viable? Actually, Reichenbach's version already used a weak form of PSR (in Rowe's sense), and others follow suit as we will see.

---

[121]Rowe, *Philosophy of Religion*, 31-32.
[122]See the discussion in Rowe, *Cosmological Argument*, 78-88.

2.3.6 Richard Gale and Alexander Pruss. Richard M. Gale (1932–
2015) held a PhD from New York University and taught for most of his
career at the University of Pittsburgh. His 1991 book *On the Nature and
Existence of God* was intended to be, and certainly is, a careful response
to the contemporary revival of philosophical theism by, especially,
Alvin Plantinga, William Alston, and Richard Swinburne. This includes an extensive treatment of the cosmological argument. Our only
interest here is his final summary argument for rejecting it. It is simply
this: The argument concludes to a being that exists necessarily and is
morally good. This conclusion, however, must contradict the premise
that there are evils that occur in this world. Specifically, he argues that
the conclusion of any cosmological argument will be that "in the actual
world, *N* [a necessary being] is both maximally excellent and necessarily existent" and is therefore "an unsurpassably great being."[123] From
this, it must follow that *N* "both exists and has omnibenevolence,
omniscience, and sovereignty in every possible world."[124]

However, theists must also hold, as part of their theodicy, that
persons are free and therefore can do what is morally wrong, and hence
that there "is a possible world in which every free person always freely
does what is morally wrong."[125]

These two contradicting propositions, he asserts, "constitute ontological disproofs of the existence of the very sort of being whose
existence is asserted in the conclusion of every version of the
cosmological argument, thereby showing that these arguments are
radically defective."[126]

Then, in 1999, Richard Gale and his student Alexander Pruss
(b. 1973), who finished his PhD in 2001 at the University of Pittsburgh,

---

[123]Richard Gale, *On the Nature and Existence of God* (Cambridge: Cambridge University Press,
1991), 284.
[124]See Gale, *On the Nature and Existence of God*, 231.
[125]Gale, *On the Nature and Existence of God*, 230.
[126]Gale, *On the Nature and Existence of God*, 230.

and who now teaches at Baylor University, published something rather surprising: a new and valid version of the argument. This was, it turns out, a highly complex argument with seventeen steps that concludes to (18): "It is contingently true that there exists a necessary supernatural being who is very powerful, intelligent, and good and freely creates the actual world's universe."[127]

Not only does this new version resolve a number of other difficulties Gale had seen in various forms of the argument, but, most importantly, it handles the overriding and "most serious problem" related to God's apparent involvement in the occurrence of evil.[128]

> The most serious problem concerns the moral attributes of our "very powerful and intelligent supernatural necessary being that freely causes the existence of the cosmos in the actual world." If we cannot show that this being is at least a very good being, our argument may very well have created a Frankenstein, for this being will not be a suitable object of worship and thus will not meet the needs of the working theist.
>
> To begin with, our creator God is not shown to be such as to have the essential property of always having to do the best, and thus our God logically could do wrong in the actual world. . . . Moreover, our God was not even shown to be perfectly good in every possible world, and for this reason the God of our argument's conclusion will not fully satisfy the hopes and wants of all theists. What matters foremost to the working theist, however, is not whether it is *logically* possible (which is a concept that she does not have) that God do what is morally wrong, but whether God is capable of doing so in the actual world, in which *capable* is understood in terms of what a being has the capacity, knowledge, and opportunity to do. God could be said to be incapable in the *actual* world of doing wrong in the sense that he could not get himself to do so, that he is above temptation, that we can place absolute

---

[127]Richard Gale and Alexander Pruss, "A New Cosmological Argument," *Religious Studies* 35 (1999): 467.

[128]Several of these difficulties have to do with the allegedly difficult reach from first cause to God. Gale and Pruss responded to many of these objections in a follow-up article, "A Response to Oppy, and to Davey and Clifton," *Religious Studies* 38 (2002): 89-99.

confidence in him. This does not require that it be logically impossible that God does wrong.

The most serious problem with our argument is not whether its God is essentially benevolent but whether he is *actually* benevolent. And this is of primary concern to the working theist. It is here that our argument becomes quite vulnerable. To meet this problem we'll have to marshal all of the extant theodicies for God's permitting all of the known evils of the world, again showing the need for making out a global case for theism. This battery of theodicies will still leave countless apparently gratuitous evils, and it is at this point that faith must enter in that God has morally exonerating reasons for permitting these evils, even if we cannot access these reasons.[129]

The real point here is that the problem of evil cannot be smuggled in after the game has ended as a defeater for an argument already shown to be sound. Sufficiently powerful defenses are available to defeat this objection; however, even if they were not, it is still irrelevant to the logic of the argument itself. We should note that this holds for all forms of the cosmological argument, not just PSR types.

2.3.7 Richard Swinburne's inductive version. One of the strongest voices on the matter of God's existence has been Oxford University's Richard Swinburne (b. 1934). His book *The Existence of God* has at this point seen three editions, the first in 1979.[130] In addition, there is a shorter and more accessible version titled *Is There a God?*[131] and an even shorter and even more accessible one called *Evidence for God.*[132]

Swinburne's approach, though based ultimately on Leibniz, is inductive, both in terms of the derivation of PSR, and in the overall format of his full cosmological argument. This makes for a quite different-looking argument, and one that is not susceptible to any of

---

[129]Gale and Pruss, "New Cosmological Argument," 470.
[130]Richard Swinburne, *The Existence of God* (Oxford: Clarendon, 1979; rev. ed., 1991; 2nd ed., 2004).
[131]Richard Swinburne, *Is There a God?*(Oxford: Oxford University Press, 1996; rev. ed., 2010).
[132]Richard Swinburne, *Evidence for God* (Oxford: Mowbray Press, 1986).

Rowe's complaints about PSR. It has a weak PSR that simply calculates probability and is not necessary. It is, however, still intended to apply to the entire universe; and it is still cosmological in that it seeks an explanation of the existence of contingent things.

Here, then, is Swinburne's summation of the argument, after six long chapters explaining "explanation":

> As we saw at some length . . . the supposition that there is a God is an extremely simple supposition; the postulation of a God of infinite power, knowledge, and freedom is the postulation of the simplest kind of person that there could be. . . . The existence of the universe is less simple, and so less to be expected a priori than the existence of God. Hence, if there is no God, the existence of a complex physical universe is not much to be expected; it is not a priori very probable at all. . . .
>
> Yet, if there is a God, clearly he can create a universe; and he will do so in so far as his perfect goodness makes it probable that he will. I argued . . . that God has good reason to create humanly free agents. . . . I argued that it would be an equal best act to create or not to create such creatures, and so we should suppose the logical probability that God should create such creatures to be 1/2. I argued that these creatures would need to have bodies, and so there would need to be a physical world. So for this reason alone the probability that a God will create a physical world will be no less than 1/2. . . . Yet, of course, our judgments as to what a perfectly good God might do may be in error, because our views of moral goodness are limited; and, as I emphasize throughout this book, we cannot often give more than the roughest of values to the probabilities that I discuss. Nevertheless, if the moral intuitions about what a perfectly good God would do that I am commending to my readers are in any way close to the truth, we must conclude that the logical probability that, if there is a God, there will be a physical universe is quite high.[133]

So, what follows for Swinburne is a simple probability comparison. The likelihood of a universe as we know it (i.e., contingency) with its

---

[133]Swinburne, *Existence of God*, 2nd ed., 150-51.

observable causal connections (i.e., PSR) simply existing by itself is rather low, whereas it is "rather more likely that God would exist uncaused."[134] On that basis, and with that conclusion's strength, this is a solid inductive argument. While it by itself does not leave us overwhelmed by deductive convincingness, it is certainly at least a gateway to a larger case.

The only real objection to this argument is to deny that "God + universe" is a simpler explanation of things than just "universe"—by itself. There is quite a bit of literature on this point, but Swinburne's original response to this objection remains, I think, unanswered. An infinite God is a perfectly simple intelligence and therefore always a simpler solution than the complexity of an evolutionary universe that is somehow caused and governed by mathematics and quantum mechanics so that it operates autonomously and automatically.

Further Reading

On Leibniz and Clarke see H. G. Alexander, *The Leibniz-Clarke Correspondence* (Oxford: University of Manchester Press, 1956).

My interest here in Gale and Pruss has been the matter of the objection from evil as stated in Gale's original argument. For the full argument, which itself involves a weak form of the principle of sufficient reason that avoids Rowe's objections, see Richard Gale and Alexander Pruss, "A New Cosmological Argument," *Religious Studies* 35 (1999): 461-476. For a good discussion of the Gale-Pruss argument see Bruce Reichenbach, "The Cosmological Argument," in *Stanford Encyclopedia of Philosophy*, ed. Edward N. Zalta, fall 2019 ed., esp. sec. 5, https://plato.stanford.edu/archives/fall2019/entries/cosmological -argument/. For a follow-up by Gale and Pruss see "A Response to Oppy, and to Davey and Clifton," *Religious Studies* 38 (2002): 89-99.

On Richard Gale see Paul Helm, "Gale on God," *Religious Studies* 29, no. 2 (1993): 245-55.

For a much more detailed critique of PSR see William Rowe, *The Cosmological Argument* (New York: Fordham University Press, 1998), chaps. 2 and 3.

For the extended version of Swinburne's argument see *The Existence of God* (Oxford: Clarendon, 2004), chaps. 1-7. More on induction can be found in

---

[134]Swinburne, *Existence of God*, 152.

Swinburne, *The Justification of Induction* (Oxford: Oxford University Press, 1974) and Swinburne, *Bayes's Theorem* (Oxford: Oxford University Press, 2005). On the issue of simplicity as a criterion for explanations and its application to God, including the recent conversation, see his *The Coherence of Theism*, 2nd ed. (Oxford: Oxford University Press, 2016).

For more on both Rowe's and Swinburne's discussion, including a good bibliography of objectors and responders, see Reichenbach's above-mentioned "The Cosmological Argument." One detailed response to Swinburne's simplicity argument is John Ostrowick, "Is Theism a Simple, and Hence Probable, Explanation for the Universe?," *South African Journal of Philosophy* 31, no. 1 (2012): 305-19.

For more on the fallacy of composition as related to the cosmological argument, see Rem Edwards, *Philosophy of Religion* (New York: Harcourt, Brace, Jovanovich, 1972). See also Mortimer Adler, *How to Think About God: A Guide for the Twentieth-Century Pagan* (New York: Simon & Schuster, 1980).

On the matter of "necessity" in this argument see Reichenbach, *The Cosmological Argument*, chap. 6, and, as mentioned above, John Hick, "God as Necessary Being," *Journal of Philosophy* 57, nos. 22-23 (1960): 725-33. For a more recent, fairly advanced examination see Alexander Pruss and Joshua Rasmussen, *Necessary Existence* (Oxford: Oxford University Press, 2018).

2.4 Where We Are Now

2.4.1 Tim Bayne. Tim Bayne (b. 1972), holds a PhD from the University of Arizona, taught at Oxford University, and is now at Monash University in Melbourne, Australia. He has recently provided a succinct assessment of the current state of the cosmological argument in his *A Very Short Introduction to Philosophy of Religion*.[135] Bayne begins with the kalam argument, primarily that of al-Ghazali, but in general the temporal version. He gives the following argument:

(1) The universe began to exist.

(2) Everything that begins to exist has a cause of its existence.

---

[135]Tim Bayne, *A Very Short Introduction to Philosophy of Religion* (Oxford: Oxford University Press, 2018), chap. 3.

(3) The universe has a cause of its existence. (From (1) and (2).)

(4) If the universe has a cause, then that cause must be personal—that is, it must be God.

(5) Therefore, there is a God.[136]

This, he thinks, suffers from three problems. First, there is the matter of actual infinites. Current mathematicians regard all infinite sets as having the same number of members. So the set of positive integers has the same size as the set of positive even integers. Hence, we have good reasons to believe that the intuitions we have about the oddities of infinite sets when we apply them to actual worlds must be dismissed, and so actual infinites are possible.[137]

This, however, simply ignores the difference between mathematical possibility and actual reality. As we have seen many times, we cannot simply draw inferences from one to the other. The paradoxes that occur with actual infinites still stand, and metaphysical criteria have to take precedence over mathematical.

Second, he notes it is unclear whether "the very existence of the universe is something that has a causal explanation."[138] This issue has been addressed several times as well. The chief problem is that in the kalam argument it is not the existence of the universe per se that is to be explained, but rather the cause of the beginning or initial state of the universe. Now we are back to the whole point of the argument—namely, whether and under what conditions a causal series can begin *ex nihilo*.

Third, there is the problem of the argument's very general conclusion: It simply asserts that there is a cause of the universe's beginning, not a personal agent. Now this is an issue that everyone since Aristotle was well aware of, and I have frequently noted how the argument has been extended to infer various qualities of the "first uncaused cause" that

---

[136]Bayne, *Very Short Introduction*, 27.
[137]Bayne, *Very Short Introduction*, 29
[138]Bayne, *Very Short Introduction*, 30.

entitle us to conclude that this is God. So, again, there is nothing new or compelling here.

Bayne then moves on to the atemporal argument of Thomas Aquinas but also, he says, of Leibniz. This can be stated as follows:

(1) The universe is contingent.

(2) There is an explanation for the existence of all contingent entities.

(3) The existence of contingent entities can be explained only by appeal to a necessary being.

(4) There is at least one necessary being. (From (1), (2), and (3).)

(5) That necessary being is God.[139]

This argument also sustains three telling objections. The first is that the supposed need for an explanation of the universe exists only if we assume PSR. I covered this in the previous section and do not need to repeat it here. In any case, this discussion only attaches to the argument of Clarke and Leibniz, and it has no reference to Thomas's. Thomas is not concerned with the whole universe, nor does he employ or require a version of PSR.

The second objection is that the argument concludes to a necessary being, and "we don't have a good grasp of *how* the actions of a necessary being such as God might account for the existence of contingent entities."[140] Now this is a truly odd objection, since the argument never purports to explain *how* God causes; it simply concludes that there must *be* a cause of the contingent entities in question. In fact, Thomas's argument only refers to a being that exists necessarily in the metaphysical sense; it concludes that there must be an "uncaused" being—that is, a *non*contingent entity.[141] So this objection seems to have no

---

[139]Bayne, *Very Short Introduction*, 31.

[140]Bayne, *Very Short Introduction*, 32.

[141]It was Immanuel Kant who famously objected—in his *Critique of Pure Reason*—that "necessary being" refers to logical necessity, and that it is borrowed from the ontological argument and is illegitimate. This criticism, as we saw it in Bertrand Russell, is still brought to the cosmological

claim on the Aristotelian-Thomistic argument at all.[142] In fact, while it no doubt poses an interesting puzzle for theism in general, it has no bearing on the PSR argument either. It, too, does not need to explain *how* a necessary being acts; it only needs to show validly that he *does*.

The third objection is one we have also seen before. Bayne asks why God's existence itself does not need an explanation. He insists that theists simply claim that his existence requires no explanation. But, of course, they do not merely claim it. It is precisely the conclusion of the argument. To ask what causes the uncaused cause is just to miss the whole point of the cosmological argument.

A real problem with Bayne's discussion of the atemporal argument is the confusion of the arguments of Leibniz and Thomas. Some of what he asserts has some bearing on the PSR argument, but Thomas's argument is quite unlike what Bayne gives us, and it will not be so easily dismissed. It is not about the whole universe, only specific observations. It does not appeal to a universal PSR; it simply observes that some entities we see are caused or contingent, and that there can be no infinite regress of such entities if they are causally connected in sequence.

Nor does it require a prior concept of necessary being as an explanation; it simply concludes to a first uncaused being. This is critical to the contingency form of the argument. While it is true that Thomas, like Aristotle, held to an observation-based causality principle, it plays no role in this argument. The burden of the argument is borne by the subargument against an infinite regress. That is what leads to the conclusion that there can only ever be a finite regress of contingent causes of existence, and hence a first and therefore uncaused cause of the existence of all the contingently existing items in any sequence.

---

argument by some, and perhaps in part here by Bayne. But this is wrong. The argument uses "necessary" only in the sense of "not-contingent"—that is, a metaphysical not a logical necessity. More on Kant's objection in the chapter on the ontological argument.

[142]A good discussion of how the necessary can cause the contingent and he can be free can be found in most any of the commentators on Thomas, most notably in Eleonore Stump's masterful work *Aquinas, Arguments of the Philosophers* (New York: Routledge, 2003), 103-15.

So too the concept of necessary being is neither an assumption nor the conclusion of the argument. As we have seen, the conclusion is simply the negation of contingent cause: uncaused. Granted, other components of necessary being follow from the Parmenidean subarguments, but then they are well grounded.

I conclude that the cosmological argument, in all three of its primary forms, contingency, kalam, and (weak) PSR, is still on good footing. While Bayne's book is, of course, only a brief treatment, it nevertheless should be expected that he brings forward at least the most formidable recent and current objections. If so, then the argument stands and theists who defend this argument are still clearly on sound rational ground.

Further Reading

An excellent assessment of the current (2017) state of the argument, including a detailed discussion of objections and rejoinders, is, again, Bruce Reichenbach, "The Cosmological Argument," in *Stanford Encyclopedia of Philosophy*, ed. Edward N. Zalta, fall 2019 ed., https://plato.stanford.edu/archives/fall2019/entries/cosmological-argument/. The bibliography is especially helpful.

A good source of objections to the cosmological argument is the previously mentioned book by Michael Martin, *Atheism: A Philosophical Justification* (Philadelphia: Temple University Press, 1990).

For the full discussion of the meaning of "necessary" in this argument see John Hick, "God as Necessary Being," *Journal of Philosophy* 57, nos. 22-23 (1960): 725-33. A more recent, highly technical discussion is Alexander Pruss and Joshua Rasmussen, *Necessary Existence* (Oxford: Oxford University Press, 2018). This will be especially helpful in responding to several of Bayne's objections.

CHAPTER 3

Teleological Arguments

3.1 Phase One: Simple Design Arguments

The cosmological argument codifies the most basic form of puzzling about God and how the very existence of our world is to be explained. I do think, though, that our amazement at the order, beauty, and symmetry—the sheer fit of the universe we experience—is the oldest and most common form of questioning. As a philosophical argument, however, the teleological argument does not seem to flourish until after Aristotle.

The combined weight of Socrates, Plato, and Aristotle put an end to most of the rampant skepticism that had pervaded Greek thinking for half a century before them. But what follows them almost immediately is a shift to a less metaphysical and much more practical as well as observational and scientific mood. Philosophy now seeks to answer the question of how life is to be lived. *What is the good life?*

This concern with practical ethics, not surprisingly, leads to a different thought sequence regarding God's reality. How—maybe better, *why*—does our world make sense, fit together, seem so suited to our needs and wants? Indeed, why can we do science at all?

The teleological argument moves from fit, order, functionality, and temporal sequence; aesthetic qualities like beauty and elegance; and also epistemic qualities like rationality, knowableness, mathematical precision, and repeatability, to an intelligent creative source. This is always an inductive argument: from evidence to explanation. In fact, its earliest phase is simply a generalization argument. Later phases are more complex but still inductive in format.

The result is that teleological arguments always share the general features of induction. First, there are always multiple possible conclusions: different explanations of the evidence are always conceivable and each with different quantifiers, including some, more, many, most, all, and so on. Second, each possible conclusion will have a different probability or likelihood. Third, given these two factors, there are no 100 percent inductive arguments. The evidence may in some cases be insurmountable and yield a patently obvious conclusion; still, there are always other conclusions that may have negligible but still measurable probability.

We begin with phase-one arguments—that is, arguments that move from our ordinary observations of functional complexity to the explanation of an intelligent source. And what better place to start than Socrates?

3.1.1 Socrates. Plato's great teacher, Socrates (470–399 BC), gave us one of the first examples of a teleological argument.

> Does it not strike you then that he who made man from the beginning did for some useful end furnish him with his several senses, giving him eyes to behold the visible word, and ears to catch the intonations of sound? Or again, what good would there be in odors if nostrils had not been bestowed upon us? What perception of sweet things and pungent, and of all the pleasures of the palate, had not a tongue been fashioned in us as an interpreter of the same? And besides all this, do you not think this looks like a matter of foresight, this closing of the delicate orbs of sight with eyelids as with folding doors, which, when there is need to use them for any purpose, can be thrown wide open and firmly closed again in sleep? And, that even the winds of heaven may not visit them too roughly, this planting of the eyelashes as a protecting screen? This coping of the region above the eyes with cornice-work of eyebrow so that no drop of sweat fall from the head and injure them? Again this readiness of the ear to catch all sounds and yet not to be surcharged? This

capacity of the front teeth of all animals to cut and of the "grinders" to receive the food and reduce it to pulp? The position of the mouth again, close to the eyes and nostrils as a portal of ingress for all the creature's supplies? And lastly, seeing that matter passing out of the body is unpleasant, this hindward direction of the passages, and their removal to a distance from the avenues of sense? I ask you, when you see all these things constructed with such show of foresight can you doubt whether they are products of chance or intelligence?[1]

Several words here mark this as a teleological argument. The evidence for design is characterized by a number of observations that show functionality. It is "useful" implies that there is some end. Likewise, rationality involves "foresight"—that is, its functioning involves the ability to plan the future: to think about what could be but is not. That is the very essence of design. The conclusion allows a choice between two alternate explanations for the evidence, seen here as "products." The first, "chance," is given little likelihood, while the second, "intelligence," appears to Socrates to be beyond reasonable doubt.

We will see these ideas develop as we trace the evolution of this argument. The idea that networks of means and ends demand a capacity to plan future outcomes provides the basic definition of "design," which becomes the key term for this argument. Hence it is often referred to as the argument from design. It is important to see that from the start "design" had a definition in specific types of observation. This is not, as often alleged, a circular argument that just assumes design and then magically pulls a designer out of the hat.

3.1.2 Zeno. This argument became a staple among the Stoic philosophers. The founder of this school in Athens, Zeno of Citium (334–262 BC), produced a pantheistic metaphysics heavily influenced by Heraclitus. So what drives the universe (God) is the divine fire that is

---

[1]Xenophon, *Memorabilia* 4.3, in *The Memorabilia: Recollections of Socrates*, trans. H.G. Dakyns (New York, 1897; Project Gutenberg, 2008).

governed by the Logos. What is unique in Zeno, and what came to define the characteristic social ethic of the Stoics, is the doctrine of universal reason, Logos, as present in every human being. This unites us as one people and gives us a shared virtue ethic.

We know of Zeno's writing only from quotations and references in later Stoics. Like virtually all of the Greek and Roman philosophers, Plato and Aristotle being notable exceptions, Zeno writes in a poetic style rather than argumentative. Here is a teleological argument as repeated by Cicero:

> Zeno, then, defines nature by saying that it is artistically working fire, which advances by fixed methods to creation. For he maintains that it is the main function of art to create and produce, and that what the hand accomplishes in the productions of the arts we employ, is accomplished much more artistically by nature, that is, as I said, by artistically working fire, which is the master of the other arts.[2]

We find these sorts of statements in all the early Stoics, including Zeno's successor as head of the school, Cleanthes (330–230 BC). What is an interesting development here is the notion that human productions are imitations of nature's designs. Rather than attributing design to nature based on what is known about our own intelligent designing, they argue the reverse. Cleanthes, in his "Hymn to Zeus," calls us all his children who imitate him. We will see this logic more explicitly in Cicero and discuss it there.

3.1.3 Epictetus. A slave to Nero's secretary in Rome, Epictetus (55–135) was exiled by Emperor Domitian in 93 and founded a philosophical school in Nicopolis in western Greece. He had studied Stoic philosophy for many years, and we see in him the real height of Stoic development. While we have no writings directly from him, we do have the *Discourses*, written down by his student Arrian around the year 108:

---

[2]Cicero, *De natura deorum*, trans. Francis Brooks (London: Methuen, 1896), II.22.

Each single thing that comes into being in the universe affords a ready ground for praising Providence, if one possesses these two qualities—a power to see clearly the circumstances of each, and the spirit of gratitude therewith. Without these, one man will fail to see the usefulness of nature's products and another though he see it will not give thanks for them. If God had created colours and, in general, all visible things, but had not created a faculty to behold them, of what use would they be? None at all. If on the other hand He had created this faculty, but had not created objects of such a nature as to fall under the faculty of vision, even so of what use would it be? None at all. If again He had created both these, and had not created light, even so there would be no use in them. Who is it then that has adapted this to that, and that to this? . . . Surely the very structure of such finished products leads us commonly to infer that they must be the work of some craftsman, and are not constructed at random. Are we to say then that each of these products points to the craftsman, but that things visible and vision and light do not? Do not male and female and the desire of union and the power to use the organs adapted for it—do not these point to the craftsman? But if these things are so, then the fact that the intellect is so framed that we are not merely the passive subjects of sensations, but select and subtract from them and add to them, and by this means construct particular objects, nay more, that we pass from them to others which are not in mere juxtaposition—I say are not these facts sufficient to rouse men's attention and to deter them from leaving out the craftsman? If it be not so, let them explain to us what it is which makes each of these things, or how it is possible that objects so marvellously designed should have come into being by chance and at random?

Again, are these faculties found in us alone? Many in us alone— faculties which the rational creature had special need of—but many you will find that we share with irrational creatures. Do they also then understand events and things? No—for using is one thing, and understanding is another. God had need of them as creatures dealing with impressions, and of us as dealing with them and understanding them as well. . . . What is my conclusion? God makes one animal for eating, and another for service in farming, another to produce cheese, and others for

different uses of a like nature, for which there is no need of understanding impressions and being able to distinguish them; but He brought
man into the world to take cognizance of Himself and His works, and
not only to take cognizance but also to interpret them. Therefore it is
beneath man's dignity to begin and to end where the irrational creatures
do: he must rather begin where they do and end where nature has ended
in forming us; and nature ends in contemplation and understanding and
a way of life in harmony with nature. See to it then that ye do not die
without taking cognizance of these things.[3]

While this is again the typical simple inference from design to designer, there are some remarkable features in this argument. First, he
discusses the ethics of knowledge. We are ethically obligated to carry
out our capacities to reason and to abide by their conclusions. But,
second, he argues that it is precisely this capacity that is itself evidence
of nature's fine-tuning.

3.1.4 Marcianus Aristides.

One of the first, as best we know, Christian
apologists was Marcianus Aristides (d. 133/134). We know little about
him, other than that he was active in Athens and clearly demonstrates
good philosophical training. He wrote his *Apology* to Emperor Hadrian
in about 125.[4] Here is the opening section:

I, O king, by the grace of God came into this world; and when I had
considered the heaven and the earth and the seas, and had surveyed the
sun and the rest of creation, I marveled at the beauty of the world. And
I perceived that the world and all that is therein are moved by the power
of another; and I understood that he who moves them is God, who is
hidden in them, and veiled by them. And it is manifest that that which
causes motion is more powerful than that which is moved. But that I
should make search concerning this same mover of all, as to what is his

---

[3]Epictetus, *Discourses* 1.6., trans. P. E. Matheson (Oxford: Clarendon Press, 1916).

[4]There is some possibility it was written in 140 to Emperor Antoninus Pius, but most scholars
agree on Hadrian. At about the same time, Quadratus, the bishop of Athens from 125 to 129, also
wrote an apology to Hadrian. He was likely older, born in the late first century and died in 129,
and so usually gets credit for being the first Christian apologist.

nature (for it seems to me, he is indeed unsearchable in his nature), and
that I should argue as to constancy of his government, so as to grasp it
fully—this is a vain effort for me; for it is not possible that a man should
fully comprehend it. I say, however, concerning this mover of the world,
that he is God of all, who made all things for the sake of mankind. And
it seems to me that this is reasonable, that one should fear God and
should not oppress men.[5]

One might think of this as a cosmological argument, and it certainly
betrays Aristotelian causal language, but what makes this a design argument is Aristides's reference not only to beauty but especially to the
"constancy of his government."

It is interesting that Aristides here makes no reference to Jewish or
Christian Scriptures, but pursues a philosophical argument entirely on
the basis of reason. He concedes that we can know nothing of God's
nature, at least from this argument, though he does proceed to give us
a few conclusions in addition to God's existence. Constancy in government certainly indicates God's creative activity over time. Nevertheless, there is no doubt that the teleological argument, even in its
most fully developed form, tells us very little of God's nature.

3.1.5 Theophilus. Similar arguments, usually more expanded, were
common among the early Christian thinkers. They typically begin with
a simple comparison argument that pushes us to conclude to an intelligence—that is, God. That is followed by a lot of evidence to back up
the conclusion. Here is Theophilus, patriarch of Antioch (d. ca. 184):

> For as the soul in man is not seen, being invisible to men, but is per-
> ceived through the motion of the body, so God cannot indeed be seen
> by human eyes, but is beheld and perceived through His providence and
> works. For, in like manner, as any person, when he sees a ship on the sea
> rigged and in sail, and making for the harbour, will no doubt infer that

---

[5]Marcianus Aristides, *Apology*, in *The Ante-Nicene Fathers*, vol. 9, trans. D. M. Kay, ed. Allan
Menzies and Alexander Roberts (New York: Christian Literature, 1896).

there is a pilot in her who is steering her; so we must perceive that God is the governor of the whole universe, though He be not visible to the eyes of the flesh, since He is incomprehensible. For if a man cannot look upon the sun, though it be a very small heavenly body, on account of its exceeding heat and power, how shall not a mortal man be much more unable to face the glory of God, which is unutterable? For as the pomegranate, with the rind containing it, has within it many cells and compartments which are separated by tissues, and has also many seeds dwelling in it, so the whole creation is contained by the spirit of God, and the containing spirit is along with the creation contained by the hand of God.

Consider, O man, His works,—the timely rotation of the seasons, and the changes of temperature; the regular march of the stars; the well-ordered course of days and nights, and months, and years; the various beauty of seeds, and plants, and fruits; and the divers species of quadrupeds, and birds, and reptiles, and fishes, both of the rivers and of the sea; or consider the instinct implanted in these animals to beget and rear offspring, not for their own profit, but for the use of man; and the providence with which God provides nourishment for all flesh, or the subjection in which He has ordained that all things subserve mankind.[6]

3.1.6 Lactantius. To my mind the best of these early Christian arguments comes from Lucius Caecillius Firmianus Lactantius (ca. 250–ca. 325). A North African, well educated in philosophy and a teacher of rhetoric in Nicomedia, he became a Christian in 300. He served as advisor to several emperors, but especially to Constantine, who made him private tutor to his son Crispus. In his work *Treatise on the Anger of God* he interacts with virtually all of the prior philosophers as well as current schools including the Peripatetics, Epicureans, and Stoics. What I find most fascinating is how well he addresses twenty-first-century naturalistic objections, which he knows in the form of the atomism of Lucretius and Democritus:

---

[6]Theophilus of Antioch, *Ad Autolycus* 1.5-6, in *The Ante-Nicene Fathers*, vol. 3, trans. Marcus Dods, ed. Alexander Roberts and James Donaldson (Edinburgh: T&T Clark, 1867).

They who do not admit that the world was made by divine providence, either say that it is composed of first principles coming together at random, or that it suddenly came into existence by nature, but hold, as Straton does, that nature has in itself the power of production and of diminution, but that it has neither sensibility nor figure, so that we may understand that all things were produced spontaneously, without any artificer or author. Each opinion is vain and impossible. But this happens to those who are ignorant of the truth, that they devise anything, rather than perceive that which the nature of the subject requires.

. . . Lucretius, as though forgetful of atoms, which he was maintaining, in order that he might refute those who say that all things are produced from nothing, employed these arguments, which might have weighed against himself.

For he thus spoke:

"If things came from nothing, any kind might be born of anything; nothing would require seed."

Likewise afterwards:

"We must admit, therefore, that nothing can come from nothing, since things require seed before they can severally be born, and be brought out into the buxom fields of air."

. . . Why should I speak of animals, in whose bodies we see nothing formed without plan, without arrangement, without utility, without beauty, so that the most skillful and careful marking out of all the parts and members repels the idea of accident and chance? But let us suppose it possible that the limbs, and bones, and nerves, and blood should be made up of atoms. What of the senses, the reflection, the memory, the mind, the natural capacity: from what seeds can they be compacted? He says, From the most minute. There are therefore others of greater size. How, then, are they indivisible?

In the next place, if the things which are not seen are formed from invisible seeds, it follows that those which are seen are from visible seeds. Why, then, does no one see them? But whether any one regards the invisible parts which are in man, or the parts which can be touched, and which are visible, who does not see that both parts exist in accordance with design? How, then, can bodies which meet together without design effect anything reasonable? For we see that there is nothing in the whole world which has not in itself very great and wonderful design. And since this is above the sense and capacity of man, to what can it be more rightly attributed than to the divine providence? If a statue, the resemblance of man, is made by the exercise of design and art, shall we suppose that man himself is made up of fragments which come together at random? And what resemblance to the truth is there in the thing produced, when the greatest and most surpassing skill can imitate nothing more than the mere outline and extreme lineaments of the body? Was the skill of man able to give to his production any motion or sensibility?

But, as others say, the world was made by Nature, which is without perception and figure. But this is much more absurd. If Nature made the world, it must have made it by judgment and intelligence; for it is lie that makes something who has either the inclination to make it, or knowledge. If nature is without perception and figure, how can that be made by it which has both perception and figure, unless by chance any one thinks that the fabric of animals, which is so delicate, could have been formed and animated by that which is without perception, or that that figure of heaven, which is prepared with such foresight for the uses of living beings, suddenly came into existence by some accident or other, without a builder, without an artificer?

"If there is anything," says Chrysippus, "which effects those things which man, though he is endowed with reason, cannot do, that assuredly is greater, and stronger, and wiser than man." But man cannot make heavenly things; therefore that which shall produce or has produced these things surpasses man in art, in design, in skill, and in power. Who, therefore, can it be but God? But Nature, which they suppose to be, as it were, the mother of all things, if it has not a mind, will effect nothing, will contrive nothing; for where there is no reflection there is neither motion nor efficacy. But if it uses counsel for the commencement of anything, reason for its arrangement, art for its accomplishment, energy for its consummation, and power to govern and control, why should it be called Nature rather than God? . . . But ought not atoms to have come together to effect these things, since they leave no position untried?

For concerning Nature, which has no mind, it is no wonder that it forgot to do these things. What, then, is the case? It is plain that God, when He commenced this work of the world . . . Himself made the things which could not be made by man. . . .

But if in the commonwealth of this world, so to speak, there is no providence which rules, no God who administers, no sense at all prevails in this nature of things. From what source therefore will it be believed that the human mind, with its skill and its intelligence, had its origin? For if the body of man was made from the ground, from which circumstance man received his name; it follows that the soul, which has intelligence, and is the ruler of the body, which the limbs obey as a king and commander, which can neither be looked upon nor comprehended, could not have come to man except from a wise nature. But as mind and soul govern everybody, so also does God govern the world. For it is not probable that lesser and humble things bear rule, but that greater and highest things do not bear rule.

In short, Marcus Cicero, in his *Tusculan Disputations*, and in his *Consolation*, says: "No origin of souls can be found on earth. For there is nothing, he says, mixed and compound in souls, or which may appear to be produced and made up from the earth; nothing moist or airy, or of the nature of fire. For in these natures there is nothing which has the force of memory, of mind and reflection, which both retains the past and foresees the future, and is able to comprise the present; which things alone are divine. For no source will ever be found from which they are able to come to man, unless it be from God."

For whatever exists which has reason, must have arisen from reason. Now reason is the part of an intelligent and wise nature; but a wise and intelligent nature can be nothing else than God.[7]

What is especially noteworthy here is that Lactantius sees the argument as a best-explanation strategy, and as having three options: God, nature itself, and chance. The chance option is ruled out by the intricacy

---

[7]Lactantius, *On The Anger Of God* 10, in *Ante-Nicene Fathers*, vol. 7, trans. William Fletcher, ed. Alexander Roberts, James Donaldson, and Cleveland Coxe (Buffalo, NY: Christian Literature, 1886). Excerpts are from chap. 10. I have left a good deal of this argument out.

of the design. He has no knowledge of probability theory as such, but it is clear to him that the odds of producing this kind of functional complexity will just not work.

The nature option is just as current. We would call it evolution: In some way, the process of the universe—or multiverse—guided by quantum physics or simply the laws of nature becomes the functional complexity in which we now live. Lactantius here gives the same argument that is still in use: atoms cannot produce intelligence. Only intelligence can produce intelligence. Only reason can produce reason.

Democritus had tried to avoid the force of this by holding that mind was composed of extremely fine atoms. Lactantius will have none of that. Atoms are atoms. There is no machine intelligence. There is only one option left: God.

Similar though less sophisticated arguments can be found in Irenaeus (130–202), Athenagoras (133–190), Minucius Felix (d. ca. 250), Gregory of Nyssa (335–394), and Gregory the Great (540–604). We have to assume that these philosophically educated theologians both received from and gave back to Stoic philosophers during this time period. Their format and content is much the same. So let us turn instead to the Roman Stoics next.

3.1.7 Marcus Tullius Cicero and Marcus Aurelius. Cicero (106–43 BC), the great Roman statesman, lawyer, orator, poet, and philosopher, gives us another example of Stoic argument. It is interesting in the fact that it already rests on a comparison of natural and human productions, but also that it uses a clock example. As we will see, this becomes something of a standard example of complex functionality that cannot occur without intelligent engineering:

> If, then, the things achieved by nature are more excellent than those achieved by art, and if art produces nothing without making use of intelligence, nature also ought not to be considered destitute of intelligence.

If at the sight of a statue or painted picture you know that art has been
employed, and from the distant view of the course of a ship feel sure that
it is made to move by art and intelligence, and if you understand on
looking at a horologe, whether one marked out with lines, or working by
means of water, that the hours are indicated by art and not by chance,
with what possible consistency can you suppose that the universe which
contains these same products of art, and their constructors, and all things,
is destitute of forethought and intelligence? Why, if any one were to carry
into Scythia or Britain the globe which our friend Posidonius has lately
constructed, each one of the revolutions of which brings about the same
movement in the sun and moon and five wandering stars as is brought
about each day and night in the heavens, no one in those barbarous
countries would doubt that that globe was the work of intelligence.[8]

This is in many ways a typical example of a simple design argument.
We see the same design in one object of which we know the source
(Posidonius's horologe or orrery) and one of that we do not (the
heavens). Hence, we conclude that the latter needs a similar—that is, an
intelligent—source. But what is different is that here the artifact is not
just another designed object in an inductive argument but a scale model
of a natural object. So, if the uncivilized Brits recognize that the horologe has to have had an intelligent craftsman, how much more do the
heavens demand one? This avoids issues of analogous comparisons,
which will be problematic for later arguments. The comparison is legiti-
mized by being imitation or model.[9]

Emperor Marcus Aurelius (AD 121–180) was the final of only five
emperors historians have generally regarded as good. His principal
writing, a collection of his philosophical thoughts about life, is the
Meditations, in which he gives several examples of teleological-type arguments. They are characterized by their higher degree of abstractness
compared to other Stoics.

---

[8]Cicero, *De natura deorum* 2.35, trans. Francis Brooks (London: Methuen, 1896).
[9]See the discussion of this point in Graeme Hunter, "Cicero's Neglected Argument from Design,"
British Journal for the History of Philosophy 17, no. 2 (2009): 235-45.

> Every instrument, tool, vessel, if it does that for which it has been
> made, is well, and yet he who made it is not there. But in the things
> which are held together by nature there is within and there abides in
> them the power which made them; wherefore the more is it fit to rev-
> erence this power, and to think, that, if thou dost live and act ac-
> cording to its will, everything in thee is in conformity to intelligence.
> And thus also in the universe the things which belong to it are in
> conformity to intelligence.[10]

This is a clear statement of the Stoic doctrine of Logos. The same rationality carries through all of nature, including ourselves, because it is
sourced in nature. Again here, we are merely imitators in our productions, and the real source of creative intelligence is what we know first.
As in Cicero, we are—in his case the Brits are—persuaded of the
intelligent source only because we recognize the status of human productions as *models* of natural things.

3.1.8 Medieval Design arguments. This basic tradition is known and
continued by both Christian and Islamic thinkers during the medieval
centuries. Let us first consider a few examples from Islamic sources.

3.1.8.1 Al-Ghazali. We have encountered al-Ghazali (1058–1111)
before. As a Sunni, he was opposed to philosophy, authoring his famous
The Incoherence of the Philosophers, but he did admit that commonsense
observations allow us to recognize God. So, we are able to understand
a very basic teleological argument:

> It should be apparent to anyone with the minimum of intelligence . . . if
> he looks at the wonders in God's creation on earth and in the skies and
> at the wonders in animals and plants, that this marvelous, well-ordered
> system cannot exist without a maker who conducts it, and a creator who
> plans and perfects it. Indeed, human nature itself seems to testify that it
> is subjected to the Creator's direction, and directed according to His

---

[10]Marcus Aurelius, *Meditations* 6.40, trans. George Long (1862; New York: Washington Square
Press, 1964). See also 7.75 and 8.20.

management. Hence God most high said: "Is there any doubt regarding God, the Originator of the heavens and the earth?"[11]

3.1.8.2 Averroes. Averroes, or Ibn Rushd, (1126–1198) defended the use of philosophy as warranted by the Qur'an. He responded to al-Ghazali in his *The Incoherence of the Incoherence*. Nevertheless, he limited his arguments for God's existence to what he held that the Qur'an actually supported. He does give a simple design argument, but the following is interesting in that it goes beyond mere design and argues from fitness. Thus it is an early form of a fine-tuning argument. That is, we observe that there is an order to things that serves to produce an environment that allows, even fosters, the existence and life of other things. Ultimately, we have a context that furthers human life. This harmony of the whole universe is intentional and so cannot be thought to have occurred by chance.

> We would say that the method which the Divine Book has adopted, and by which it has invited all to believe, is, when thoroughly investigated from the Quran, dependent upon two principles. The one is a knowledge of God's solicitude for man, and the creation of everything for his sake. We would call this the argument of solicitude. The second is the creation of the essences of the existent things, as for example, the creation of life in the minerals, and feeling and intelligence. We would call this method the "argument of creation." The first method is founded upon two principles: first that all the existent things suit man; secondly, that this suitability must have existed in the mind of the Maker before He intended to make the object in question, for it cannot be obtained by chance alone. Now their suitability for the existence of man can be easily ascertained by the suitability of day and night, sun and moon, for the existence of man. Such is also the case with the suitability of the four seasons, and of the place in which he lives, that is, the earth. It is also apparent with respect to animals, vegetables, and minerals; and many other

---

[11]Al-Ghazali, *The Jerusalem Tract*, trans. Al Tibawi, *Islamic Quarterly* 9 (1965): 67. The ending quote is from Qur'an 14:10.

things, such as rain, rivers, seas, the whole of the earth, water, fire and air. It is also evident from the different members of his body, on account of their suitability for the preservation of his life and existence. On the whole, a knowledge of the benefit derived from all the existent things may be included in it. So it is necessary for a man who wants to know God perfectly, to investigate the benefits derived from existent things. In the argument of creation is included the existence of the animal world, the plant world, and the heavens. . . . So it is right to say from the two foregoing principles that for every existent thing there is an inventor. There are many arguments, according to the number of the created things, which can be advanced to prove this premise. Thus it is necessary for one who wants to know God as He ought to be known, to acquaint himself with the essence of things, so that he may get information about the creation of all things. For who cannot understand the real substance and purpose of a thing, cannot understand the minor meaning of its creation.[12]

The argument as Averroes summarizes it is this:

(1) The universe evidences fitness: it is suited for a single purpose.

(2) When something complex is suited for a single purpose it must be intentionally so ordered.

(3) There is, therefore, an intentional creator of the universe, namely, God.

This remains a powerful argument. It can be bypassed really only two ways. The first would be to insist that chance is still an option. That demands some method of minimizing what turn out to be overwhelming probabilities. The second is to find some universe machine that somehow produces fine-tuning. But we are getting ahead of ourselves here.

3.1.8.3 John Scotus Eriugena. John Scotus Eriugena (815–877) was an Irish Christian theologian and philosopher. It was typical for commentators on the prologue of the Gospel of John, in John 1, to use this as an

---

[12]Averroes, *An Exposition of the Methods of Argument Concerning the Doctrines of the Faith*, trans. Mohammad Jamil-ub-Behman (Baroda: Manibhai Mathurbhal Gupta, 1921), 120-23.

excuse to do a bit of philosophy, especially to answer the epistemological question as to just how God is known to us. Here he *is* Word.
John Scotus's argument is intriguing in that it uses biological, legal-
moral, and geometric examples of complex ordering as evidence in a
simple generalization to an intelligent source.

> If you want to know how, or by what reason, all things that are made
> through the Word thus subsist vitally, causally, and in the same manner
> in him, consider examples chosen from created nature. Learn to know
> the maker from those things that are made in him and by him. "For the
> invisible things of him," as the Apostle says, "are clearly understood by
> the intelligence, being understood from the things that are made."
>
> Consider the infinite, multiple power of the seed—how many grasses,
> fruits, and animals are contained in each kind of seed; and how there
> surges forth from each a beautiful, innumerable multiplicity of forms.
> Contemplate with your inner eye how in a master the many laws of an
> art or science are one; how they live in the spirit that disposes them.
> Contemplate how an infinite number of lines may subsist in a single
> point, and other similar examples drawn from nature.
>
> From the contemplation of such as these, raised above all things by
> the wings of natural contemplation, illuminated and supported by divine
> grace, you will be able to penetrate by the keenness of your mind the
> secrets of the Word and, to the extent that it is granted to the human
> being who seeks signs of God, you will see how all things made by the
> Word live in the Word and are life: "For in him," as the Sacred Scripture
> says, "We live and move and have our being."[13]

3.1.8.4 Thomas Aquinas. Thomas Aquinas (1225–1274) provides another example of a commentary on John. What is remarkable here is
the fine-tuning component, as well as Thomas's note that teleology is
the easiest way to see God's creative authority:

> Some attained to a knowledge of God through his authority, and this is
> the most efficacious way. For we see the things in nature acting for an

---

[13]John Scotus Eriugena, *Homily on the Prologue to the Gospel of St. John*, trans. Christopher Bam-
ford (Hudson, NY: Lindisfarne Press, 1990).

end, and attaining to ends which are both useful and certain. And since they lack intelligence, they are unable to direct themselves, but must be directed and moved by one directing them, and who possesses an intellect. Thus it is that the movement of the things of nature toward a certain end indicates the existence of something higher by which the things of nature are directed to an end and governed. And so, since the whole course of nature advances to an end in an orderly way and is directed, we have to posit something higher which directs and governs them as Lord; and this is God. This authority in governing is shown to be in the Word of God when he says, Lord. Thus the Psalm (88:10) says: "You rule the power of the sea, and you still the swelling of its waves," as though saying: You are the Lord and govern all things. John shows that he knows this about the Word when he says below (1:11), "He came unto his own," i.e., to the world, since the whole universe is his own.[14]

Two aspects of design stand out here. First is the matter of functional complexity, not just individual things, but the "whole course of nature" itself. Second, there is here again the argument that intelligence comes only from intelligence.

I omit here any discussion of Thomas's fifth way since it is included under the cosmological argument. It does make use of harmony, and so it is often included in histories of design arguments. But harmony and teleology appear in the fifth way only as indicators of contingency, and so it is properly a form of cosmological argument. The above, however, is more clearly an example of teleological reasoning from Thomas.

Further Reading

On these Stoic arguments see Myrto Dragona-Monachou, *The Stoic Arguments for the Existence and the Providence of God* (Athens: National and Capodistrian University of Athens, 1976).

On Lactantius see Robert Eustace, *A Treatise on the Anger of God: Lactantius* (Whitefish, MT: Kessinger, 2006).

---

[14]Thomas Aquinas, *Commentary on the Gospel Of St. John*, trans. James Weisheipl (Albany, NY: Magi Books, 1998), prologue, 3.

On John Scotus I suggest starting with Dermot Moran, "John Scottus Eriugena" in *Stanford Encyclopedia of Philosophy*, ed. Edward N. Zalta, winter 2019 ed., https://plato.stanford.edu/archives/win2019/entries/scottus-eriugena/. This contains an excellent bibliography.

On the medievals, I recommend starting with Frederick Copleston, *A History of Philosophy*, vol. 2 (London: A&C Black, 2003).

3.2 Phase Two: Analogy Arguments

3.2.1 David Hume and William Paley. We have seen the use of human productions as illustrations of design in Stoic arguments. Here they are really just a subset of natural objects with functional complexity that need explanation. In the modern discussion, which I will call phase two, natural and human productions are juxtaposed in quite a different way. They form an analogical argument. This type of argument was popular in the late seventeenth and the eighteenth centuries among both deists and Christians, and the use of the clock as the basis of analogy was common. In fact, the image of clockworks was a popular picture of the universe in general.[15]

Analogical arguments are a kind of inductive argument with the following form:

1. *S* is similar to *T* in certain (known) respects.

2. *S* has some further feature *Q*.

3. Therefore, *T* also has the feature *Q*, or some feature *Q** similar to *Q*.[16]

This type of reasoning may be, in fact, one of the most frequent in the sciences. Charles Darwin used an analogical argument as the basis for natural selection:

---

[15]On this see James Sire, *The Universe Next Door*, 5th ed. (Downers Grove, IL: InterVarsity Press, 2009), chap. 3.

[16]This is taken from Paul Bartha, "Analogy and Analogical Reasoning," in *Stanford Encyclopedia of Philosophy*, ed. Edward N. Zalta, spring 2019 ed., https://plato.stanford.edu/archives/spr2019/entries/reasoning-analogy/.

Why may I not invent the hypothesis of Natural Selection (which from the analogy of domestic productions, and from what we know of the struggle of existence and of the variability of organic beings, is, in some very slight degree, in itself probable) and try whether this hypothesis of Natural Selection does not explain (as I think it does) a large number of facts.[17]

In relation to God's existence, the classic confrontation over the analogical form of the teleological argument is that of David Hume (1711–1776) and William Paley (1743–1805). Hume was a Scottish politician, historian, and philosopher. His writings include the massive *History of England*, which became a bestseller and made him a wealthy man. He is best known today, however, for his *Dialogues Concerning Natural Religion*, though at the time it was not well received and sold poorly. It is here that we find the most trenchant critique of design arguments. Hume is representative of the first backlash against this argument. It is not a denial of the basic logic, but more a reaction to an overreaching conclusion. So it will produce, in Paley for example, a much humbler outcome.

Paley, English clergyman, moral philosopher, and apologist, first interacted with Hume during his undergraduate studies at Christ College, Cambridge. He would go on to be a lecturer in moral philosophy at Cambridge University, and this led to his publication of *The Principles of Moral and Political Philosophy*. In 1782 he became the archdeacon of Carlisle. In 1802, he published his *Natural Theology; or, Evidences of the Existence and Attributes of the Deity*.

The history of this analogical argument in England goes back to the blossoming of biology and astronomy in the seventeenth century. A good example is John Ray (1627–1705) and his 1691 book, *The Wisdom of God Manifested in the Works of the Creation*. He begins by rejecting

---

[17]Charles Darwin, "To J. S. Henslow 8 May [1860]," www.darwinproject.ac.uk/letter/DCP-LETT -2791.xml. Also contained in several collections of Darwin's correspondence, including *More Letters of Charles Darwin*, ed. Francis Darwin (New York: D. Appleton, 1903).

Aristotle's view of eternal matter and the chance hypothesis of Democritus and Epicurus, instead arguing that Cicero got it right. He then proceeds with over two hundred pages of examples from nature that exhibit the sort of complexity in human productions, like clocks, known to occur only by intelligent creativity.

Similar analogical arguments and collections of scientific evidence can be found in Ralph Cudworth (1678), Henry More (1668), and many others.[18] So Paley stands in a long tradition of argument, as does Hume. There is really nothing new here, but it is the culmination of two centuries of discussion and dialogue and it rightly deserves to have become the standard example of analogical design argumentation. I will keep this in chronological order and begin with Hume.

Hume's 1776 *Dialogues* is precisely that: a dialogue. It is staged between three fictional characters: Cleanthes, empiricist and advocate of the teleological argument; Demea, the fideist who accepts the deductive cosmological argument but rejects evidential arguments; and Philo, who, while not an atheist, does not think human reason can ascertain detailed knowledge of (the Christian) God. Which one is Hume? Most scholars think Philo is the most likely candidate, but Hume's actual position, as seen in earlier writings, is somewhere between Philo and Cleanthes, with a little of Demea thrown in.[19] He himself is neither a participant nor the narrator. This is Hume's own internal dialogue.

First, however, we need to look at his 1757 *Natural History of Religion*, where Hume clearly accepted a simplified form of design argument. He is perfectly well aware that human beings pervert their theistic conceptions, and that religions have done monstrous things in God's name,

---

[18]Ralph Cudworth, *The True Intellectual System of the Universe: The First Part Wherein All the Reason and Philosophy of Atheism Is Confuted and Its Impossibility Demonstrated* (London: Thomas Tegg, 1845); and Henry More, *Divine Dialogues containing sundry disquisitions & instructions concerning the attributes and providence of God* (Glasgow: Robert Foulis, 1743).

[19]Much ink has been spilled on this question. I think a good place to begin is with Jordan Sobel, *Logic and Theism* (Cambridge: Cambridge University Press, 2004), sec. 7.5-6.

and even that in our early history we may not have come to this idea immediately.[20] Nevertheless, design in nature leads to theism, at least a weak and broad form of it.

> Though the stupidity of men, barbarous and uninstructed, be so great that they may not see a sovereign author in the more obvious works of nature, to which they are so much familiarized; yet it scarcely seems possible that any one of good understanding should reject that idea, when once it is suggested to him. A purpose, an intention, a design, is evident in everything; and when our comprehension is so far enlarged as to contemplate the first rise of this visible system, we must adopt, with the strongest conviction, the idea of some intelligent cause or author. The uniform maxims, too, which prevail throughout the whole frame of the universe, naturally, if not necessarily, lead us to conceive this intelligence as single and undivided, where the prejudices of education oppose not so reasonable a theory. Even the contrarieties of nature, by discovering themselves everywhere, become proofs of some consistent plan, and establish one single purpose or intention, however inexplicable and incomprehensible. . . .
>
> The universal propensity to believe in an invisible, intelligent power, if not an original instinct, being at least a general attendant of human nature, may be considered as a kind of mark or stamp, which the divine workman has set upon his work; and nothing surely can more dignify mankind than to be thus selected from all the other parts of the creation, and to bear the image or impression of the universal Creator. But consult this image, as it appears in the popular religions of the world. How is the deity disfigured in our representations of him! What caprice, absurdity, and immorality are attributed to him! How much is he degraded even below the character which we should naturally, in common life, ascribe to a man of sense and virtue!
>
> What a noble privilege is it of human reason to attain the knowledge of the supreme Being; and, from the visible works of nature, be enabled to infer so sublime a principle as its supreme Creator?[21]

---

[20]As we have seen, late nineteenth-century anthropology will show Hume to be wrong about this.

[21]David Hume, *The Natural History of Religion* (London: A. & H. Bradlaugh Bonner, 1889), sec. 15, pp. 72-74.

Granted, this was twenty years earlier than the *Dialogues*, but there is no indication that Hume had changed his mind on this matter. In any case, Hume is not an atheist, though current atheists often portray him as such. Then again, neither is Philo for that matter. But Hume clearly does want to show that design will not give us the full Christian God as many in his time had attempted to do.

The discussion in part two of the *Dialogues* begins with Cleanthes's statement of a traditional analogical design argument:

> All these various machines, and even their most minute parts, are adjusted to each other with an accuracy which ravishes into admiration all men who have ever contemplated them. The curious adapting of means to ends, throughout all nature, resembles exactly, though it much exceeds, the productions of human contrivance; of human designs, thought, wisdom, and intelligence. Since, therefore, the effects resemble each other, we are led to infer, by all the rules of analogy, that the causes also resemble; and that the Author of Nature is somewhat similar to the mind of man.[22]

What follows is a series of objecting statements put forward by Philo in pursuit of his conclusion that the analogy underlying the teleological argument is weak. I leave out much of the elaboration, as well as the interspersed responses and affirmations by Cleanthes and Demea:

> But wherever you depart, in the least, from the similarity of the cases, you diminish proportionably the evidence; and may at last bring it to a very weak analogy, which is confessedly liable to error and uncertainty. . . .
>
> If we see a house, CLEANTHES, we conclude, with the greatest certainty, that it had an architect or builder; because this is precisely that species of effect which we have experienced to proceed from that species of cause. But surely you will not affirm, that the universe bears such a resemblance to a house, that we can with the same certainty infer a similar cause, or that the analogy is here entire and perfect. The

---

[22]David Hume, *Dialogues Concerning Natural Religion* (London: Longmans, Green, 1898), part 2.

dissimilitude is so striking, that the utmost you can here pretend to is a guess, a conjecture, a presumption concerning a similar cause; and how that pretension will be received in the world, I leave you to consider.[23]

The first objection is that the two sides of the analogy are dissimilar. Now Philo argues that the analogy could only show that a human-like mind is needed, including the option of pantheism.

> Order, arrangement, or the adjustment of final causes, is not of itself any proof of design; but only so far as it has been experienced to proceed from that principle. For aught we can know a priori, matter may contain the source or spring of order originally within itself, as well as mind does; and there is no more difficulty in conceiving, that the several elements, from an internal unknown cause, may fall into the most exquisite arrangement, than to conceive that their ideas, in the great universal mind, from a like internal unknown cause, fall into that arrangement. The equal possibility of both these suppositions is allowed.[24]

Philo then proceeds to argue that the analogy does not permit us to say anything about the universe as a whole, based only on our knowledge of some of the parts:

> But, allowing that we were to take the operations of one part of nature upon another, for the foundation of our judgment concerning the origin of the whole (which can never be admitted), yet why select so minute, so weak, so bounded a principle, as the reason and design of animals is found to be upon this planet? What peculiar privilege has this little agitation of the brain which we call thought, that we must thus make it the model of the whole universe? Our partiality in our own favour does indeed present it on all occasions; but sound philosophy ought carefully to guard against so natural an illusion.
>
> So far from admitting . . . that the operations of a part can afford us any just conclusion concerning the origin of the whole, I will not allow

---

[23]Hume, *Dialogues Concerning Natural Religion*, part 2.
[24]Hume, *Dialogues Concerning Natural Religion*, part 2.

any one part to form a rule for another part, if the latter be very remote from the former.[25]

By extension, Philo argues, we can say nothing about other worlds. We would have to visit and observe them, most of them in fact, and of course we have no such observations. (Remember it is 1776!) So he concludes part two by noting that

> in this cautious proceeding of the astronomers, you may read your own condemnation, CLEANTHES; or rather may see, that the subject in which you are engaged exceeds all human reason and inquiry. Can you pretend to show any such similarity between the fabric of a house, and the generation of a universe? Have you ever seen nature in any such situation as resembles the first arrangement of the elements? Have worlds ever been formed under your eye; and have you had leisure to observe the whole progress of the phenomenon, from the first appearance of order to its final consummation? If you have, then cite your experience, and deliver your theory.[26]

In part five, Philo raises a number of limiting factors to any conclusion from design. The analogy can only demonstrate what it can demonstrate.

> First, By this method of reasoning, you renounce all claim to infinity in any of the attributes of the Deity. For, as the cause ought only to be proportioned to the effect, and the effect, so far as it falls under our cognisance, is not infinite. . . .
>
> Secondly, You have no reason, on your theory, for ascribing perfection to the Deity, even in his finite capacity, or for supposing him free from every error, mistake, or incoherence, in his undertakings. There are many inexplicable difficulties in the works of Nature, which, if we allow a perfect author to be proved a priori, are easily solved, and become only seeming difficulties, from the narrow capacity of man, who cannot trace infinite relations.

---

[25]Hume, *Dialogues Concerning Natural Religion*, part 2.
[26]Hume, *Dialogues Concerning Natural Religion*, part 2.

But were this world ever so perfect a production, it must still remain uncertain, whether all the excellences of the work can justly be ascribed to the workman. . . . Many worlds might have been botched and bungled, throughout an eternity, ere this system was struck out; much labour lost, many fruitless trials made; and a slow, but continued improvement carried on during infinite ages in the art of world-making. In such subjects, who can determine, where the truth lies; nay, who can conjecture where the probability lies, amidst a great number of hypotheses which may be proposed, and a still greater which may be imagined?

And what shadow of an argument, continued PHILO, can you produce, from your hypothesis, to prove the unity of the Deity? A great number of men join in building a house or ship, in rearing a city, in framing a commonwealth; why may not several deities combine in contriving and framing a world?

To multiply causes without necessity, is indeed contrary to true philosophy. . . .

But further, CLEANTHES: men are mortal, and renew their species by generation; and this is common to all living creatures. The two great sexes of male and female, says MILTON, animate the world. Why must this circumstance, so universal, so essential, be excluded from those numerous and limited deities?

Why not assert the deity or deities to be corporeal, and to have eyes, a nose, mouth, ears, &c.?

In a word, CLEANTHES, a man who follows your hypothesis is able perhaps to assert, or conjecture, that the universe, sometime, arose from something like design: but beyond that position he cannot ascertain one single circumstance.[27]

Throughout the rest of the *Dialogues,* Hume's Philo raises other issues. In part eight he notes that we cannot eliminate the possibility, at least on the basis of this analogy, that the design is actually just a chance arrangement of atoms. In parts ten and eleven he brings up the problem of evil. Ultimately, Philo rejects it, arguing that Christians have good

---

[27]Hume, *Dialogues Concerning Natural Religion*, part 5.

responses to the presence of evil in the world, but he does conclude that evil weakens our ability to ascribe *omni*benevolence to God.

These objections can be summarized in two categories. As with all analogical arguments, you can go wrong by basing the comparison on either *insufficient* or on *biased* sampling. We simply do not have enough evidence to reach a well-defined conclusion. We cannot, for example, show that God is infinite, and the presence of evil prevents us from concluding his omnibenevolence. Worse yet, we only have this *one* universe. And our evidence is too biased or selective to show that there is a solidly based comparison here. The universe is just not much like a machine.

We should note that Philo several times affirms both his belief in God and his acceptance of the design argument as a weak analogy that does allow the inference to a creative intelligence. This is especially clear at the end of the *Dialogues*. This is also Hume's conclusion. We cannot infer the Christian religion or any other religion from this argument. But we can start here. Natural theology is possible:

> If the whole of Natural Theology, as some people seem to maintain, resolves itself into one simple, though somewhat ambiguous, at least undefined proposition, That the cause or causes of order in the universe probably bear some remote analogy to human intelligence: If this proposition be not capable of extension, variation, or more particular explication: If it affords no inference that affects human life, or can be the source of any action or forbearance: And if the analogy, imperfect as it is, can be carried no further than to the human intelligence, and cannot be transferred, with any appearance of probability, to the other qualities of the mind; if this really be the case, what can the most inquisitive, contemplative, and religious man do more than give a plain, philosophical assent to the proposition, as often as it occurs, and believe that the arguments on which it is established exceed the objections which lie against it?
>
> To be a philosophical Sceptic is, in a man of letters, the first and most essential step towards being a sound, believing Christian.[28]

---

[28]Hume, *Dialogues Concerning Natural Religion*, part 12.

Paley's design argument follows the familiar pattern. The actual argument is nothing more than a summary conclusion to a story. In Cicero's case it was about showing a clock (horologe) to savage Britons. This story is about a now famous walk in the heath: the grassy, rock-strewn hills of England. Suppose that as you walk along you stumble across a rock. What do you think? Well, nothing really. There are lots of them around, and they got there by some random natural sequence of events. Suppose, however, that you stumble upon a watch. Now what do you think, especially after examining it carefully, taking it apart, and so on? Well, at the very least you think that this is the result of some intelligence-directed and intentional process, and so now you *do* wonder how this could have got here.

Paley concludes the story by observing, "Every indication of contrivance, every manifestation of design, which existed in the watch, exists in the works of nature; with the difference, on the side of nature, of being greater and more, and that in a degree which exceeds all computation."[29] So it, too, must have an intelligent source. That is the argument.

Most of this first chapter of *Natural Theology*, however, consists of Paley's responses to eight objections, including, I think, all of Philo's:

> Nor would it, I apprehend, weaken the conclusion, that we had never seen a watch made; that we had never known an artist capable of making one; that we were altogether incapable of executing such a piece of workmanship ourselves, or of understanding in what manner it was performed. . . . Nor can I perceive that it varies at all the inference, whether the question arise concerning a human agent, or concerning an agent of a different species, or an agent possessing, in some respects, a different nature.
>
> Neither, secondly, would it invalidate our conclusion, that the watch sometimes went wrong, or that it seldom went exactly right. The purpose of the machinery, the design, and the designer, might be evident, and in

---

[29]William Paley, *Natural Theology* (London: Faulder, 1802), 3 (introduction).

the case supposed would be evident, in whatever way we accounted for the irregularity of the movement, or whether we could account for it or not. It is not necessary that a machine be perfect, in order to show with what design it was made: still less necessary, where the only question is, whether it were made with any design at all.

Nor, thirdly, would it bring any uncertainty into the argument, if there were a few parts of the watch, concerning which we could not discover, or had not yet discovered, in what manner they conduced to the general effect; or even some parts, concerning which we could not ascertain, whether they conduced to that effect in any manner whatever. For, as to the first branch of the case; if by the loss, or disorder, or decay of the parts in question, the movement of the watch were found in fact to be stopped, or disturbed, or retarded, no doubt would remain in our minds as to the utility or intention of these parts. . . . Then, as to the second thing supposed, namely, that there were parts which might be spared, without prejudice to the movement of the watch, and that we had proved this by experiment—these superfluous parts, even if we were completely assured that they were such, would not vacate the reasoning which we had instituted concerning other parts. The indication of contrivance remained, with respect to them, nearly as it was before.

Nor, fourthly, would any man in his senses think the existence of the watch, with its various machinery, accounted for, by being told that it was one out of possible combinations of material forms; that whatever he had found in the place where he found the watch, must have contained some internal configuration or other; and that this configuration might be the structure now exhibited, viz. of the works of a watch, as well as a different structure.

Nor, fifthly, would it yield his inquiry more satisfaction to be answered, that there existed in things a principle of order, which had disposed the parts of the watch into their present form and situation. He never knew a watch made by the principle of order; nor can he even form to himself an idea of what is meant by a principle of order, distinct from the intelligence of the watchmaker.

Sixthly, he would be surprised to hear that the mechanism of the watch was no proof of contrivance, only a motive to induce the mind to think so.

And not less surprised to be informed, that the watch in his hand was nothing more than the result of the laws of *metallic* nature. It is a perversion of language to assign any law, as the efficient, operative cause of anything. A law presupposes an agent. . . .

Neither, lastly, would our observer be driven out of his conclusion, or from his confidence in its truth, by being told that he knew nothing at all about the matter. He knows enough for his argument: he knows the utility of the end: he knows the subserviency and adaptation of the means to the end. These points being known, his ignorance of other points, his doubts concerning other points, affect not the certainty of his reasoning. The consciousness of knowing little, need not beget a distrust of that which he does know.[30]

Paley continues to examine one further possibility. Suppose it turns out that the watch has the uncanny ability to reproduce itself. Now what should one think?

He would reflect, that though the watch before him were, *in some sense*, the maker of the watch, which was fabricated in the course of its movements, yet it was in a very different sense from that, in which a carpenter, for instance, is the maker of a chair; the author of its contrivance, the cause of the relation of its parts to their use. With respect to these, the first watch was no cause at all to the second: in no such sense as this was it the author of the constitution and order, either of the parts which the new watch contained, or of the parts by the aid and instrumentality of which it was produced. We might possibly say, but with great latitude of expression, that a stream of water ground corn: but no latitude of expression would allow us to say, no stretch of conjecture could lead us to think, that the stream of water built the mill, though it were too ancient for us to know who the builder was. What the stream of water does in the affair, is neither more nor less than this; by the application of an unintelligent impulse to a mechanism previously arranged, arranged independently of it, and arranged by intelligence, an effect is produced, viz. the corn is ground. But the effect results from the arrangement. The

---

[30]Paley, *Natural Theology* 1, I-VIII.

force of the stream cannot be said to be the cause or author of the effect, still less of the arrangement. Understanding and plan in the formation of the mill were not the less necessary, for any share which the water has in grinding the corn: yet is this share the same, as that which the watch would have contributed to the production of the new watch, upon the supposition assumed in the last section. Therefore,

Though it be now no longer probable, that the individual watch, which our observer had found, was made immediately by the hand of an artificer, yet doth not this alteration in anywise affect the inference, that an artificer had been originally employed and concerned in the production. The argument from design remains as it was.[31]

So, Paley concludes that an intervening process, even one that proceeds by itself—automatically—does nothing to mitigate the need for an original designer. In fact, it increases the demand, since we now need a source for the causal connections in the process that maintain the design, as well as the build-in of the process (the assembly line) into the original product. Reproducer watches are more complexly functional than nonreproducers, and so are humans, hippos, and hydrangeas.

What is the takeaway from this debate? Certainly Hume-type objections have validity. There are severe limitations on what the argument can give us as to the nature of the intelligent source of design. This argument does not, for example, give us infinity, simplicity, singularity, changelessness, timelessness, immateriality—none of the Parmenidean qualities. Nor does it guarantee perfect goodness. Evil, after all, needs intelligent design too.[32] Nevertheless, nothing here disputes the need for an extremely creative and intelligent source.

On the other hand, Paley-type responses leave us with two conclusions. First, all of Philo's limiting objections are irrelevant to the final conclusion. Most importantly, the problem of evil is just not a defeater

---

[31]Paley, *Natural Theology* 2.2-3.

[32]For what it is worth, Hume's argument is the only philosophical argument I know of for the reality of an actual intelligent source of the evils in this world, an idea present in almost all religious traditions, and certainly in the Jewish/Christian/Islamic idea of Satan.

to the need for an intelligent source. If all the universe were disorder, chaos, and suffering (actually, suffering would demand prior order), and there is *only one* single example of good and functional ordering, then that would still be enough to require an intelligent source. In that sense, any actual universe at all would be enough evidence. It only takes one watch!

Second, the design arguments can say nothing about the process that mediates between designer(s) and designed. I like car analogies here. When I see the brand-new lineup of cars at my local dealer, full of computer-controlled operating and safety features, I am quite entitled to the conclusion that there is a sophisticated design team behind it. But I know nothing about the process in between that brought the finished car to the showroom. I cannot even conclude that there is one. Perhaps there is no assembly line at a factory at all. Maybe the design team just snaps their fingers and the cars magically come together and are teleported to the showroom instantaneously. Or maybe there is an extended assembly-line process in which cars are laboriously put together piece by piece and transported by truck thousands of miles to the showroom. There is nothing in the argument that stipulates which, if any, process is involved, nor, in turn, does anything about the properties of the process have any effect back on the argument.

In addition, there is nothing that stipulates that the original design plan is successfully carried out in this process. Perhaps all sorts of errors are made. Perhaps a year later we find out that these cars have been recalled multiple times, many people have been injured, some even killed. The original conclusion still stands. The point is just that the teleological argument is immune to all of these matters. They are, no doubt, essential to one's respective theology, and so we will demand a theodicy of some sort. However, all of this is irrelevant to the argument for God's existence. That is Paley's point. The argument, as he says, remains as it is.

3.2.1.1 James Orr, George F. Wright, and Henry Beach. Paley proved
to be quite prophetic here. He clearly foresees something like evolution—Darwin was born only four years after Paley died—and rightly
reckons it ineffective as a defeater. So did Christians in the wake of
Darwin. *The Fundamentals: A Testimony to the Truth* was first published
as quarterly pamphlets between 1910 and 1915 by the leading theologians and philosophers of conservative Christianity.[33] It includes three
essays on the topic of science and religion by James Orr, George F.
Wright, and Henry Beach.

None of them see evolution as a challenge. They do, of course, have
quarrels with Darwinism, especially the attempt to account for human
intentionality by way of a mechanical physical process. Orr especially
notes that evolution, seen just as a process, *does* not and *can* not account
for original design, nor for the large jumps to life, consciousness, intelligence, and morality that follow it.[34] The real issue, he argues, is whether
there exists a (theistic) God who can direct this process, not the nature
of the process itself.[35] He even insists that by the time all of the necessary
qualifiers and additions are added to evolution, especially an accounting
for large jumps and the uniformity of natural law, "evolution" has
become just "a new name for 'creation,' only that the creative power now
works from *within*, instead of . . . in an *external*, plastic fashion."[36]

But in the end, Darwin somehow wins the cultural argument. It will
seem to most intellectuals and academicians that evolution destroys the
need for God. As Darwin himself says in his autobiography,

> The old argument of design in nature, as given by Paley, which formerly
> seemed to me so conclusive, fails, now that the law of natural selection

---

[33]Published ultimately by the Bible Institute of Los Angeles (now Biola University) in 1917. It was
reprinted by Baker Books (Grand Rapids, MI) in 2003.

[34]See the discussion in James Orr, "Science and Christian Faith," *The Fundamentals: A Testimony to
the Truth*, ed. R. A. Torrey, A. C. Dixon et al. (1917; repr., Grand Rapids, MI: Baker Books,
2003), 1:346.

[35]Orr, "Science and Christian Faith," 1:339.

[36]Orr, "Science and Christian Faith," 1:346.

had been discovered. We can no longer argue that, for instance, the beautiful hinge of a bivalve shell must have been made by an intelligent being, like the hinge of a door by man. There seems to be no more design in the variability of organic beings and in the action of natural selection, than in the course which the wind blows. Everything in nature is the result of fixed laws.[37]

3.2.2 Charles Sanders Peirce. Frequently noted as the father of pragmatism, the American philosopher Charles Peirce (1839–1914) is best known for identifying a third type of logical argument in addition to induction and deduction: abduction. His "Neglected Argument for the Reality of God" is a good example of this. There is here no direct line of inference, but a simple jump from the evidence to the obviously best explanation. This is actually the most common form of reasoning we perform on an average day: with only a brief weighing of all the possibilities, we conclude to the most likely. Looking at the conditions of our universe, any normal, as Peirce puts it, person will come to believe this conclusion. In this case, there is clearly an underlying analogy at work, but it is hardly worth mentioning for Peirce. In that respect, this is not much more than Cicero's argument: just updated evidence.

He refers here to the three universes of experience. He means by that the realms of ideas, of actuality, and of signs—that is, all those things that mediate between mind and objects. So here is the neglected but obvious argument, or process of thought, that produces a specified belief:

> Let the Muser, for example, after well appreciating, in its breadth and depth, the unspeakable variety of each Universe, turn to those phenomena that are of the nature of homogeneities of connectedness in each; and what a spectacle will unroll itself! As a mere hint of them I may point out that every small part of space, however remote, is bounded by

---

[37]Charles Darwin, *Life and Letters of Charles Darwin*, ed. Francis Darwin (New York: D. Appleton, 1887), 1:279.

just such neighbouring parts as every other, without a single exception throughout immensity. The matter of Nature is in every star of the same elementary kinds, and (except for variations of circumstance) what is more wonderful still, throughout the whole visible universe, about the same proportions of the different chemical elements prevail. Though the mere catalogue of known carbon-compounds alone would fill an un-wieldy volume, and perhaps, if the truth were known, the number of amido-acids alone is greater, yet it is unlikely that there are in all more than about 600 elements, of which 500 dart through space too swiftly to be held down by the earth's gravitation, coronium being the slowest-moving of these. This small number bespeaks comparative simplicity of structure. Yet no mathematician but will confess the present hope-lessness of attempting to comprehend the constitution of the hydrogen-atom, the simplest of the elements that can be held to earth.

From speculations on the homogeneities of each Universe, the Muser will naturally pass to the consideration of homogeneities and connections between two different Universes, or all three. Especially in them all we find one type of occurrence, that of growth, itself consisting in the homogeneities of small parts. This is evident in the growth of motion into displacement, and the growth of force into motion. In growth, too, we find that the three Universes conspire; and a universal feature of it is provision for later stages in earlier ones. This is a specimen of certain lines of reflection which will inevitably suggest the hypothesis of God's Reality. It is not that such phenomena might not be capable of being accounted for, in one sense, by the action of chance with the smallest conceivable dose of a higher element; for if by God be meant the *Ens necessarium*, that very hypothesis requires that such should be the case. But the point is that that sort of expla-nation leaves a mental explanation just as needful as before. Tell me, upon sufficient authority, that all cerebration depends upon move-ments of neurites that strictly obey certain physical laws, and that thus all expressions of thought, both external and internal, receive a physical explanation, and I shall be ready to believe you. But if you go on to say that this explodes the theory that my neighbour and myself are gov-erned by reason, and are thinking beings, I must frankly say that it will not give me a high opinion of your intelligence. But however that may be, in the Pure Play of Musement the idea of God's Reality will be sure sooner or later to be found an attractive fancy, which the Muser will develop in various ways. The more he ponders it, the more it will find response in every part of his mind, for its beauty, for its supplying an ideal of life, and for its thoroughly satisfactory explanation of his whole threefold environment.

The hypothesis of God is a peculiar one, in that it supposes an infinitely incomprehensible object, although every hypothesis, as such, supposes its object to be truly conceived in the hypothesis. This leaves the hypothesis but one way of understanding itself; namely, as vague yet as true so far as it is definite, and as continually tending to define itself more and more, and without limit. The hypothesis, being thus itself inevitably subject to the law of growth, appears in its vagueness to represent God as so, albeit this is directly contradicted in the hypothesis from its very first phase. But this apparent attribution of growth to God, since it is ineradicable from the hypothesis, cannot, according to the hypothesis, be flatly false. Its implications concerning the Universes will be maintained in the hypothesis, while its implications concerning God will be partly disavowed, and yet held to be less false than their denial would be. Thus the hypothesis will lead to our thinking of features of each Universe as purposed; and this will stand or fall with the hypothesis. Yet a purpose essentially involves growth, and so cannot be attributed to God. Still it will, according to the hypothesis, be less false to speak so than to represent God as purposeless.

Assured as I am from my own personal experience that every man capable of so controlling his attention as to perform a little exact thinking will, if he examines Zeno's argument about Achilles and the tortoise, come to think, as I do, that it is nothing but a contemptible catch, I do not think that I either am or ought to be less assured, from what I know of the effects of Musement on myself and others, that any normal man who considers the three Universes in the light of the hypothesis of God's Reality, and pursues that line of reflection in scientific singleness of heart, will come to be stirred to the depths of his nature by the beauty of the idea and by its august practicality, even to the point of earnestly loving and adoring his strictly hypothetical God, and to that of desiring above all things to shape the whole conduct of life and all the springs of action into conformity with that hypothesis. Now to be deliberately and thoroughly prepared to shape one's conduct into conformity with a proposition is neither more nor less than the state of mind called Believing that proposition, however long the conscious classification of it under that head be postponed.[38]

Peirce allows for two possible objections here, but considers them not worthy of our intelligence: that this is all the result of chance, and that this might be the result of a physical process consisting of a sequence of small steps. Neither can dissuade us of the need for a purposeful intelligence. And so the beauty and the "august practicality" of this conclusion will, in the end, lead us to belief.

3.2.3 Mohandas Karamchand Gandhi. Known best by his honorific title, Mahatma, Mohandas Gandhi (1869–1948) was the leader of the independence movement in India. He remained a Hindu throughout his life but had great respect for and read widely in other religious traditions. In a series of articles in the weekly journal he published from 1919 to 1931, *Young India*, titled "God Is," Gandhi discussed a number of the arguments in response to agnostic letters he had received. They included the cosmological, moral, religious experience, and *consensus gentium* arguments. But he seems particularly attracted to the teleological, and sees it as evident from natural law, the course of history, and the moral law:

> I do feel . . . that there is an orderliness in the universe, there is an unalterable Law governing everything and every being that exists or lives. It is not a blind Law; for no blind law can govern the conduct of living beings. . . . That Law then which governs all life is God. Law and Lawgiver are one.

---

[38]Charles S. Peirce, "A Neglected Argument for the Reality of God," *Hibbert Journal* (1908): secs. 1-2.

I do dimly perceive that whilst everything around me is ever-changing, ever-dying, there is underlying all that change a living power that is changeless, that holds all together, that creates, dissolves and recreates. That informing power or spirit is God.[39]

While God transcends our senses, nevertheless our reason can know something of him. One way comes from our observation that the cosmos is not chaos. But this lawfulness is seen as part of the larger law that governs everything and does so in a way that relates to intelligent and free persons. It follows for Gandhi that God must be intellect as well.

Further Reading

On Hume: Start with William Lad Sessions, *Reading Hume's Dialogues: A Veneration for True Religion* (Bloomington: Indiana University Press, 2002). On Paley, start with Martin L. Clarke, *Paley: Evidences for the Man* (Toronto: University of Toronto Press, 1974).

For a good study of the debate in its historical context see Niall O'Flaherty, "William Paley's Moral Philosophy and the Challenge of Hume: An Enlightenment Debate?," *Modern Intellectual History* 7, no. 1 (2010): 1-31.

For a good discussion of Peirce's work and abduction see Douglas R. Anderson, *Strands of System: The Philosophy of Charles Peirce* (West Lafayette, IN: Purdue University Press, 1995).

On Gandhi, see Rama Shanker Srivastava, *Contemporary Indian Philosophy* (Delhi: Munshi Ram Manohar Lal, 1965), chaps. 26-27. Gandhi's own writings are available online (in facsimile) at the Gandhi Heritage Portal, https://www.gandhiheritageportal.org/.

3.3 Phase Three: Probability and Fine-Tuning Arguments

As I said, Darwin changed everything! Even though, in fact, evolution has no real bearing on the teleological argument,[40] that was certainly

---

[39] *Young India*, October 11, 1928, 340, https://www.gandhiheritageportal.org/journals-by-gandhiji/young-india. This, along with most of Gandhi's writings, can be accessed at the Gandhi Heritage Portal, gandhiheritageportal.org.

[40] For a good discussion of this point see C. Stephen Evans and R. Zachary Manis, *Philosophy of Religion: Thinking About Faith*, 2nd ed., Contours of Christian Philosophy (Downers Grove, IL: InterVarsity Press, 2009), 83-87.

not the common perception, nor the general understanding in academic circles. Especially the rise of the death-of-God movement in the
mid-twentieth century and the New Atheism of the late twentieth
century proclaimed to the world is that evolution has replaced God.[41]
As a result, many—but certainly not all—creationists from every religion and culture retreated into their own fideist hideouts.[42]

This is hardly surprising. Theists in philosophy had all but lost their
place in the 1930s, 1940s, and into the 1950s, at least in Europe and
North America. There were good voices at Catholic universities, and at
a few Protestant Christian colleges as well, but no one in the larger
society was listening. The aftermath of World War II continued the
dominance of evolutionary atheism in academic circles in the United
States, though it eventually brought new life to the discussion of God's
existence. But it yielded only more despair in most of Europe for at least
a decade longer. When I was in high school in Germany in the early
1960s, Sartre and Camus were kings, most of my friends were atheists,
and by the later years of that decade they had, in an attempt at finding
some hope for the future, become Marxists.

The April 8, 1966, cover of *Time* asked the question: "Is God
Dead?"[43] It featured several of the death-of-God theologians, espe-
cially Thomas Altizer (1927–2018), who had published *The Gospel of
Christian Atheism* that same year.[44] Perhaps the epitome of the brash

---

[41]See my "Evil and the New Atheism," in *God and Evil: The Case for God in a World Filled with
Pain*, ed. Chad Meister and James K. Dew Jr. (Downers Grove, IL: InterVarsity Press,
2013), 197-213.

[42]That is not to say that there were not—or are not—strong voices against autonomous evolution
itself. Of course there have been many. It is dangerous to even start, but here are a few names of
scientists in that number: Karl Heim (1874–1958), Eberhard Bertsch (b. 1949), and Siegfried
Scherer (b. 1955) in Germany; A. E. Wilder Smith (1915–1995) in England; Matti Leisola (b. 1947)
in Finland; Willem Ouweneel (b. 1944) in the Netherlands; Duane Gish (1921–2013) and Michael
Behe (b. 1952) in the United States. In the text I give some examples of scientists who have argued
specifically against the demise of God at the hands of evolution, which is a quite different matter.
And, of course, there are many more of those as well.

[43]The article, by John T. Elson, is actually titled "Toward a Hidden God," *Time*, April 8, 1966, http://
time.com/vault/issue/1966-04-08/page/98/.

[44]Thomas Altizer, *The Gospel of Christian Atheism* (Philadelphia: Westminster, 1966).

and often contemptuous New Atheism that developed in the last decades of the millennium is found in Richard Dawkins. Ever since *The Selfish Gene* in 1976, he has been preaching the death of God at the hands of Evolution, though more ardently in *The Blind Watchmaker* (1986) and much more so in *The God Delusion* (2006).[45] Here is the key text from the latter, showing how illusory he thinks teleological considerations are:

> The whole argument turns on the familiar question "Who made God?" . . . A designer God cannot be used to explain organized complexity because any God capable of designing anything would have to be complex enough to demand the same kind of explanation in his own right. God presents an infinite regress from which he cannot help us to escape. This argument . . . demonstrates that God, though not technically disprovable, is very very improbable indeed.
>
> The argument from improbability is the big one. In the traditional guise of the argument from design, it is easily today's most popular argument offered in favour of the existence of God and it is seen, by an amazingly large number of theists, as completely and utterly convincing. It is indeed a very strong and, I suspect, unanswerable argument—but in precisely the opposite direction from the theist's intention. The argument from improbability, properly deployed, comes close to proving that God does *not* exist. My name for the statistical demonstration that God almost certainly does not exist is the Ultimate Boeing 747 gambit.
>
> The creationist misappropriation of the argument from improbability always takes the same general form. . . . Some observed phenomenon—often a living creature or one of its more complex organs, but it could be anything from a molecule up to the universe itself—is correctly extolled as statistically improbable. Sometimes the language of information theory is used: the Darwinian is challenged to explain the source all the information in living matter, in the technical sense of information content as a measure of improbability or "surprise value." . . . However

---

[45]Richard Dawkins, *The Selfish Gene* (Oxford: Oxford University Press, 1976). Dawkins, *The Blind Watchmaker* (New York: Norton, 1986). It is interesting that he admits a watchmaker, even if blind. Dawkins, *The God Delusion* (Boston: Houghton Mifflin, 2006).

statistically improbable the entity you seek to explain by invoking a designer, the designer himself has got to be at least as improbable. God is the Ultimate Boeing 747.[46]

So Dawkins wants to turn the teleological argument against the theist. For now, just note that, in the process, he admits all the evidence, both the presence of information and the high improbability of the organized complexity. Nevertheless, he concludes that "people of a theological bent are often chronically incapable of distinguishing what is true from what they'd like to be true."[47] Dawkins's books have been hugely successful bestsellers, and he became Oxford University's Professor for Public Understanding of Science from 1995 until he retired in 2008.

The result of this dominant evolutionary atheism is that the teleological argument has had to become much more sophisticated throughout the late twentieth century and into the twenty-first. Phase three has been shaped more than anything else by the advances in mathematics, in statistics, and especially probability calculation, not to speak of huge advances in theoretical physics and cosmology. What was a simple analogy based on intuitive insight has now become an intricate probability or likelihood comparison. Furthermore, these arguments are increasingly about some condition of the universe as a whole, rather than individual complexly functional items within the universe: fine-tuning arguments. I will look at a series of these, including from agnostics, starting with some fairly simple examples.

Fine-tuning is not a new concept. An early voice is actually Darwin's co-discoverer of natural selection, Alfred Russell Wallace (1823–1913). For Wallace the history of evolution is so strangely designed and prepared to produce human life that it evidences an intelligent mastermind.

---

[46]Dawkins, *The God Delusion*, 136-38. Chapter 3 in its entirety is taken up with discrediting all of the arguments for God's existence. Chapter 4 concentrates on the teleological argument. None of his arguments are philosophically novel or even interesting.

[47]Dawkins, *The God Delusion*, 135.

After over three hundred pages examining the precise conditions of the universe, the solar system, and earth's evolution, he concludes,

> All nature tells us the same strange, mysterious story, of the exuberance of life, of endless variety, of unimaginable quantity. All this life upon our earth has led up to and culminated in that of man. It has been, I believe, a common and not unpopular idea that during the whole process of the rise and growth and extinction of past forms, the earth has been preparing for the ultimate—Man. Much of the wealth and luxuriance of living things, the infinite variety of form and structure, the exquisite grace and beauty in bird and insect, in foliage and flower, may have been mere by-products of the grand mechanism we call nature—the one and only method of developing humanity.[48]

Interestingly, Wallace's understanding of fitness leads him to a call for ecological reform during the worst of the environmental pollution of runaway industrialization in the late 1800s. He actually championed a crusade for "pure air and pure water."[49] We find this idea of fitness again in the chemist John Henderson's *The Fitness of the Environment* in 1913. Most importantly for our story, it was picked up by other scientists, especially in physics, working on the parameters of the universe in the 1960s.

3.3.1 Frederick Hoyle and Chandra Wickramasinghe. A good example of perhaps the simplest form of these probability comparisons is that of physicist Sir Frederick Hoyle (1915–2001). Hoyle's great contribution as a physicist was the theory of stellar nucleosynthesis. He actually coined the term "big bang" for the view he rejected in favor of a steady-state theory of the universe. While he appears to have remained agnostic, he did see the power of a design argument and concludes that there must be some intelligent input. Here is the argument from his 1984 popular-level *Evolution from Space: A Theory of Cosmic Creationism* written with

---

[48]Alfred Russell Wallace, *Man's Place in the Universe* (New York: McClure, Phillips, 1903), 316-17.
[49]Wallace, *Man's Place in the Universe*, 257.

mathematician and astronomer Chandra Wickramasinghe (b. 1938), an authority on interstellar matter.[50] The argument itself can be quickly summarized in three points:

1. The probability of simple life forms (just the enzymes) occurring randomly is beyond reasonable science = 1 in $10^{40,000}$.

2. Any theory with a probability of being correct greater than 1 in $10^{40,000}$ is superior to random sampling.

3. The theory that life was assembled by an intelligence has a probability vastly higher than that it occurred randomly.[51]

They then conclude, "Indeed, such a theory is so obvious that one wonders why it is not widely accepted as being self-evident. The reasons are psychological rather than scientific."[52]

The basic logic here seems unassailable. Clearly the probability of an intelligent source for this functional complexity is higher than its occurring randomly. But we are left with the two limitations of teleological arguing we have noted before. First, lower probability never actually rules out an explanation. Sometimes the least likely explanation turns out to be correct. Sometimes the least simple explanation is the right one. Remember *Murder on the Orient Express*? So it is crucial that the difference in probabilities be extreme, and that the evidence clearly single out the need for creative and intentional intelligence. Their best evidence for this from within the system is the human capacity to alter biology as seen in genetic engineering.[53]

Second, the conclusion is pretty thin: intelligence-capable-of-causally-informing-the-structure-of-a-universe. For Hume this was no more than a supreme being. For Hoyle it was an idealized intelligence.[54] Not much!

[50]Fred Hoyle and N. C. Wickramasinghe, *Evolution from Space: A Theory of Cosmic Creationism* (New York: Simon and Schuster, 1984).

[51]See Hoyle and Wickramasinghe, *Evolution from Space*, 24-31.

[52]Hoyle and Wickramasinghe, *Evolution from Space*, 129-30.

[53]See Hoyle and Wickramasinghe, *Evolution from Space*, 33.

[54]Hoyle and Wickramasinghe, *Evolution from Space*, 143-45.

On the other hand, if the probability gap is sufficient, and especially if the probability of a random solution is negligible (it cannot, of course, be zero), then this is a powerful argument despite the limitations. Even if the conclusion is no more than a creative intelligence, that would be enough to rule out atheism, as well as any form of reductive materialism or physicalism. In general, it will show any worldview defined as naturalism, including, certainly, atheistic evolutionism, to be insufficient in explaining our reality.

3.3.2 Francis Collins. Another straightforward argument can be found in Francis Collins's *The Language of God*. Collins (b. 1950), with an MD from University of North Carolina and PhD in chemistry from Yale, worked with James Watson on the Human Genome Project and eventually became its director. Upon its completion he was named to head the National Institutes of Health in 2009 and was renewed in 2017.

This passage is a simple statement of a design argument that comes at the end of a section showing how similar human and chimpanzee DNA are, and how easily mutations that successfully modify a species can occur. It is important to his argument to take into account that Collins is an evolutionist, but that is exactly what strengthens the argument. Clearly, detailing the machinery of the universe does not tell us its source.

> If humans evolved strictly by mutation and natural selection, who needs God to explain us? To this, I reply: I do. The comparison of chimp and human sequences, interesting as it is, does not tell us what it means to be human. In my view, DNA sequence alone, even if accompanied by a vast trove of data on biological function, will never explain certain special human attributes, such as the knowledge of the Moral Law and the universal search for God. Freeing God from the burden of special acts of creation does not remove Him as the source of the things that make humanity special, and of the universe itself. It merely shows us something of how He operates.[55]

---

[55]Francis Collins, *The Language of God* (New York: Simon and Schuster, 2006), 140-41.

3.3.3 Richard Swinburne. We have encountered Richard Swinburne before. He is, I suspect, the leading voice on the subject of God's existence. His trilogy, *The Coherence of Theism* (1977), *The Existence of God* (1979), and *Faith and Reason* (1981) pretty much constitute the standard in the discipline of philosophy of religion. He is especially well known for his work on the teleological argument. In his more popular book *Is There a God?*, Swinburne lays out the argument as a best-explanation strategy.[56]

He begins his actual argument (in chapter four) with a comprehensive look at the complexity of the world's order, from the natural laws that codify the regularities of the universe, to the intricate ordering of animal and human bodies. From this he concludes,

> So there is our universe. It is characterized by vast, all-pervasive temporal order, the conformity of nature to formula, recorded in the scientific laws formulated by humans. It started off in such a way (or through eternity has been characterized by such futures) as to lead to the evolution of animals and humans. These phenomena are clearly things "too big" for science to explain. They are where science starts. They constitute the framework of science itself. I have argued that it is not a rational conclusion to suppose that explanation stops where science does, and so we should look for a personal explanation of the existence, conformity to law, and evolutionary potential of the universe. Theism provides just such an explanation. That is strong grounds for believing it to be true. . . . Note that I am not postulating a "God of the gaps," a god merely to explain the things which science has not yet explained I am postulating a God to explain what science explains; I do not deny that science explains, but I postulate God to explain why science explains. The very success of science in showing us how deeply orderly the natural world is provides strong grounds for believing that there is an even deeper cause of that order.[57]

---

[56]Richard Swinburne, *The Coherence of Theism* (Oxford: Oxford University Press, 1977); Swinburne, *The Existence of God* (Oxford: Oxford University Press, 1979); Swinburne, *Faith and Reason* (Oxford: Oxford University Press, 1981); Swinburne, *Is There a God?* (Oxford: Oxford University Press, 1996).

[57]Swinburne, *Is There a God?*, 68.

Then Swinburne turns in the next chapter to the special evidence found in the human mind and its relationship to the body, and draws a similar conclusion:

> The evidence deployed . . . suggests that the existence of souls and their connections to bodies are not due to the physical processes codified in natural laws. Some new powers have been given to foetal brains and to the souls to which they are joined, powers which do not have a scientific explanation. The existence of God, a simple hypothesis which leads us with some probability to expect the phenomena discussed in the last chapter, also leads us to expect these phenomena. Although the powers of the brain and its liability to exercise these when it receives certain nerve impulses from the eye provide a full explanation of my having a blue image when I do, those powers are created and conserved by God, and so his action provides the ultimate explanation of the occurrence of the blue image. God's action also provides the ultimate explanation of there being a soul (and it being my soul rather than yours) which is joined to this body.[58]

In sum, Swinburne's argument is that God is the simplest and best explanation for the evidence we find—namely, the phenomena of our universe and ourselves. Science by itself, and therefore naturalistic atheism, describes and hence explains to some level but has no power to provide ultimate explanation. In particular, it cannot explain science itself, let alone our uniquely human capacity to do science. That will require *personal explanation*—that is, the presence of intentionality, the capacity to design complex means to fit a future end.

What is crucial is that God *does* explain all of this. His unlimited capacities easily allow for such complex design, even of whole universes. And furthermore, precisely as a single and simple infinite being—a being without parts—God is by definition the simplest possible explanation.[59] A finite evolutionary process would be vastly more complex

---

[58]Swinburne, *Is There a God?*, 93-94.
[59]Swinburne, *Is There a God?*, chap. 3, discusses at length the matter of God's simplicity.

a machine, but worse, it lacks any intentionality. It is therefore severely limited in what it can explain, though no doubt it can explain at lower levels, so that its probability is not zero, but only slightly above. In any case, the probability of theism as an explanation is much greater. As Swinburne concludes, all the evidence of our universe "make it significantly more probable than not that there is a God."[60]

3.3.4 Stephen Jay Gould. A popular spokesperson for the cause of evolution, Stephen Jay Gould (1941–2002) is best known for his theory of punctuated equilibrium—that is, that evolution consists of long periods of stability interrupted by sudden rapid and large-scale changes. He spent most of his career as a paleontologist at Harvard University. It may seem strange to include Gould here since he actually opposed design arguments.[61] But Gould also remained an agnostic, claiming that the physical evidence of evolutionary science by itself is powerless to decide matters of the "superintendence" of nature. So I include him here because he makes the same point as Collins:

> To say it for all my colleagues and for the umpteenth millionth time: Science simply cannot by its legitimate methods adjudicate the issue of God's possible superintendence of nature. We neither affirm nor deny it; we simply can't comment on it as scientists. . . . Science can work only with naturalistic explanations; it can neither affirm nor deny other types of actors (like God) in other spheres (the moral realm, for example). Forget philosophy for a moment; the simple empirics of the past hundred years should suffice. Darwin himself was agnostic . . . , but the great American botanist Asa Gray, who favored natural selection and wrote a book entitled *Darwiniana*, was a devout Christian. Move forward 50 years: Charles D. Walcott, discoverer of the Burgess Shale Fossils, was a convinced Darwinian and an equally firm Christian, who

---

[60]Swinburne, *Is There a God?*, 139. Pages 25-26 give a brief but helpful discussion of the criteria for a good explanation.

[61]See here, for example, Stephen Jay Gould, *The Flamingo's Smile: Reflections in Natural History* (New York: Norton, 1985), 392-402.

believed that God had ordained natural selection to construct the history of life according to His plans and purposes. . . . Either half my colleagues are enormously stupid, or else the science of Darwinism is fully compatible with conventional religious beliefs—and equally compatible with atheism.

So those who choose to be atheists must find some other basis for taking that position. Evolution won't do.[62]

So again, the point here is that the raw data of science, including its mechanics, will only tell us about the process itself: it will describe the causal connections. It is only in that specific sense an "explanation." It is helpless to do anything else. If you want to know how a laptop works so that the movements of the keys produce letters on the screen, we need only to talk about the mechanics and electronics that connect them. It is not until there is a meaningful text on the screen that we need to talk about some superintendence. And so the evolutionist who wants to draw atheistic conclusions directly from scientific observation is just not entitled to them.

Gould's mistake lies in not pursuing a fuller explanation. In his collection of papers *The Panda's Thumb* (1980), he is content to bring up examples of apparent bad design—like said thumb—and then offer his theory of intermittent environmental stress buildup, which leads to large catastrophic changes that account for the big jumps that creationists keep bringing up, but also return things to a "punctuated equilibrium."[63] But this only adds another detail to the details of the process and provides no help in fully explaining the design.

3.3.5 Robin Collins. These sorts of probability calculations and comparisons, however, brought about a more sophisticated form of

---

[62]Stephen Jay Gould, "Impeaching a Self-Appointed Judge," *Scientific American* 267 (1992): 118-21. This is actually a review of Phillip Johnson's book *Darwin on Trial* (Downers Grove, IL: InterVarsity Press, 1991).

[63]Stephen Jay Gould, *The Panda's Thumb: More Reflections in Natural History* (New York: Norton, 1980).

argument when applied to the very conditions of the universe itself. This pattern of teleological argument came to be known as the fine-tuning argument (FTA).

I am leaving out many examples, but no doubt the current expert on the FTA, both the physics and the philosophical components, is Robin Collins (b. 1978), who teaches at Messiah College. He earned his PhD in philosophy from University of Notre Dame under Alvin Plantinga, preceded by two years of doctoral work in physics at the University of Texas at Austin.

Collins has published an extensive list of articles and chapters in books on the subject of FTA. His most thorough is "The Teleological Argument: An Exploration of the Fine-Tuning of the Universe."[64] The argument itself is rather simple. I will simplify it even more and remove the abbreviations and symbolization.

1. Given the fine-tuning evidence, a life-permitting universe is very, very epistemically unlikely under the naturalistic single-universe hypothesis.

2. Given the fine-tuning evidence, a life-permitting universe is not unlikely under theism.

3. Theism was advocated prior to the fine-tuning evidence (and has independent motivation).

4. Therefore, by the restricted version of the Likelihood Principle, a life-permitting universe strongly supports theism over the naturalistic single-universe hypothesis.[65]

We could just simply say that the evidence from fine-tuning strongly supports theism over naturalism given there is a life-permitting universe. There are, however, several caution flags raised here that demand

---

[64]Robin Collins, "The Teleological Argument: An Exploration of the Fine-Tuning of the Universe," in *The Blackwell Companion to Natural Theology*, ed. William Lane Craig and J. P. Moreland (Oxford: Wiley-Blackwell, 2009), 202-81.
[65]Collins, "Teleological Argument," 207.

the careful wording in Collins's argument. Note, first, that the argument does not apply, as is, to multiverse scenarios. Collins gets back to this later. Second, there is the matter of premise (3) and the independence of theism that restricts the likelihood principle.

Likelihood is simply a way of referring to the relative degree of expectation of a state of affairs. This is different from measuring the probability of a state of affairs. Now why should there be independent motivations for expecting a state of affairs apart from the evidence? Let me use Collins's illustration, somewhat paraphrased. Suppose I role a die twenty times and it gives the sequence 26431564321624413661. Now suppose I say that this is the favorite number of a demon I know, and that is why the die came up in this sequence. It was to be expected. It might appear that this is better than chance, but it is clearly too ad hoc to act as any sort of real confirmation:

> Now consider a modification of the demon case in which, prior to my rolling the die, a group of occultists claimed to have a religious experience of a demon they called "Groodal," who they claimed revealed that her favorite number was 2643156432162441366, and that she strongly desired that number be realized in some continuous sequence of die rolls in the near future. Suppose they wrote this all down in front of many reliable witnesses days before I rolled the die. Certainly, it seems that the sequence of die rolls would count as evidence in favor of the Groodal hypothesis over the chance hypothesis. The relevant difference between this and the previous case is that in this case the Groodal hypothesis was already advocated prior to the rolling of the die, and thus the restricted Likelihood Principle implies that the sequence of die rolls confirms the Groodal hypothesis.[66]

Collins's point is that the second hypothesis is independent—that is, was believed prior to the evidence. In the FTA case, theism is not an I-told-you-so, ad hoc hypothesis, but a well-established and prior

---

[66]Collins, "Teleological Argument," 206.

one for which the evidence can legitimately count. So there being a life-permitting universe supports theism, given the evidence of fine-tuning.[67]

We can now consider the actual evidence. I promised to avoid the science and stick to the logic, however, and so I will just mention three categories. First, there are the laws of nature: the universal attractive force, the strong nuclear force, and so forth. Second are the constants of physics, such as the gravitational constant G, and the cosmological constant Ë. Third, there are the initial conditions of the universe, such as the mass density of the early universe, the precise strength of the big bang, and much more.[68] Taken together, these factors require an initial state of enormous fine-tuning or specialness that demands explanation.

Collins's conclusion is straightforward but quite limited. It is simply the claim that "various features of the universe offer strong evidence in favor of T[heism] over its naturalistic alternatives."[69] I noted earlier that Collins's argument is initially intended for single-universe options. We will examine multiverse scenarios under phase four. Spoiler alert! They fare no better.

3.4 Counters to Probability and Fine-Tuning Arguments

In the following discussion I want to focus on philosophical and logical objections to FTA. I do not know of anyone who questions the science anymore. In fact, "fine-tuning" originated as a scientific way of designating certain constants that appeared necessary for the formation of a universe. I will focus here on the three primary objections that have arisen. There are others, but they seem easy to deal with.

---

[67]For a critique of Collins's argument, see Mark Saward, "Collins' Core Fine-Tuning Argument," *International Journal for Philosophy of Religion* 76, no. 2 (2014): 209-22. He gives two objections, but both, especially this matter of prior independence, are already well handled by Collins in the 2009 essay.

[68]See the lengthy discussion in Collins, "Teleological Argument," 211-22.

[69]Collins, "Teleological Argument," 209.

3.4.1 Antony Flew. I think Antony Flew (1923–2010) was likely the most capable overall defender of atheism in the twentieth century. He was educated at Oxford and taught at Oxford, Aberdeen, Keele, and Reading University in England, and York University in Canada. Born into a conservative pastor's home, Flew was a lifelong atheist until his shocking announcement in 2004 that he had accepted the evidence for fine-tuning. In one way at least, this was not a surprise to those of us who knew him, because he was always open to the evidence, always eager to discuss it, and then to change his mind accordingly.

Here, however, is the younger Flew, whose 1966 book, *God and Philosophy*, was a model of fair and careful philosophical argument. It was also the constitution of atheism for that whole generation of young philosophy students (like me, who took my first philosophy course in that same year) to wrestle with.

Flew here does not try to minimize the evidence, and he is quick to point out that Christians do not use the teleological argument to produce a God-of-the-gaps conclusion. He does argue, however, that the argument still falls prey to Hume's most telling objection: insufficient evidence.

> Once more it is the necessary uniqueness of the universe which makes the crux; even before the questions begin to arise from the uniquenesses of the postulated Designer. In this most peculiar context the basis for the usual contrasts between chance and its opposites disappears, and the familiar questions lose their peculiar force and application. It is put that it must be immeasurably improbable that there could be so much order without Design. A hearer who failed to catch the sound of the capital "D" might fairly and truly reply: "Well, fancy that! And yet, of course, we know that nearly all order *is* without design." But we, alerted by that capital, ask: "How does he know what is probable or improbable about universes?" For his question, like the earlier overweening assertion about the tendencies which things possess or lack "of themselves" . . . , presupposes that he knows something which not merely does he not

know, but which neither he nor anyone else conceivably ever could know. No one could acquire an experience of universes to give him the necessary basis for this sort of judgment of probability or improbability; for the decisive reason that there could not be universes to have experience of. Indeed the whole idea of contrasting, on the one hand, chance as randomness with, on the other hand, what seems to demand explanation breaks down in this limiting case. Yet if this fundamental antithesis ceases to apply, how much more inapplicable the relatively sophisticated antithesis between chance as the absence of purpose and what calls for that rather special sort of explanation which involves planners and plans. It is, therefore, not a matter here of having to choose between the prongs of either fork. Instead the difficulty is to appreciate that and why neither choice can arise. "Universes," as C. S. Peirce remarked, "are not as plentiful as blackberries."[70]

It would be almost fifty years later that Flew finally accepted the fine-tuning evidence and became a theist. That we have only observed one universe does not hinder us from conceptualizing other possible worlds. Paley and others had already answered this one.

3.4.2 Richard Dawkins. Another frequent objection to FTAs is the result of the application of the principle of simplicity. Certainly one of the guidelines for pursuing a scientific explanation is that the simplest is preferable. Dawkins has long maintained that on those grounds alone no theistic explanation can be considered. In *The God Delusion*, he narrates an encounter with some theologians at a Cambridge conference.

> I challenged the theologians to answer the point that a God capable of designing a universe, or anything else, would have to be complex and statistically improbable. The strongest response I heard was that I was brutally foisting a scientific epistemology upon an unwilling theology. Theologians had always defined God as simple. Who was I, a scientist, to dictate to theologians that their God had to be complex?[71]

---

[70]Antony Flew, *God and Philosophy* (New York: Dell, 1966), sec. 3.29, pp. 73-74.
[71]Dawkins, *God Delusion*, 183.

We can put this challenge even more plainly. On any account of God, "universe + God" is a more complex—that is, less simple—explanation than just "universe." If nothing else, the universe by itself is simpler by one. If God is regarded as complex, then the situation is even more severely out of balance, but even if we use the Aristotelian-Thomistic account of God as infinite and therefore of ultimate simplicity, the explanation still fails the simplicity challenge.

The response to this objection is nothing new. Swinburne makes the case this way:

> The supposition that there is a God is an extremely simple supposition; the postulation of a God of infinite power, knowledge, and freedom is the postulation of the simplest kind of person that there could be. God is an unextended object, the divine properties fit together, and they are properties of infinite degree; we saw . . . that infinite degrees of a property have a simplicity lacked by large finite degrees of the same property. *A priori* the existence of anything at all logically contingent, even God, may seem vastly improbable, or at least not very probable. . . . Yet whether this is so or not, the existence of the universe is less simple, and so less to be expected *a priori* than the existence of God. Hence, if there is no God, the existence of a complex physical universe is not much to be expected; it is not *a priori* very probable at all—both because . . . it is vastly improbable *a priori* that there would be anything at all; and because, if there is anything, it is more likely to be God than an uncaused complex physical universe. . . .
>
> Yet, if there is a God, clearly he can create a universe; and he will do so in so far as his perfect goodness makes it probable that he will.[72]

So, a complex physical universe like ours is always less likely on its own than an infinite God plus that contingent universe.

3.4.3 Elliott Sober. A frequent participant in the discussion of FTA, Elliot Sober (b. 1948) holds a PhD from Harvard University and

---

[72]Richard Swinburne, *The Existence of God*, 2nd ed. (Oxford: Oxford University Press, 2004), 150-51.

presently teaches at the University of Wisconsin. In his chapter "The Design Argument" in *The Blackwell Guide to the Philosophy of Religion*, he gives a good overview of objections to fine-tuning.[73]

In the end, however, it appears to be Hume's—or better, Philo's—objection that has to be taken seriously. The form of the objection that really carries the weight of Sober's critique takes us in a new direction: We are embedded *participants* in the only universe there is. We therefore have no neutral way of observing multiple universes in such a way that we could form any kind of objective judgments as to the relative degree of design that is or was needed for our universe. We suffer from "observational selection effect," or OSE.[74] Any FTA will have to begin with an assessment of fine-tuning factors, noting that they fall within the very narrow limits that will allow conscious life to develop. It can then conclude that, since we humans—conscious life, that is—*do* exist, the constants of fine-tuning must be right, and there must be a designer.

The problem here is that we lack any basis for this conclusion, Sober argues. Suppose, he says, we had a million universes created by a designer god and a million brought about by a chance process, and suppose that the proportion of universes in which the constants are right is higher among the former. Does it not follow that our universe must be designed? No, he says. We simply have no observation base on which to form this judgment. For all we know, this is what chance can produce, and universes created by a designer god have much better fine-tuning.[75]

To illustrate this point, Sober turns to a story that has been frequently used to argue *for* FTA. He quotes Swinburne's version:

> On a certain occasion the firing squad aim their rifles at the prisoner to be executed. There are twelve expert marksmen in the firing squad, and they fire twelve rounds each. However, on this occasion all 144 shots

---

[73]Elliott Sober, "The Design Argument," in *The Blackwell Guide to the Philosophy of Religion*, ed. William E. Mann (Malden MA: Blackwell, 2004), 117-47.

[74]Sober, "Design Argument," 134.

[75]Sober, "Design Argument," 136.

miss. The prisoner laughs and comments that the event is not something requiring any explanation because if the marksmen had not missed, he would not be here to observe them having done so. But of course, the prisoner's comment is absurd; the marksmen all having missed is indeed something requiring explanation; and so too is what goes with it—the prisoner's being alive to observe it. And the explanation will be either that it was an accident (a most unusual chance event) or that it was planned (e.g., all the marksmen had been bribed to miss). Any interpretation of the anthropic principle which suggests that the evolution of observers is something which requires no explanation in terms of boundary conditions and laws being a certain way (either inexplicably or through choice) is false.[76]

But Sober thinks Swinburne is wrong on this. Remember first that this is about determining whether an event is chance or design. While his being alive to know he is alive is, of course, evidence to the prisoner that he is in fact alive, it plays no role in deciding chance or design. The prisoner is subject to an OSE.

> To assess the claim that the prisoner has made a mistake, it is useful to compare the prisoner's reasoning with that of a bystander who witnesses the prisoner survive the firing squad. The prisoner reasons as follows: "given that I now am able to make observations, I must be alive, whether my survival was due to intelligent design or chance." The bystander says the following: "given that I now am able to make observations, the fact that the prisoner is now alive is made more probable by the design hypothesis than it is by the chance hypothesis." The prisoner is claiming that he is subject to an OSE, while the bystander says that he, the bystander, is not. Both, I submit, are correct.[77]

The bystander, Sober argues, is right in using his observation that the prisoner is still alive to conclude, given all the evidence he has about

---

[76]Sober, "Design Argument," 137. This is from Richard Swinburne, "Argument from the Fine-Tuning of the Universe," in *Physical Cosmology and Philosophy*, ed. John Leslie (New York: Macmillan, 1990), 171.

[77]Sober, "Design Argument," 138.

executions, that design is more likely responsible than chance. But the prisoner is not in that position.

> The basic idea of an OSE is that we must take account of the procedures used to obtain the observations when we assess the likelihoods of hypotheses. . . . What may seem strange about my reading of the firing squad story is my claim that the prisoner and the bystander are in different epistemic situations, even though their observation reports differ by a mere pronoun. After the marksmen fire, the prisoner thinks "I exist" while the bystander thinks "he exists"; the bystander, but not the prisoner, is able to use his observation to say that design is more likely than chance, or so I say.[78]

So Sober concludes that FTA fails as a claim about likelihoods. We have no way to calculate probabilities here—Hume, he thinks, was right—because we are embedded in the only universe context we know of. We can only estimate likelihoods but without any basis on which to distinguish chance and design.

Now I myself think that this is the most interesting objection to FTA. Especially in the there-is-only-one-universe form left us by Hume's Philo, it has been around for a long time, though clearly Hume himself did not consider it formidable enough to reject design arguments. And the OSE problem that complicates the objection has been around a long time too.[79] Clearly it cannot be too daunting either. After all, we *always* observe from within our own standpoint and from within this universe, and we do just fine telling green lights from red, and much more, including reading this book. It does, of course, have an effect on our observation of electrons, the relative speeds of passing objects, and so on.

---

[78]Sober, "Design Argument," 138. Sober has since changed his position on this. See his "Absence of Evidence and Evidence of Absence," *Philosophical Studies* 143 (2009): 63-90. He now thinks that FTA, but not the firing-squad example, are open to OSE objections. Jonathan Weisberg had argued that neither are, and I tend to agree. See Jonathan Weisberg, "Firing Squads and Fine-Tuning—Sober on the Design Argument," in *British Journal for the Philosophy of Science* 56 (2005): 809-21.

[79]Sober gives a brief account in "Design Argument," 134.

Nevertheless, it is just a footnote in our overall epistemology that does not prevent objective observing.

3.4.4 Michael Rota. There have been many responders to Sober's objection, often called the "anthropic objection," but I like this one from Michael Rota (b. 1975). Rota has a PhD from St. Louis University and is presently a professor of philosophy at the University of St. Thomas in St. Paul, Minnesota. His book *Taking Pascal's Wager* has a long section on FTA.[80]

Clearly something has gone wrong here, he notes, because we only have to exaggerate the story to see its point more clearly. Imagine that there are not just twelve marksmen firing—and missing—twelve times each, but hundreds going at it persistently all day—and still all missing. Sooner or later, it has to be obvious, not just to the bystander, but to the prisoner as well, that some *design* is in play. Okay, but then what exactly is wrong with Sober's analysis of the firing-squad story?

> The short version . . . is that the anthropic objection asks us to focus on an irrelevant probability; the probability that the universe is life permitting given that the universe is the result of a blind physical process *and* we're here to observe it. True, if we're here to observe it, it must be life permitting. But we might very well have never been here to observe anything! Without a Fine-Tuner in the picture, what is likely is that we would never have been here at all. Since we are here, we have evidence for a universe designer.[81]

So Sober is certainly right that the prisoner should not be surprised at being alive because he has to be alive in order to be surprised at being alive. But the prisoner certainly *is* right to be surprised at the marksmen's failure that allows him to be alive. That most certainly demands an explanation, and after 144 shots by marksmen at close range, some

---

[80]Michael Rota, *Taking Pascal's Wager: Faith, Evidence and the Abundant Life* (Downers Grove, IL: InterVarsity Press, 2016).
[81]Rota, *Taking Pascal's Wager*, 111.

intentional and intelligent design is much more likely than chance. So the anthropic objection, at least Sober's version of it, fails.

3.5 Phase Four: Multiverse Arguments

3.5.1 The early history. Phase four in the development of the teleological argument comes with the arrival of theories of multiple universes, which in turn produces a new twist to the argument. The multiverse idea actually goes back to the ancient Greeks. Anaximander's plural-universe cosmology influenced the atomists, and they influenced the Epicureans and Stoics. Anaximander is not an outright theist. More of a pantheist really. His argument combines the idea that the universe is eternal and full, and that only a limited number of possibilities can be actualized in a small, finite world like our own. This gives us the plenitude argument:

1. The initiating and actualizing cause of the universe is unbounded.

2. An individual universe is a limited set of possible space-time existents.

3. Therefore, it is both plausible and likely that there are multiple universes, together representing the full range of possibles as actualized by an unlimited source.[82]

3.5.1.1 Basil of Caesarea. This doctrine and its supporting argument can be found in the Pythagoreans, who passed it on to the atomists, Leucippus and Democritus, who in turn influenced the Epicurean Lucretius in his *On the Nature of Things*.[83] This in turn became an extremely important resource for early Christian thinkers like Origen

---

[82]See the discussion of the history of this argument in W. David Beck and Max Andrews, "God and the Multiverse," *Philosophia Christi* 16, no. 1 (2014): 101-15.

[83]Pythagoras held that there were 183 worlds arranged in a perfect triangle (of course!). A good discussion of the atomists' doctrine and their influence is Karl Marx's dissertation at the University of Jena (1841): "The Difference Between the Democritean and Epicurean Philosophy of Nature." This can be found on numerous websites full-text free. For a discussion of Lucretius's influence see Stephen Greenblatt, *The Swerve: How the World Became Modern* (New York: Norton, 2009).

and Basil the Great. Basil (330–379), bishop of Caesarea Mazaca in Cappadocia, makes several important points in the process of dealing with the naturalistic philosophers of his own day, including that God is a superior explanation of a (possible) multiverse. What is especially clever is his use of bubbles as an illustration, since it is one that is often used today:

> Does the firmament that is called heaven differ from the firmament that God made in the beginning? Are there two heavens? The philosophers, who discuss heaven, would rather lose their tongues than grant this. There is only one heaven, they pretend; and it is of a nature neither to admit of a second, nor of a third, nor of several others. The essence of the celestial body quite complete constitutes its vast unity. Because, they say, every body which has a circular motion is one and finite. And if this body is used in the construction of the first heaven, there will be nothing left for the creation of a second or a third. Here we see what those imagine who put under the Creator's hand uncreated matter; a lie that follows from the first fable. But we ask the Greek sages not to mock us before they are agreed among themselves. Because there are among them some who say there are infinite heavens and worlds. When grave demonstrations shall have upset their foolish system, when the laws of geometry shall have established that, according to the nature of heaven, it is impossible that there should be two, we shall only laugh the more at this elaborate scientific trifling. These learned men see not merely one bubble but several bubbles formed by the same cause, and they doubt the power of creative wisdom to bring several heavens into being! We find, however, if we raise our eyes towards the omnipotence of God, that the strength and grandeur of the heavens differ from the drops of water bubbling on the surface of a fountain. How ridiculous, then, is their argument of impossibility![84]

3.5.1.2 Giordano Bruno. Lucretius was especially critical for Renaissance scientists like Giordano Bruno (1548–1600), for whom this plenitude now becomes sourced in an infinite God as the very basis of

---

[84]Basil, *Hexaemeron*, trans. B. Jackson, *Nicene and Post-Nicene Fathers*, vol. 8, series 2, ed. Philip Schaff and Henry Wace (Buffalo, NY: Christian Literature, 1895), 1461b-1463.

science. In his dialogue *On the Infinite Universe and Worlds*, two of his participants conclude as follows:

> Philotheo. I declare God to be completely infinite because he can be associated with no boundary and his every attribute is one and infinite. And I say that God is all-comprehensive infinity because the whole of him pervades the whole world and every part thereof comprehensively and to infinity.
>
> Theophilo. Then, by virtue of all those arguments by which this world understood as finite is said to be expedient, good and necessary, so also should all the innumerable other worlds be named expedient and good; and to them by the same argument Omnipotence doth not grudge being.[85]

Bruno is part of a long line of plural-world advocates, from Copernicus to Huygens and Cusanus. And the argument is always that the infinity of God's goodness and power demands an infinity of finite worlds.

3.5.1.3 Immanuel Kant. The scientists of the nineteenth century learned the plural-universe option from the young Immanuel Kant's (1724–1804) commentary on Isaac Newton, published in 1755 and titled *The Theory of the Heavens*:

> The doctrine which I have brought forward opens up for us a view of the boundless expanse of creation and offers a picture of God's works appropriate to the boundlessness of the great Masterbuilder. If the size of the planetary structure—within which the Earth can barely be seen as if a grain of sand—fills the understanding with astonishment, how pleasantly astounded we will be when we see the boundless amount of worlds and systems which fill the whole Milky Way. Our astonishment will grow even more when we become aware that all these immeasurable orderings of stars again make up another unified structure, the end of which we do not know, and which is likely, as was the previous one, unimaginably large, and then, all over again, forms the unity of a whole new structure. . . . The wisdom, the goodness, and the power which has revealed itself is boundless.[86]

---

[85]Giordano Bruno, *On the Infinite Universe and Worlds* 1.2, trans. Dorothea Singer, in Dorothea Singer, *Giordano Bruno: His Life and Thought* (New York: Henry Schuman, 1950), 261-62.

[86]Immanuel Kant, *Allgemeine Naturgeschichte und Theorie des Himmels* [Universal natural history and the theory of the heavens] 1.2 (my translation).

I recount this history primarily to make the point that there is nothing new about multiverse theory and that no one, at least not among theists, has thought that it in any way argues against the existence of God. Quite the contrary: it seemed to many a natural consequence of the fullness—plenitude—of God's being and creative omnipotence. Nevertheless, its current reincarnation seems to have spooked many theists. I think we can attribute that to the actual intention of many of those who have been promoting it to show once and for all that the teleological argument for God is dead in the water.

3.5.2 *The current scene.* Multiverse theory comes these days in four quite different versions. Max Tegmark, who has championed perhaps the most prominent versions of the multiverse,[87] distinguishes four levels. Level one is just space beyond the observable universe. If we go to the edge of the universe, there would continue to be more space, but only one system is involved and all of space starts with the same big bang. A level-two multiverse consists of "bubble" universes that emerge from a cosmic landscape in inflationary cosmology. This version predicts that different universes can exhibit different actual values for the variables in the laws of physics, though the formulas of those laws will remain the same and it may not be the case that there is an infinite set of universes. The level-three multiverse is Hugh Everett's many-worlds interpretation of quantum physics. It is a mathematically simple model that argues that everything that can happen does happen. It is this version that is most popular with current physicists. Level four is Max Tegmark's all-encompassing version where mathematically possible existence is equivalent to actual physical existence. Mathematical structures are thus physically real and the

---

[87]Max Tegmark, "Parallel Universes," *Scientific American* 288 (2003): 40–51. See his discussion for much more detail and bibliography on the various theories and their creators. For an extensive and highly technical discussion see his *Our Mathematical Universe* (New York: Alfred A. Knopf, 2014). Much of this summary paragraph was done by Max Andrews for our "God and the Multiverse," 101-15.

entire human language we use to describe it is merely a useful approximation for describing our subjective perceptions. It is curious how Platonic Tegmark sounds here. It is quite literally mathematics that generates universes—that *is* universes.[88]

Two things are important about all of these options. First, they all hold that universes emerge from the same big bang; they have a common origin. Second, when you look at all the requirements, it turns out that the variation is quite limited. It is not the case that just *everything* happens, at least in some universe. Rather, only what is *possible* happens. And in turn, possibles are limited by mathematics and the laws of quantum physics. This places a considerable restriction on possibilities. In particular, it leaves the whole of probability theory intact. What is highly probable in one universe is highly probably in every other universe. What has negligible probability in one has negligible probability in all. And, of course, what is metaphysically necessary or impossible in one is metaphysically necessary or impossible in all. Hence, an event with the probability of $1/10^{40,000}$ to 1 has that same probability in all universes. Which is to say that it will not occur, ever, in *any* universe.

In a paper published a month after he died, Stephen Hawking admitted this severe restriction that results from the universality of quantum theory: "Our conjecture strengthens the intuition that holographic cosmology implies a significant reduction of the multiverse to a much more limited set of possible universes. This has important implications for anthropic reasoning. In a significantly constrained multiverse discrete parameters are determined by the theory."[89]

With all that said, we can go on to look at several attempts to show that the teleological argument has now finally been discredited by multiverse theory.

---

[88] On this see especially Tegmark, *Our Mathematical Universe*, chap. 12, and the summary on 357.
[89] Stephen Hawking, "A Smooth Exit from Eternal Inflation?," *Journal of High Energy Physics* 147, no. 4 (April 2018).

3.5.2.1 Victor Stenger. Victor Stenger (1935–2014) was an accomplished particle physicist at the University of Hawaii, and held research positions at several universities around the world. He has also published a number of popular-level books promoting the New Atheism, including his last: *God and the Multiverse: Humanity's Expanding View of the Cosmos.*[90] In a previous book, *The Fallacy of Fine-Tuning*, he said this:

> Cosmologists have proposed a very simple solution to the fine-tuning problem. Their current models strongly suggest that ours is not the only universe but a part of a *multiverse* containing an unlimited number of individual universes extending an unlimited distance in all directions and for an unlimited time in the past and future. If that's the case, we just happen to live in that universe which is suited for our kind of life. The universe is not fine-tuned to us; we are fine-tuned to our particular universe. . . . [In] fact, a multiverse is more scientific and parsimonious than hypothesizing an unobservable creating spirit and a single universe.[91]

So, apart from avoiding problems with fine-tuning, the real value of the multiverse lies in its simplicity. In particular, it eliminates the need for a selection mechanism that produces our fine-tuned universe, because every universe just happens randomly, including ours.

3.5.2.2 Max Tegmark. A PhD from Berkeley, Max Tegmark (b. 1967) is professor of physics at MIT. He has authored over two hundred technical papers in his field and has been an ardent proponent of multiverse theory. But he has also written several more popular-level books laying out a full cosmology.

In *Our Mathematical Universe*, Tegmark develops a level-four multiverse, in which mathematics produces universes. In fact, mathematical

[90]Victor Stenger, *God and the Multiverse: Humanity's Expanding View of the Cosmos* (Amherst, NY: Prometheus, 2014).
[91]Victor Stenger, *The Fallacy of Fine-Tuning: Why the Universe Is Not Designed for Us* (Amherst, NY: Prometheus, 2011), 22-23.

existence just is physical existence, and there is no need for something outside of the system to create the system, nor could there be. His website includes an FAQ. In a section he calls "Multiverse Philosophy" he responds to the following question.

> Q: *Is it in your opinion possible to imagine a "scientific theology," based on the assumption that in an infinite universe all is possible and even necessary, also the evolution of some intelligent life until a level that we usually consider typical of God?*
>
> A: An interesting question. I certainly believe the laws of physics in our universe allow life forms way more intelligent than us, so I'd expect that they have evolved (or been built) somewhere else, even at Level I. I think many people wouldn't be happy to call them "God," though, since they would be outside of our cosmic horizon and thus completely unable to have any effect on us, however smart they are (assuming there are no spacetime wormholes). However, perhaps they can create their own "universe," for instance by simulating it, playing God to its inhabitants in a more traditional sense. And perhaps we ourselves live in such a created/simulated universe.[92]

So for Tegmark, mathematics is the real creator, and any "God" would have to be within the system, though beyond our horizon. Thus there could be individual universes within the multiverse, including ours, that are simulations of highly intelligent life forms. So perhaps we are "living" in a computer-generated game world. Mathematics just *is* the real reality.

3.5.2.3 Lawrence Krauss. The theoretical physicist Lawrence Krauss (b. 1954) did his doctoral work at MIT, and was, until his retirement in 2018, a professor at Arizona State University, formerly at Yale University and Case Western Reserve University. He is an authority on dark matter and has written numerous books and articles in his field. He has also written a number of more popular books in cosmology, including

---

[92]You can find this at Max Tegmark, "Max' Multiverse FAQ: Frequently Asked Questions," The Universes of Max Tegmark, http://space.mit.edu/home/tegmark/crazy.html.

A Universe from Nothing, in 2012, and *The Greatest Story Ever Told—So Far*, in 2017.[93]

In the final chapter of *A Universe from Nothing*, titled "Brave New Worlds," Krauss dismisses the arguments for a first cause and suggests that a simple answer to this question of origins might just be that "empty space or the more fundamental nothingness from which empty space may have arisen" is eternal.[94] He continues, "One thing is certain, however. The metaphysical 'rule,' which is held as an ironclad conviction by those with whom I have debated the issue of creation, namely that *'out of nothing nothing comes,'* has no foundation in science."[95] Not only do theologians and philosophers have no grounds for this rule; it is, he argues, self-defeating since it would have to apply to God as well. It would be purely arbitrary, and without any empirical basis, to exempt God from the rule. Now what is curious is that Krauss had just noted that there is no logical basis to exclude God, but this would leave us with a deistic god, which, he thinks, has no connection to any of the world's religions.[96] Now I suspect he is right about that; nevertheless, he admits that God is a logically possible solution here.

So we are left with a solution that is advanced purely on empirical grounds of simplicity—that is, that nothing outside of or in addition to the universe is needed to account for its origin and operation:

> Our modern understanding of the universe provides another plausible and, I would argue, far more physical solution to this problem, however, which has some of the same features of an external creator—and moreover is logically consistent.
>
> I refer here to the multiverse. The possibility that our universe is one of a large, even possibly infinite set of distinct and causally separated

---

[93]Lawrence Krauss, *A Universe from Nothing: Why There Is Something Rather than Nothing* (New York: Free Press, 2012); Krauss, *The Greatest Story Ever Told—So Far: Why Are We Here?* (New York: Atria, 2017).

[94]Krauss, *A Universe from Nothing*, 174.

[95]Krauss, *A Universe from Nothing*, 174.

[96]Krauss, *A Universe from Nothing*, 173.

universes, in each of which any number of fundamental aspects of physical reality may be different, opens up a vast new possibility for understanding our existence.

Under the general principle that anything that is not forbidden is allowed, then we would be guaranteed, in such a picture, that some universe would arise with the laws that we have discovered. No mechanism and no entity is required to fix the laws of nature to be what they are. They could be almost anything. Since we don't currently have a fundamental theory that explains the detailed character of the landscape of a multiverse, we cannot say.

In fact, there may be no fundamental theory at all.[97]

3.5.3 Responses to multiverse objections. What then is there to say in response to these objections that a multiverse cosmology, by allowing all possibles to occur, defeats the teleological argument in all its forms? The point of these objections, to sum up the last section, is that regardless of how improbable an event might be, it does happen in some universe. So, even if the evolutionary steps—especially the really large jumps to life, consciousness, self-consciousness, and so on—carry only a negligible probability, there is no demand for a designer or intelligent agent to "fill the gap."

A number of responses have come back from theists. In the following discussion, I want to largely avoid the physics of multiverse theory. Here and there some will be unavoidable, but my concern is the logic of this proposal. Does the multiverse displace God?

3.5.3.1 Jeffrey Koperski. First, perhaps the most obvious response is that multiverse theory is merely an unproved hypothesis for which there is little and maybe no real evidence. That it is the current hot topic among physicists, especially a few vocal atheists, makes it interesting but hardly worth getting excited—or paranoid—about. But is it testable science?

---

[97]Krauss, *A Universe from Nothing*, 174-77.

Jeffrey Koperski (b. 1965), whose PhD dissertation from Ohio State University in 1997 was on chaos theory, begins his discussion in *The Physics of Theism* by noting the following:[98]

> The most important naturalistic explanation proposed for fine-tuning is that this universe is not the only one. Our observable universe is one of many, perhaps infinitely many, all within a massive *multiverse*. Instead of one chance to get the FTCs to line up just so, nature has had many chances. Each universe has its own values for the constants and initial conditions we have discussed and so most of the multiverse will be lifeless. On this view at least one universe, our own, had all the right values and so here we are. While it might be unusual to get two royal flushes in a row, such an event is inevitable if one plays in trillions of poker tournaments. The same goes for life in the multiverse. . . .
>
> Enthusiasm for the multiverse seems to have peaked as a growing number of physicists see it as untestable.
>
> . . . Some have questioned whether the multiverse is a scientific proposal. Increasingly physicists say no; it's not a testable hypothesis and therefore cannot be science. John Polkinghorne calls it a metaphysical posit. While [Ernan] McMullin was not a multiverse advocate, he did believe that it is scientific, a case of inferring a cause from its effect. . . . The real question is not whether the multiverse and/or design count as science. Demarcation arguments unsuccessfully try to force precision onto an intrinsically fuzzy issue. The right question is whether they count as *good* science. Both the multiverse and theistic design are explanatory, and that's good. Neither is directly testable, and that's bad. Hence, if a testable explanation for fine-tuning were to come along, it would tend to trump both design and the multiverse.[99]

---

[98]Jeffrey Koperski, *The Physics of Theism: God, Physics, and the Philosophy of Science* (Hoboken, NJ: Wiley-Blackwell, 2015). See also Jeffrey Koperski and Del Ratsch, "Teleological Arguments for God's Existence," in *Stanford Encyclopedia of Philosophy*, ed. Edward N. Zalta, summer 2020 ed., https://plato.stanford.edu/archives/sum2020/entries/teleological-arguments.

[99]Koperski, *Physics of Theism*, 75, 77, 81. FTC stands for "fine tuning constant." For more on John Polkinghorne see *The Polkinghorne Reader: Science, Faith, and the Search for Meaning*, ed. Thomas Jay Oord (London: SPCK; West Conshohocken, PA: Templeton Press, 2010). For Ernan McMullin's argument see his "Tuning Fine-Tuning," in *Fitness of the Cosmos for Life: Biochemistry and Fine-Tuning*, ed. John D. Barrow (Cambridge: Cambridge University Press, 2008), 70-96.

That the multiverse is not directly testable is precisely why many question whether it is even science. The problem here, I add, is that this is a serious issue for empirical naturalists, for whom testable science is all there is. At the same time, of course, theistic design is untestable in the same sense. We cannot observe God designing. Koperski has more telling arguments against the multiverse as making God unnecessary, but this is an important starting point.

Note this from Hans Halvorsen at Princeton University:

> An omnipotent God would get to choose the laws of nature, and hence the standard measure on initial configurations of the universe. Therefore, if the standard measure says that the chances of life are practically nil, then a theist who believes contemporary physics should think that the chances of life are practically nil, as a result of the laws that God chose. But then the theist and the atheist are in exactly the same epistemic situation: both are puzzled by the fact that we exist.[100]

I take it that means that the testability objection is something of a draw. But that only means that we have to look at the big-picture explanatory power. In terms of the larger case, theistic design in the form of creative intelligence has strong evidential argument backing it, and it is clearly the better explanation. That is why Hume concludes that he cannot simply discard the teleological argument. The naturalist's multiverse, on the other hand, has nothing but problems.

3.5.3.2 Michael Rota. A second response is that multiverse theory simply repeats the gambler's fallacy, though in a different form. This fallacy, as normally understood, is committed when one thinks the odds get better each time a predictable event fails to happen. If I don't roll double sixes the first time, surely the odds are better the next time, even better the next, and so on. Wrong! The odds are always the same.

---

[100]This is the concluding paragraph in Hans Halvorsen, "A Probability Problem in the Fine-Tuning Argument," September 2, 2014, available online at: https://www.researchgate.net/publication/279265485_A_probability_problem_in_the_fine-tuning_argument.

I will, of course, roll it eventually, but that is because 1 in 36 are easily obtainable odds.

The same is also true if I have multiple sets of dice that I roll all at the same time. If I roll thirty-six pairs together at the same time, I am bound to get double sixes. Well, again, that is likely since 1 in 36 are very good odds, but the fact is that the odds remain the same for *each* pair of dice *every* time. Thus, if there are multiple universes and multiple times in each that a particular event might occur, its likelihood is *always* the same.[101] And given what we know about fine-tuning probabilities, it will *always* be far more likely that there is a God than not, regardless of how many universes there are.

Rota, whom we met previously, makes the point this way:

> No one knows for sure whether or not there are many universes, but we do know this: either ours is the only universe, or there is a multiverse. On the one hand, if ours is the only universe, it is much more likely that the universe was designed than that it just happened to be life-permitting by chance. . . . So if there is only one universe, the evidence of fine-tuning favors the view that our universe was designed. On the other hand, our universe may exist within a multiverse. But even then, either theism or atheism may be true. (God may have wanted to create many universes.) If we exist in an atheistic multiverse, then the proportion of life-permitting universes will be *very* small. But if we exist in a multiverse created by God, we should expect the proportion of life-permitting universes to be not nearly so small. (Since life is a good, any intelligent being has a reason to value it, and thus God would have some reason to create more of it.) So the proportion of life-permitting universes will be much higher in a theistic multiverse than in an atheistic multiverse. This in turn implies that the epistemic probability that our universe would be life-permitting is much higher on a theistic version of the multiverse hypothesis than on an atheistic version. So if there are many universes, the evidence of fine-tuning favors theism

---

[101] Arguing backward from an improbable event to a multiverse is a case of the inverse gambler's fallacy.

over atheism. Either way, considerations of fine-tuning strongly favor the existence of a universe designer.

The key step in this argument is the claim that if we are in a multiverse, then the fine-tuning of our universe is strong evidence that we are in a theistic multiverse rather than an atheistic multiverse. Three main ideas lend support to this claim. First, God might very well want to create many universes. Second, the reasons to create many universes which God would have are also reasons to think that a significant proportion of universes created by God would be life-permitting universes. Third, this fact about proportions implies that it is much more likely that the universe we are in fact in would have a life-permitting cosmological constant given a theistic multiverse hypothesis than given an atheistic multiverse hypothesis. Let's look at each of these three ideas in order.

The thought that God might create many universes may seem odd and unfamiliar. Upon reflection, though, nothing about the notion of God implies that God would make only a small number of living beings, or a small number of different kinds of living beings. According to Christian tradition, God has not only brought about the existence of large numbers of individual living physical beings and a large number of *kinds* of living physical beings, he has also created a vast number of intelligent living non-physical beings (the angels). So the idea that God's creation of life was vast is not a new idea. The main difference introduced with a theistic multiverse is the great spatial separation between the various products of God's creative activity—these other universes are so distant (or otherwise separated from us) that there's no chance of travel between them. But if God wanted to create very many more physical living things than, say, can exist on Earth, then it seems likely that at some point so much space would have to be provided that any given set of physical beings would have to be separated from most of the others. There's only so many elephants you can fit in one place.

So, God and the multiverse aren't incompatible.[102]

3.5.3.3 Don Page.

3.5.3.3 *Don Page.* Another example of this point comes from Don Page (b. 1948). Page was Stephen Hawking's graduate assistant at

---

[102]Rota, *Taking Pascal's Wager*, 128-29.

Cambridge, and they are jointly known for their discovery of the "Hawking-Page phase transition."[103] He is currently a professor of physics at the University of Alberta:

> One might still ask whether the multiverse explanation always works, assuming that it has enough universes. . . . Is it sufficient to explain what we see by a multiverse theory in which there are enough different conditions that ours necessarily occurs somewhere?
>
> I would say no, but rather that there is the further requirement that the conditions we observe should not be too rare out of all the conditions that are observed over the entire multiverse. A theory making our observations too rare should not be considered a good theory.
>
> Good theories should be intrinsically plausible and fit observations.[104]

Multiverse theory may well provide a universe-generating machine that produces a variety of universes, and therefore initially explains how our universe has contingently arrived at the possibilities it has. Nevertheless, it does not alter probabilities, and so "rare" or highly improbable events will still not likely occur in any universe. Quantum theory, gravity, and mathematics govern the multiverse. And that means that there is intelligent ordering that needs accounting. Hawking's "grand design" did not happen by *random* process.

3.5.3.4 Richard Swinburne. A third response is that the multiverse does not provide a completed or ultimate explanation. One example comes from Richard Swinburne, who argues that the multiverse fails to explain in the same way that any physicalistic scientific account fails to *ultimately* explain anything:

> Even if there is a large range of possible multiverses tuned for life (in the sense of producing a universe tuned for life), and the proportion of the range of possible multiverses tuned for life is vastly greater than the

---

[103]See Don Page and Stephen Hawking, "Thermodynamics of Black Holes in Anti-de Sitter Space," *Communications in Mathematical Physics* 87, no. 4 (1982): 577-88.

[104]Don N. Page, "Does God So Love the Multiverse?," in *Science and Religion in Dialogue*, ed. Melville Y. Stewart (Hoboken, NJ: Wiley-Blackwell, 2010), 1:385.

proportion of the range of single universes so tuned, this holds only because the former range includes very complex multiverses that are intrinsically very improbable. So I stick by my point that it is intrinsically very improbable that there be a universe tuned for life (whether it is a sole universe, or a universe produced by a universe-generating mechanism). Yet it may well be that this improbability is less than the improbability that a single universe would be tuned for life.

A God however . . . has good reason for bringing about free rational . . . beings, such as human beings appear to be; and so, on the hypothesis of theism, it is moderately probable that the universe will be tuned—that is, such as to make significantly probable the existence of human bodies.[105]

The process of a universe-generating machine superimposed on quantum physics, itself superimposed on evolution, might appear to be a fuller explanation of fine-tuning. Swinburne allows that it might be. Nevertheless, it remains merely an enhanced accounting of the process. We still have an—even more—random sequence of events. God, as a personal intelligent agent, will always be far more probable, and so provide a real explanation. Intentionality in the source yields an ultimate explanation of fine-tuning.

3.5.3.5 William Dembski. William Dembski (b. 1960) holds two PhDs, one in mathematics from the University of Chicago and one in philosophy from the University of Illinois at Chicago. He refers to this strategy of burying one incomplete explanation within another larger incomplete explanation as "information displacement":

Constraining the search of an original space by employing information does not provide a nonteleological, design-free explanation for the success of that search. Instead, the solution found in the original space merely reflects the solution already in hand in a higher-order informational space. And if the one solution exhibits complex specified

---

[105]Richard Swinburne, "The Argument to God from Fine-Tuning," in Stewart, *Science and Religion in Dialogue*, 1:231.

information, then so does the other (this follows from the simple fact that any information that identifies complex specified information is itself complex specified information . . .). In particular, when nonteleological processes output complex specified information, it is because they take preexisting complex specified information and merely re-express it. They are not generating it for free or from scratch. To claim otherwise is like filling one hole by digging another. If the problem was to be rid of holes period (i.e., design), then the problem hasn't been resolved but merely relocated. . . . Displacement implies that if you have some naturalistic process whose output exhibits complex specified information, then that process was front-loaded with complex specified information.[106]

That is, when we take explanatory information to a higher level *that itself needs explanation*, we have accomplished nothing. For example, suppose we explain the design information in a car by referring to the assembly line that produces it. Now that does explain the production of the car, but it does not eliminate the need to explain the design of the car. In fact, it only adds to the overall explanation the need to explain the design of the assembly line itself, such that it can produce precisely this car. That was my earlier point that evolution gets us only deeper into the hole.

The multiverse, as a universe-generating machine, just takes us to one more level in explanatory information displacement. It is as if we explain the design of the assembly line by referring to the computer program that details and, in effect, produces it. Are we now done? Clearly not: we have only displaced the information that is the design of the car one more time. The multiverse, as an explanation of the design of the universe, may well be true, but it only adds to the demand for a designer of the universe, or maybe now: universes. We are left with a much greater demand for an ultimate designer. I now have to explain

---

[106]William Dembski, "An Information-Theoretic Design Argument," in *To Everyone an Answer: The Case for the Christian Worldview*, ed. Francis J. Beckwith, William Lane Craig, and J. P. Moreland (Downers Grove, IL: InterVarsity Press, 2004), 92-93.

a universe-generating machine that is so fine-tuned (by quantum physics, mathematics, gravity, etc.) that it produces fine-tuned machines—randomly!

3.5.3.6 David Albert. A fourth response is to address specifically the problem that if the multiverse is to be a full accounting of things, then it must explain the first event in space-time. As we have seen, for example in Krauss, the preferred answer is to argue that particles can appear out of nothing, and hence the multiverse itself might have emerged out of the Nothing.

David Albert (b. 1954), a philosopher of science at Columbia University, answered Krauss's attempt this way, in a review of *A Universe from Nothing* in the *New York Times Review of Books*:

> The fundamental physical laws that Krauss is talking about in "A Universe from Nothing"—the laws of relativistic quantum field theories—are no exception. . . . The particular, eternally persisting, elementary physical stuff of the world, according to the standard presentations of relativistic quantum field theories, consists (unsurprisingly) of relativistic quantum fields. And the fundamental laws of this theory take the form of rules concerning which arrangements of those fields are physically possible and which aren't, and rules connecting the arrangements of those fields at later times to their arrangements at earlier times, and so on—and they have nothing whatsoever to say on the subject of where those fields came from, or of why the world should have consisted of the particular kinds of fields it does, or of why it should have consisted of fields at all, or of why there should have been a world in the first place. Period. Case closed. End of story. . . . What on earth, then, can Krauss have been thinking?[107]

The most important takeaway from this is what we have seen many times now: science—in this case quantum theory—cannot fully, ultimately explain anything. It only describes connections. Multiverse(s)

---

[107]David Albert, "On the Origin of Everything," *New York Times Book Review*, March 25, 2012, BR20.

emerging from nothing is not even interesting science, and certainly not a final accounting of things.

3.5.3.7 Don Page—again. The conclusion to all this, is, I think, well stated by Don Page. After an analysis of multiverse theory for a collection of essays on science and religion, Page says this:

> In conclusion, multiverses are serious ideas of present science, though certainly not yet proven. They can potentially explain fine-tuned constants of physics but are not an automatic panacea for solving all problems; only certain multiverse theories, of which we have none yet in complete form, would be successful in explaining our observations. Though multiverses should not be accepted uncritically as scientific explanations, I would argue that theists have no more reason to oppose them than they had to oppose Darwinian evolution when it was first proposed. God might indeed so love the multiverse.[108]

There simply is nothing new here. Multiverse options do not change the fundamental dynamics of teleological arguments. Granted, as I have noted, this type of argument has serious limitations. It is never more than a probability argument, and so other explanations of the grand design are possible, however negligible the probability. And the conclusion is thin. A creative intelligence still leaves open various finite God options, including perhaps some form of pantheism, at least panentheism, though they can be ruled out on other grounds. Nevertheless, naturalistic atheism, or naturalism in any form, does not seem to remain a reasonable choice. The more we learn about our cosmos, the more the evidence cries out for an intelligent and intentional source. A grand design demands a grand Designer.

Further Reading

A good source of objections to the teleological argument in general is the previously mentioned book by Michael Martin, *Atheism: A Philosophical Justification* (Philadelphia: Temple University Press, 1990).

---

[108]Page, "Does God So Love the Multiverse," 395.

An excellent response to Dawkins's objections to the teleological and other arguments is Keith Ward, *Why There Almost Certainly Is A God* (Oxford: Lion
Hudson, 2008).

For the most recent conclusions by Elliott Sober see his *The Design Argument*
(Cambridge: Cambridge University Press, 2019). See also his response to
Thomas Nagel, "Ending Science as We Know It," *Boston Review*, November/
December 2012, https://bostonreview.net/archives/BR37.6/elliott_sober
_thomas_nagel_mind_cosmos.php.

There is a great deal of material on the FTA, along with good bibliographies in
the two large volumes of *Science and Religion in Dialogue*, ed. Melville Stewart
(Hoboken, NJ: Blackwell, 2007). In general, I recommend starting here for
further study, both for advanced and even not-so-advanced students.

Or you can start much more quickly and simply with the excellent entry by
Kenneth Himma of Seattle Pacific University, "Design Arguments for the
Existence of God," in *Internet Encyclopedia of Philosophy*, https://www.iep
.utm.edu/design/.

A recent and fairly simply written discussion of objections to FTA is John Hawthorne and Yoaav Isaacs, "Misapprehensions About the Fine-Tuning Argument," *Royal Institute of Philosophy Supplements* 81 (2017): 133-55. See also
their "Fine-Tuning Fine-Tuning," in *Knowledge, Belief, and God: New Insights
in Religious Epistemology*, ed. Matthew A. Benton, John Hawthorne, and
Dani Rabinowitz (Oxford: Oxford University Press, 2020), 136-68.

Another good collection of essays by many leading philosophers, both atheists
and theists, on both FTA and multiverse issues, is Neil Manson, ed., *God and
Design: The Teleological Argument and Modern Science* (London: Routledge,
2003). Another good collection of earlier essays on fine-tuning is John Leslie,
ed., *Physical Cosmology and Philosophy* (New York: Macmillan, 1990). This
includes some early essays by physicists like R. H. Dicke's from 1961, which
mentions neither God nor fine-tuning, but does discuss factors like the
gravitational-coupling constant (122).

John Gribbin and Martin Rees wrote one of the earliest defenses of the FTA in
Cosmic Coincidences (New York: Bantam, 1989). Rees is Royal Astronomer
of Great Britain and professor at Cambridge. John Gribbin is an astro-
physicist from Cambridge currently teaching at University of Sussex. Both
have authored other books on this topic.

Another good example of an atheist using the there-is-only-one-universe objection is Keith Parsons. See his chapter "Is there a Case for Christian

Theism?," in *Does God Exist? The Great Debate*, ed. J. P. Moreland and Kai
Nielsen (Nashville: Thomas Nelson, 1990). For a refutation of Parsons see
Robin Collins's argument in "The Teleological Argument," in *The Blackwell
Companion to Natural Theology*, ed. William Lane Craig and J. P. Moreland
(Oxford: Wiley-Blackwell Publishing, 2009), chap. 4.

A good study that accepts the anthropic objection is John Barrow and Frank
Tipler, *The Anthropic Cosmological Principle* (Oxford: Oxford University
Press, 1988). For more that counters it, see John Leslie, *Universes* (London:
Routledge, 1989).

For more on Bruno and the other Renaissance multiple-world advocates see
Dorothea Singer, *Giordano Bruno: His Life and Thought* (New York: Henry
Schuman, 1950).

Interesting discussions from an Islamic perspective can be found in Usama
Hussan and Althar Osama, eds., *Islam and Science: Muslim Responses to
Science's Big Questions* (Islamabad, Pakistan: Muslim World Science Initiative,
2016). I especially recommend Muhammed Basile Altaie, "Has Science Killed
the Belief in God?," 130-40.

A unique but advanced discussion of mathematics as an FTA is Mark Steiner,
The Applicability of Mathematics as a Philosophical Problem (Cambridge, MA:
Harvard University Press, 1998).

For more on God and the multiverse see the excellent collection edited by Klaas
J. Kraay, *God and the Multiverse: Scientific, Philosophical, and Theological
Perspectives* (London: Routledge, 2015). This is a great place to start on this
topic, and it has good bibliographies. See also Thomas Metcalf, "Fine-Tuning
the Multiverse," *Faith and Philosophy* 35, no. 1 (2018): 3-32.

Jeffrey Koperski has recently written on God's action in the universe in *Divine
Action, Determinism, and the Laws of Nature* (London: Routledge, 2020). This
is a careful examination of the options that argues to an ingenious theistic
solution. I admit to being biased: he is a former student of mine.

An important contributor to this discussion is John Polkinghorne (b. 1930), ordained clergy in the Church of England and a retired professor of particle
physics at Cambridge University. Start with *The Polkinghorne Reader: Science,
Faith, and the Search for Meaning*, ed. Thomas Jay Oord (London: SPCK and
West Conshohocken, PA: Templeton Press, 2010). He is the author of many
books on the relationship between science and religion, including his most
recent, *Science and Religion in Quest of Truth* (London: SPCK, 2011). You can
also find debates and presentations of his on YouTube.

For more on Max Tegmark's mathematical Platonism, see his *Our Mathematical Universe* (New York: Alfred A. Knopf, 2014). This is rather advanced material, especially the physics.

3.6 Where We Are Now

3.6.1 *Thomas Nagel.* How should we sum this up? I think perhaps the final word ought to be given to Thomas Nagel. Nagel has long been one of America's best philosophers, not just because of his great skill in pursuing the logic of an argument, but also for his honesty and integrity in allowing arguments to lead where they do. Born in 1937 in Belgrade, in what was then Yugoslavia, he was educated at Harvard, Cornell, and Oxford University. He is University Professor of Philosophy and Law Emeritus at New York University, where he taught for thirty-five years until retiring in 2016.

Nagel remains an evolutionary atheist, but he surprised many, certainly me, with his 2012 book, *Mind and Cosmos: Why the Materialist Neo-Darwinian Conception of Nature Is Almost Certainly False.*[109] Here is what he says about the neo-Darwinian account of the origin and evolution of life—"the story"—as an explanation of the evident teleology in nature:

> What is lacking, to my knowledge, is a credible argument that the story has a nonnegligible probability of being true. . . . Given what is known about the basis of biology and genetics, what is the likelihood that self-reproducing life forms should have come into existence spontaneously? . . . What is the likelihood that, as a physical accident, a sequence of viable genetic mutations should have occurred that was sufficient to permit natural selection to produce the organisms that actually exist? . . .
>
> The world is an astonishing place, and the idea that we have in our possession the basic tools needed to understand it is no more credible now than it was in Aristotle's day. That it has produced you, and me, and the rest of us is the most astonishing thing about it. If contemporary research in molecular biology leaves open the possibility of legitimate

---

[109]Thomas Nagel, *Mind and Cosmos: Why the Materialist Neo-Darwinian Conception of Nature Is Almost Certainly False* (Oxford: Oxford University Press, 2012).

doubts about a fully mechanistic account of the origin and evolution of life, dependent only on the laws of chemistry and physics, this can combine with the failure of psychophysical reductionism to suggest that principles of a different kind are also at work in the history of nature, principles of the growth of order that are in their logical form teleological rather than mechanistic. I realize that such doubts will strike many people as outrageous, but that is because almost everyone in our secular culture has been browbeaten into regarding the reductive research program as sacrosanct, on the ground that anything else would not be science.[110]

This is indeed a remarkable claim from an atheist. It is even more so because Nagel has remained an atheist. While he has not yet—at least as of 2020—found a metaphysics that will do everything he wants, theism is not an option. It appears to him to be too ad hoc: a God-of-the-gaps solution. It forces us to a final explanation that is outside the system of the universe, and Nagel wants a *full* explanation of the system that is internal and involves only the system.[111]

Now I think his instincts are right. X cannot be the explanation of Y, if X is entirely separate from, unrelated to, and utterly different from Y. And theists are often represented as holding such a view. But that would not be theism at all: that would be deism on steroids. God, as defined by the cosmological argument, while infinite, and precisely because of infinity, is intimately related to all things as their uncaused cause. And his properties are analogous to ours: they find their perfection in him. So there is a sense in which God is beyond the system as infinite being, yet he is also very much the explanation for the system as its intentional cause, and therefore intimately involved in and with it.[112] And certainly the teleological argument allows for this.

---

[110]Nagel, *Mind and Cosmos*, 6-7. I give here only the conclusion, which he states up front. In the book he gives careful arguments based on consciousness, intentionality, and valuing.
[111]See Nagel, *Mind and Cosmos*, 21-33.
[112]Nagel's discussion is at *Mind and Cosmos*, 21-22. A good response is David Baggett's discussion of Nagel's problem here in "On Thomas Nagel's Rejection of Theism," *Harvard Theological Review* 106, no. 2 (April 2013): 227-38.

Nevertheless, Nagel gives us teleology in a form that demands explanation but that defies mechanistic, physicalistic explanation. And that is all we need to argue for a creative intelligence that ultimately, without remainder, explains the universe in which we live. If nature is such as to give rise to minds that can comprehend it, and comprehend themselves in the act of comprehending it, then "the intelligibility of the world is no accident."[113]

Thus, I think it is eminently reasonable to conclude that there is a creative intelligence responsible for the structuring of our universe—or perhaps multiverse. Granted, this is a thin conclusion in terms of defining God, and certainly this is an inductive argument with other possible explanations with their own probability calculations. But these other options have extremely negligible probabilities at best. So I think we should agree with Hume that the evidence demands that there is some supreme being whom we may have the privilege of knowing.

[113]Nagel, *Mind and Cosmos*, 17. Note Elliott Sober's response to Nagel, "Ending Science as We Know It," *Boston Review*, November/December 2012, https://bostonreview.net/archives/BR37.6 /elliott_sober_thomas_nagel_mind_cosmos.php.

CHAPTER 4

Moral Arguments

4.1 Early Moral-Design Arguments

The moral argument flows from our perception that we as persons with the power of free will are obligated, in some way, to lives our lives in accord with certain rules, or guidelines, or priorities in relation to the society of other persons, and even the physical world around us. This perception seems to be universal. There are, of course, those who demand to live without rules and however they please. But even they will insist that this is their right, that it belongs to everyone, and that, however extreme, there are some boundaries even here. In doing so they implicitly agree to a moral duty.

What generates an argument here, as with the previous two arguments, is the quest for an explanation. In this case there are actually two questions that need to be asked. First, how is obligation itself to be explained? What are the conditions, metaphysical and epistemic, that give rise to axiological considerations? This involves us in issues like free will, responsibility, intentionality, valuation, and many more.

Second, if obligations are real, then we immediately face the question of source. On what grounds are free persons duty-bound to act and live in certain ways and not others? Who or what obligates us? What would grant such authority? This leads to proposals regarding God.

Our concern here is principally with the second of these questions, though we cannot entirely avoid the first. In part that is because different answers to the question of what a human person actually is will determine what sort of authority would be appropriate over them. For example, if humans are only physical biological organisms living in a deterministic context, as many today hold, then evolution, as a nexus of physical determinism itself, will be a sufficient authority source. On the other hand, if persons are free and responsible for their own actions, then clearly there must be some *higher* personal authority that obligates. Again, that leads to proposals regarding God.

4.1.1 Zeno. The story of moral arguments begins with the Stoics. They included moral arguments as a variant of teleological arguments. Their emphasis on a universal Logos or Reason included the system of natural physical laws, the functional design of human reason that allows us to know them, as well as the natural social and moral law that governs our human lives. So asking for the source of moral law was closely related to asking for the source of physical law because both are part of asking for the source of law. And hence we come to use the term *natural law* to cover both.

The first of these moral/teleological arguments comes from Zeno of Citium (ca. 335–ca. 263 BC), the founder of the Stoic school. He was born in Cyprus and became a wealthy merchant, but after suffering shipwreck, he moved to Athens and lived the life of an ascetic, following his goal of living according to Logos, or as we would say today, simply and naturally.

We depend here on Sextus Empiricus (ca. AD 160–210). He is the source of much of what we know of the early Greek Stoics. The following he attributes to the Stoics in general,[1] and he also gives a similar argument based on holiness or piety:

> Why then do the Stoics assert that men have a certain just relation and connection with one another and with the Gods? . . . Because we possess

---

[1]Sextus refers to similar *prolepsis* arguments in Chrysippus and Cleanthes. They are also found in Epictetus, *Enchiridion* (AD 125) c. 31.

that reason which reaches out to one another and the Gods, whereas the irrational animals, having no share in this, will have no relation of justice toward us. So that, if justice is conceived because of a certain fellowship between men and men and between men and Gods, if Gods do not exist, it must follow that justice also is non-existent. But justice is existent; we must declare, therefore, that Gods also exist.[2]

Zeno himself is said to have given this brief version: "One may reasonably honour the Gods; but those who are non-existent one may not reasonably honour; therefore Gods exist."[3]

These all have the general format of arguing that if God does not exist, then morality (in some specific form) does not exist; morality does exist; therefore God exists. This is a kind of reductio ad absurdum argument, often called a prolepsis. What is critical here is the understanding of the Stoics, beginning with Zeno, that the universal order that must be attributed to God(s) includes a moral order. And so the existence of a moral order, in turn, demands the existence of God.

Now clearly, there is much that needs to be added to this. There is no real discussion of alternative sources of moral values, though there is a clear notion that the source must be reasoning. That would eliminate naturalist materialist sources. Nor is there any argument given for the objectivity of values, though of course that is contained in the argument for the objectivity of natural ordering in general.

4.1.2 Marcus Aurelius. We have met the good emperor Marcus Aurelius before. His *Meditations* are a prime example of later Roman Stoicism. There are a number of places in this work where moral reasoning is included in a general teleological-type argument. But in the following segment such reasoning appears by itself as an argument for the Logos. Nothing comes from nothing, and intellect comes only from intellect:

---

[2]Sextus Empiricus, *Against the Physicists*, trans. R. G. Bury, Loeb Classical Library (Cambridge, MA: Harvard University Press, 1968), 1.131, p. 71.
[3]Sextus Empiricus, *Against the Physicists* 1.133, p. 73.

If our intellectual part is common, the reason also, in respect of which we are rational beings, is common: if this is so, common also is the reason which commands us what to do, and what not to do; if this is so, there is a common law also; if this is so, we are fellow-citizens; if this is so, we are members of some political community; if this is so, the world is in a manner a state. For of what common political community will anyone say that the whole human race are members? And from thence, from this common political community comes also our very intellectual faculty and reasoning faculty and our capacity for law; or whence do they come? For as my earthly part is a portion given to me from certain earth, and that which is watery from another element, and that which is hot and fiery from some peculiar source (for nothing comes out of that which is nothing, as nothing also returns to non-existence), so also the intellectual part comes from some source.[4]

We can see here the common strains of the argument beginning to emerge. We find ourselves members of social-political groups with moral guidelines that allow us to live together. But this is a matter of reason, not simply caused behavior. Hence we must ask how we have acquired this sort of moral social reasoning, and since it cannot have come from some material causality, nor could it have come from nothing, it can only have come from some greater intellect.

Granted, there is nothing here that argues for an infinite source, though it clearly is something beyond us as humans, including the entire set of human beings. Further, it must be something with sufficient personhood to understand and relate to human persons, and even further, something with the authority to establish moral requirements—that is, obligations—for the entire human race. In the end, that is the crux of this argument: The source of moral obligation must have personhood. The Logos must have moral intelligence sufficient to understand, predict, organize, and order the society of human persons. It is

---

[4]Marcus Aurelius, *Meditations*, trans. George Long (1862; repr., New York: Washington Square Press, 1964), 4.4, pp. 22-23.

still a step, but not a huge step, to an omniscient, omnibenevolent, and omnipotent God of free persons.

4.1.3 Marcus Minucius Felix. Here is a brief but early Christian example. We know almost nothing about Marcus Minucius Felix, including his dates, but he likely died around 260. The one thing we do know is that he was a Berber from what is now Algeria in North Africa, and he was a solicitor in Rome. But we do have this paragraph from his writings referred to as the *Octavius*, actually a dialogue between a Christian and a pagan philosopher:

> Supposing you went into a house and found everything neat, orderly and well-kept, surely you would assume it had a master, and one much better than the good things, his belongings; so in this house of the universe, when throughout heaven and earth you see the marks of foresight, order and law, may you not assume that the lord and author of the universe is fairer than the stars themselves or than any portions of the entire world?[5]

Theists share with Stoics the idea of a natural law that includes, as Minucius says here, natural history, physical design, and moral law. Not surprisingly, then, the arguments look quite similar.

4.1.4 Thomas Aquinas's fourth way. The fourth of Thomas Aquinas's Five Ways in his *Summa theologiae* (written 1265–1274) is often considered to be an early form of the moral argument. Now I think that it is clear that all five of them are based on ways in which contingency evidences itself to us.[6] In the fourth way we find contingency demonstrated by the fact that the things we observe come in degrees of various properties. Some things and events are hotter than others, some are larger or smaller, yellower or bluer, and so on. These degree levels are a

---

[5]Minucius Felix, *Octavius* 18, trans. Robert Ernest Wallis, in *Ante-Nicene Fathers*, vol. 4, ed. Alexander Roberts, James Donaldson, and A. Cleveland Coxe (Buffalo, NY: Christian Literature, 1885).

[6]See my "A Fourth Way to Prove God's Existence," in *Revisiting Aquinas' Proofs for the Existence of God*, ed. Robert Arp (Leiden: Brill, 2016), 147-72.

way of expressing limitation. A cannot be more F than B, unless both A and B are limited in their F-ness. And limitation is contingency.

Nevertheless, there does seem to be a connection here to a moral argument in the one special case when the property under consideration is "goodness." So if we put Thomas's argument in syllogistic form, and insert "good" as the property to be considered, we get the following:

(1) It can be found that things have properties in degrees.

(2) Among them are more and less good, and other properties of this kind.

(3) More and less are said about different things according as they resemble in different ways something which is the maximum.

(4) There is therefore something that is most good.

(5) But what is said to be the most amount in any kind is the cause of all things that are in that kind.

(6) Therefore there is something which of all beings is the cause of their goodness, and such as you will, properties.

(7) This we say is God.[7]

Put more succinctly, Thomas argues that since (some) objects and actions have varying degrees of goodness, there must be something of maximal goodness against which they are measured, and hence something that *causes* their contingent degree of goodness. Thus there is something of maximal goodness.

This argument depends heavily on Aristotelian metaphysics. In particular, the concept of goodness in general is to be understood as a connotative property of being itself.[8] To be is to be good—that is, we

---

[7] This is based on my own translation of the text in Beck, "A Fourth Way," 148-49.

[8] That is, they are connotations of "being" as a property, not separate properties. Thomas calls them transcendent properties—that is, properties of all possible substances, just by way of their being at all.

would say, to be "good for" something. For something to exist is for it to have certain defining causal properties, and they in turn give it certain powers, capacities, and liabilities. So everything is good, but in persons, since they have free will by which they make themselves what they are, this general property becomes *moral* goodness. Maximal goodness thus includes maximal moral goodness. The maximum good is, Thomas holds, infinite good, and must therefore be God.

No doubt, to most people this seems a strange and convoluted argument—at best. I understand. Unless you accept Aristotelian metaphysics, it will make little sense. I do think, however, that this metaphysics is in accord with common sense and that the argument is quite sound.[9] So, in a broader sense, we can think of this as a moral argument, though it certainly plays little role in the bigger story of this argument.

Further Reading

On the Stoic arguments see again Myrto Dragona-Monachou, *The Stoic Arguments for the Existence and the Providence of God* (Athens: National and Capodistrian University of Athens, 1976).

For more resources on Thomas's fourth way, see the bibliography in my "A Fourth Way to Prove God's Existence," in *Revisiting Aquinas' Proofs for the Existence of God*, ed. Robert Arp (Leiden: Brill, 2016), 147-72.

4.2 Kant's Practical-Reason Argument

Immanuel Kant (1724–1804) was born into a north German family heavily influenced by the Pietist movement. Early on he rejected this conservative and literalist interpretation of Christianity and exchanged it for a very private and internal understanding in which religion in general is defined by autonomy and experience. This reimagined Christianity is outlined in his 1793 work *Religion Within the Limits of Reason Alone*. All of the standard Christian doctrines are here—the fall, sin and

---

[9]I have argued this point at much greater length in "A Fourth Way," 168-71.

salvation, heaven and hell—but they are now seen through the lens of autonomy. Christ does not alter my will and life; only I can alter my will. Actually, to be more precise, only my will can alter my will.

Here we find the roots of nineteenth- and early twentieth-century theological liberalism, but also theistic existentialism. Religion is what I do in and for myself. For the still-pious Kant, Christ is the ultimate historical example. For liberalism, however, he is reduced even further to a mere ideal without any historical reality at all. Nevertheless, Kant retains his basic beliefs about Christ, and in *The Critique of Practical Reason* in 1788 he laid the philosophical groundwork for Christianity by showing why and how we should accept free will, immortality, and God. We turn then to that argument:

> Happiness is the condition of a rational being in the world with whom everything goes according to his wish and will; it rests, therefore, on the harmony of physical nature with his whole end and likewise with the essential determining principle of his will. Now the moral law as a law of freedom commands by determining principles, which ought to be quite independent of nature and of its harmony with our faculty of desire (as springs). But the acting rational being in the world is not the cause of the world and of nature itself. There is not the least ground, therefore, in the moral law for a necessary connection between morality and proportionate happiness in a being that belongs to the world as part of it, and therefore dependent on it, and which for that reason cannot by his will be a cause of this nature, nor by his own power make it thoroughly harmonize, as far as his happiness is concerned, with his practical principles. Nevertheless, in the practical problem of pure reason, i.e., the necessary pursuit of the *summum bonum*, such a connection is postulated as necessary: we ought to endeavour to promote the *summum bonum*, which, therefore, must be possible. Accordingly, the existence of a cause of all nature, distinct from nature itself and containing the principle of this connection, namely, of the exact harmony of happiness with morality, is also postulated. Now this supreme cause must contain the principle of the harmony of nature, not merely with a law of the will of

rational beings, but with the conception of this law, in so far as they make it the supreme determining principle of the will, and consequently not merely with the form of morals, but with their morality as their motive, that is, with their moral character. Therefore, the *summum bonum* is possible in the world only on the supposition of a Supreme Being having a causality corresponding to moral character. Now a being that is capable of acting on the conception of laws is an intelligence (a rational being), and the causality of such a being according to this conception of laws is his will; therefore the supreme cause of nature, which must be presupposed as a condition of the *summum bonum* is a being which is the cause of nature by intelligence and will, consequently its author, that is God. It follows that the postulate of the possibility of the highest derived good (the best world) is likewise the postulate of the reality of a highest original good, that is to say, of the existence of God. Now it was seen to be a duty for us to promote the *summum bonum*; consequently it is not merely allowable, but it is a necessity connected with duty as a requisite, that we should presuppose the possibility of this *summum bonum*; and as this is possible only on condition of the exis-tence of God, it inseparably connects the supposition of this with duty; that is, it is morally necessary to assume the existence of God.[10]

This is a rather curious argument. In fact, many have thought that it is not really an argument at all, strictly speaking; rather, it is a postulate. Something like this: (1) Given that there is a moral duty, and (2) given that it must be the case that we freely can do what we ought to do, and (3) given, furthermore, that we cannot complete our moral duty in this life, it makes sense, or, we need to postulate, that (4) there is an afterlife. That is, there is a heaven, of sorts, in which we will find complete happiness by freely attaining complete virtue. Finally, all of this ordering of the moral life demands that (5) there is a God who can bring all of this about.

That is how practical reasoning functions for us. Now there are two problems that remain in order to turn this into a helpful and credible

---

[10]Immanuel Kant, *The Critique of Practical Reason*, 1.2.5, trans. Thomas Abbott (London: Long-mans, Green, 1898).

argument. We need to know why we should start with morality at all, and we need to see more clearly how this connects to God.

For Kant there is no real need for an argument demonstrating moral duties. Commonsense reason just establishes this in the form of what he calls the categorical imperative. Reason, acting as the unifier and sense-maker of our sensory data, tells us that we must always act in accord with that rule that we can will to become a universal law. Whatever act can, without contradiction, be turned into a universal—everyone does it—guideline is a moral duty. And in this way the categorical imperative yields a list of moral duties or moral absolutes. No further argument for objective morality is needed.

Now from here the path of logic leading to God is rather tortuous. Kant outlines it in the section above. What ultimately drives us along is the connection to happiness that demands a grand design of our world, but especially of history, including a future heaven, that only God is capable of providing. The connections here to a universal Logos or a natural law, and from there to its source in a grand Designer, is still evident. It still has the sorts of teleological overtones that Paley and Hume would have appreciated.

In general, however, the argument has not gotten much traction, either then or today. There are simply too many assumptions to be made along the way, and too many of which the atheist is not likely to grant. I would argue, though, that to most people the assumptions and internal logical connections make good sense and produce a reasonable argument. If nothing more, Kant's argument demonstrates the internal coherence of a theistic morality, in line with at least Christian, Jewish, and Islamic theologies.

Further Reading

Kant is notoriously difficult to interpret, especially on the function of reason, and practical reason in particular. And there is no end to the literature available. One good place for advanced students to start is Onora O'Neill, *Constructing Authorities: Reason, Politics and Interpretation in Kant's Philosophy* (Cambridge: Cambridge University Press, 2015). Beginners might want to start with Garrath Williams, "Kant's Account of Reason," in *Stanford Encyclopedia of Philosophy*, ed. Edward N. Zalta, summer 2018 ed., https://plato.stanford.edu/archives/sum2018/entries/kant-reason/.

A good general resource on Kant's view of God and the arguments is Peter Byrne, *Kant on God* (Aldershot, UK: Ashgate, 2007). So is Gordon Michalson, *Kant and the Problem of God* (Oxford: Blackwell, 1999).

4.3 Nineteenth-Century Moral Arguments

The aftermath of Kant's argument brings about a new and unique style of moral arguing, primarily in the second half of the nineteenth century, but continuing into the twentieth. This style owes much to the prevailing philosophical idealism of the period. If *post*modernism is actually "post-" something or other, this is it. It is the set of basic ideas that human reason is supreme, that nature—that is, the physical world—is ours to conquer, and that the outcome of this will be a world of peace, prosperity, universal morality, and the rule of human dignity. This worldview, which still has its adherents, is often called humanism.

Two events brought this moral modernity to its knees, although it would linger on for another fifty years before postmoderns finally gave it the (well-deserved) coup de grâce. The most significant of these was the so-called war to end all wars, World War I. But a few years earlier came the first devastating event, one that still has an obsessing fascination for us: the sinking of the Titanic. The idealism of the time is expressed in the editorial of the *Wall Street Journal* the next morning.

> Slowly but surely human thought is neutralizing the largely incalculable forces of Nature. . . . But the important point is that she did not sink.
>
> Man is slowly but steadily bringing into order and usefulness the devastating forces of Nature. He has conquered the air in principle; he has harnessed the lightnings to his chariot, and the cataracts obey his will.

> Man is the weakest and most formidable creature on the earth. . . . But his brain has within it the spirit of the divine, and he overcomes natural obstacles by thought, which is incomparably the greatest force in the universe.[11]

This incredible optimism about human reason in general, but centrally about our moral nature, will be replaced in philosophy by a strict empiricism that banishes moral thinking and replaces it with emotive accounts of morality. But for now, let us travel back to mid-nineteenth century and see how post-Kantian idealism shaped the moral argument.

These arguments that follow are all indebted to Kant and, with him, to Hume for their general character. First, they are *empirical*, at least in the broadly Kantian sense. That is, they locate the basis of our knowledge of the moral law in our common human experience. Second, they are *subjective*. The experience base is internal, private, individual, and yet a source we all readily recognize as common to all human persons, and observable in that sense. In essence, we can think of this period as a working out of the Kantian agenda, but in the form of a more standard deductive argument, albeit with empirical premises drawn from observation.

4.3.1 *John Henry Newman.*
An Anglican priest who converted to Catholicism, became a cardinal, and then was canonized in 2019, John Henry Newman (1801–1890) taught at Oxford until his conversion and then became the founding rector of what is now University College, Dublin. Completed after twenty years of work, his 1870 *An Essay in Aid of a Grammar of Assent* is a study of the nature and epistemology of belief, on which Newman worked for twenty years.

> Our great internal teacher of religion is . . . our Conscience. Conscience is a personal guide, and I use it because I must use myself; I am as little able to think by any mind but my own as to breathe with another's lungs.

11"Nature and Human Thought" in *The Wall Street Journal*, vol. LIX, no. 88, p. 1, April 16, 1912.

Conscience is nearer to me than any other means of knowledge. And as it is given to me, so also is it given to others; and being carried about by every individual in his own breast, and requiring nothing besides itself, it is thus adapted for the communication to each separately of that knowledge which is most momentous to him individually. . . . Conscience, too, teaches us, not only that God is, but what He is; it provides for the mind a real image of Him, as a medium of worship; it gives us a rule of right and wrong, as being His rule, and a code of moral duties. Moreover, it is so constituted that, if obeyed, it becomes clearer in its injunctions, and wider in their range, and corrects and completes the accidental feebleness of its initial teachings. Conscience, then, considered as our guide, is fully furnished for its office. . . . I am not concerned here with abstract questions.

Now Conscience suggests to us many things about that Master, whom by means of it we perceive, but its most prominent teaching, and its cardinal and distinguishing truth, is that He is our Judge. In consequence, the special Attribute under which it brings Him before us, to which it subordinates all other Attributes, is that of justice—retributive justice. We learn from its informations to conceive of the Almighty, primarily, not as a God of Wisdom, of Knowledge, of Power, of Benevolence, but as a God of Judgment and Justice; as One, who not simply for the good of the offender, but as an end good in itself, and as a principle of government, ordains that the offender should suffer for his offence. If it tells us anything at all of the characteristics of the Divine Mind, it certainly tells us this; and, considering that our shortcomings are far more frequent and important than our fulfilment of the duties enjoined upon us, and that of this point we are fully aware ourselves, it follows that the aspect under which Almighty God is presented to us by Nature, is (to use a figure) of One who is angry with us, and threatens evil. Hence its effect is to burden and sadden the religious mind, and is in contrast with the enjoyment derivable from the exercise of the affections, and from the perception of beauty, whether in the material universe or in the creations of the intellect.[12]

---

[12]John Henry Newman, *An Essay in Aid of a Grammar of Assent* (London: Burns, Oates, 1874), 389-91.

So the underlying evidence that forces us to recognize the reality of God is conscience, as an inner subjective experience. Why should we think that these internal phenomena have any evidential status? Why should we grant it objectivity? Newman advances two reasons. First, all persons share it. We attribute objectivity to emotions, fear, say, or attraction, precisely because they are shared experiences for all of us. Second, conscience is not merely a subjective feeling, but is tied to moral law, which we know as objective duties in our real world. So conscience is tied to our common human experience of a common moral law.[13]

Earlier, Newman even compares our knowledge of obligation to our knowledge of an external world. It is not just the content that links to objectivity, but the actual epistemic process parallels our normal sensory apparatus in gathering knowledge of the real world. As he said, this is not an abstract argument! No doubt his Kantian roots are showing here, but here is how Newman argues:

> Now certainly the thought of God, as Theists entertain it, is not gained by an instinctive association of His presence with any sensible phenomena; but the office which the senses directly fulfil as regards creation that devolves indirectly on certain of our mental phenomena as regards the Creator. Those phenomena are found in the sense of moral obligation. As from a multitude of instinctive perceptions, acting in particular instances, of something beyond the senses, we generalize the notion of an external world, and then picture that world in and according to those particular phenomena from which we started, so from the perceptive power which identifies the intimations of conscience . . . we proceed on to the notion of a Supreme Ruler and Judge.[14]

The final link to God is supplied here by the logic we have seen before in the Stoics. Put simply: Only minds make moral judgments, and this

---

[13]So Newman thinks of conscience in the pre-Freudian and also standard Catholic sense of *con* (with) *scientia* (knowledge): an agreement with, in this case, objective moral truth. This is the meaning it has, for example, in Luther (German: *Gewissen*), and in the American Founding Fathers' notion of the "liberty of conscience."

[14]Newman, *Grammar of Assent*, 102-3.

cannot be one of us, since "it" judges all of us. So there must be a supreme Judge. What is novel about Newman's argument is *what* the conclusion tells us about the nature of God. It shows us his angry side! It causes fear; it burdens and saddens. It threatens evil and punishment. For the Stoics, and perhaps Kant as well, the quasi-teleological pattern of the inference created awe and wonder, but not so for Newman. This is, I think, an indicator of a somewhat different kind of moral argument, important because it adds a new dimension to what we may know of God's personal nature.

4.3.2 Hastings Rashdall. While he did not himself formulate a moral argument, Henry Sidgwick (1838–1900) was the author of the highly influential *The Methods of Ethics* (1874), which sets the tone for the idealist arguments that come over the next almost hundred years. A universalistic utilitarian philosopher and economist at Cambridge University, he argued for intuitive and commonsense moral principles. His argument was that duty and happiness did largely coincide and that such must be the result of divine activity, but that conclusion, however, was not within the proper domain of philosophy. It fell to his philosophical heirs to complete this line of reasoning and formulate full arguments.

An important historian of the medieval university, Hastings Rashdall (1858–1924) was educated at Oxford and, after several other posts, returned to teach there. His most famous work was *The Theory of Good and Evil* (1907), which he wrote in honor of Henry Sidgwick. Here we get an argument based on moral conscience.

What is most interesting, however, is Rashdall's defense of the moral law. This is the project of lecture three, "God and the Moral Consciousness," of his less-known *Philosophy and Religion: Six Lectures Delivered at Cambridge.*[15] Rashdall argues here that the case for

---

[15]Hastings Rashdall, *Philosophy and Religion: Six Lectures Delivered at Cambridge* (London: Duckworth, 1909).

an objective moral law is not in any way hindered by the fact that our knowledge of it is partial, that we disagree about it, that we do not always obey it, and that we come to know it in all sorts of ways. The same, after all, is true of simple arithmetic. And, in any case, that is precisely a good argument that we are not its source.

It need hardly be pointed out that the assertion of the existence of the Moral Consciousness is not in the slightest degree inconsistent with recognising its gradual growth and development. The moral faculty, like every other faculty or aspect or activity of the human soul, has grown gradually. No rational man doubts the validity . . . of our mathematical judgments because probably monkeys and possibly primitive men cannot count, and certainly cannot perform more than the very simplest arithmetical operations. . . . Equally little do we deny a real difference between harmony and discord because people may be found who see no difference between "God save the King" and "Pop goes the Weasel." Self-evident truth does not mean truth which is evident to everybody.

It is not doubted that the gradual evolution of our actual moral ideas— our actual ideas about what is right or wrong in particular cases—has been largely influenced by education, environment, association, social pressure, superstition, perhaps natural selection—in short, all the agencies by which naturalistic Moralists try to account for the existence of Morality. Even Euclid, or whatever his modern substitute may be, has to be taught; but that does not show that Geometry is an arbitrary system invented by the ingenious and interested devices of those who want to get money by teaching it. . . . Our scientific ideas, our political ideas, our ideas upon a thousand subjects have been partly developed, partly thwarted and distorted in their growth, by similar influences. But, however great the difficulty of getting rid of these distorting influences and facing such questions in a perfectly dry light, nobody suggests that objective truth on such matters is non-existent or for ever unattainable. A claim for objective validity for the moral judgment does not mean a claim for infallibility on behalf of any individual Conscience. We may make mistakes in Morals just as we may make mistakes in Science, or even in pure Mathematics. . . . What is meant is merely that, if I am right in affirming that this is good, you cannot be likewise right in saying that it is bad: and that we have some capacity—though doubtless a variable capacity—of judging which is the true view. Hence our moral judgments, in so far as they are true judgments, must be taken to be reproductions in us of the thought of God. To show that an idea has been gradually developed, tells us nothing as to its truth or falsehood—one way or the other.

In comparing the self-evidence of moral to that of mathematical judgments, it is not suggested that our moral judgments in detail are as certain, as clear and sharply defined, as mathematical judgments, or that they can claim so universal a consensus among the competent. What is meant is merely (*a*) that the notion of good in general is an ultimate category of thought; that it contains a meaning intelligible not perhaps to every individual human soul, but to the normal, developed, human consciousness; and (*b*) that the ultimate truth of morals, if it is seen at all, must be seen immediately. . . . Moral insight is not possessed by all men in equal measure. Moral genius is as rare as any other kind of genius.[16]

4.3.3 William Sorley.

4.3.3 William Sorley. William Sorley (1855–1935), educated at Edinburgh and Cambridge University, taught at the latter for over thirty years, having succeeded Sidgwick as Knightbridge Professor. His most important contribution are the Gifford Lectures of 1914–1915, published under the title *Moral Values and the Idea of God*. Here is where he lays out the argument for the existence of God from our consciousness of moral values. It is similar to Rashdall's in that it argues from our inner experience of an absolute and binding moral law, of which we ourselves cannot be the source. So there must be some supreme mind that obligates us.

What is more interesting for our story of the argument is Sorley's argument that physicalistic evolution cannot account for morality. He is way ahead of his time on this, and it is debatable whether current naturalists have anything to say that Sorley has not already refuted. This

---

[16]Rashdall, *Philosophy and Religion*, 63-66.

argument was best presented earlier in his *The Ethics of Naturalism*, which stemmed from the 1884 Shaw Fellowship Lectures at Edinburgh University.[17] He advances here two arguments against the possibility of a naturalistic ethic:

> We might indeed speak . . . of the tendency of evolution becoming conscious in man, and then working towards its own realisation as a fixed idea. . . . Consciousness of an end is a motive to action. Thus the notion of final cause includes that of efficient cause; but the two are not convertible. The idea of an end, being conceived by reason, cannot be described simply as a tendency become conscious. It has passed into the region in which various conceptions are, or may be, competing against one another, and the resultant is decided on upon grounds which may be called subjective since they proceed from conscious determination. However the laws of this conscious determination may be expressed, they are not to be identified with the natural sequence of events as it may be conceived to exist independently of the individual consciousness. . . . In passing therefore to the working out of a rational or mental idea— such as is implied in the conception of an end—we can no longer fully represent our notions by means of the determined temporal succession called causality.
>
> Thus the empirical standpoint leaves the case incomplete. A man might quite reasonably ask why he should adopt as maxims of conduct the laws seen to operate in nature. . . . From the purely evolutionist point of view, no definite attempt has been made to solve the difficulty. When any further answer is attempted now to the question, it appears to be on hedonistic grounds.
>
> The doctrine of evolution itself, when added to empirical morality, only widens our view of the old landscape—does not enable us to pass from "is" to "ought," or from efficient to final cause, any more than the telescope can point beyond the sphere of spatial quantity.
>
> We are endeavouring to get at the idea or end of human nature in an impossible way when we attempt to reach it on purely empirical

---

[17]William Sorley, *The Ethics of Naturalism* (Edinburgh and London: William Blackwood and Sons, 1885).

lines, and think that, if we work long enough on them, we are sure to come to it.[18]

This first argument is based on our ability to think teleologically. That is, we have intentionality: the capacity to think about our experience in a way that determines what could be, and especially what ought to be. Naturalism's brain can only sort out our experience—our sense data. The brain is a machine, like the coin sorter at the bank. It can organize experiences, but it has no way of creating new ones. That would take an active mind.

Sorley's second argument is based on self-consciousness, which he considers fundamental to any understanding of human persons. Now naturalists typically admit self-consciousness, but only as feedback loops in the brain. But for Sorley it is the capacity to align knowledge and action. Morality demands this.

> From this it follows that, although, empirically, the change from the point of view of science to that of morality is a transition to a different order of facts, yet the passage may be possible transcendentally through self-consciousness. The self-consciousness which in one relation is knowledge, in another action, is thus the fundamental fact of human nature; and on it, therefore, the ethical end must be based, if that end can be disclosed by the nature of man, and is to express what is most fundamental in his nature.
>
> Yet the very notion of a finite self implies that neither such knowledge nor such activity belongs to it. In knowledge and action, as properties of the ultimate self-consciousness, human beings only participate.
>
> An end can only be made our own when conceived as necessary for realising or completing our idea of self. Conscious volition only follows a conceived want, or recognition that the self as imagined—the ideal self—is not realised in the actual self. The action is towards a fuller working out of the idea of self; and the end may therefore, in all cases of conscious action, be said to be self-realisation, though the nature of this end differs according to each man's conception of self.

---

[18]Sorley, *Ethics of Naturalism*, 269-73.

Evolution is thus not the foundation of morality, but the manifestation of the principle on which it depends. Morality cannot be explained by means of its own development, without reference to the self-consciousness which makes that development possible. However valuable may be the information we get from experience as to the gradual evolution of conduct, its nature and end can only be explained by a principle that transcends experience.[19]

What naturalism cannot provide is a means by which we can think new thoughts. We have the capacity to use experience and to go beyond it. We design new buildings, paint new worlds, write new futures; but most importantly, we change the priorities of our conduct and realize better, more moral selves. That demands more than physicalistic, evolutionary naturalism can explain.

4.3.4 Elton Trueblood. An American Quaker, David Elton Trueblood (1900–1994) held a PhD from Johns Hopkins University and was university chaplain at both Harvard and Stanford University. He spent most of his career at Earlham College, which he guided to national recognition, and he founded the Quaker seminary there. His 1957 textbook, *Philosophy of Religion*, was one of only a handful of Christian philosophy texts available in the 1950s and 1960s, especially from major publishers.[20] His version of the argument was certainly in line with the British tradition we have been looking at, and Trueblood acknowledges the influence of Sorley specifically.

Trueblood was much more sensitive to the need for a case for objective moral law. In this way he was clearly more in tune with his twentieth-century empiricist context. Further, his awareness of the issues of social morality and its progress clearly places him in the post-Holocaust context. Trueblood summarizes his argument in three premises:

---

[19]Sorley, *Ethics of Naturalism*, 284-92.
[20]Elton Trueblood, *Philosophy of Religion* (New York: Harper & Row, 1957).

1. Moral experience is a true revelation of the nature of reality.

2. Moral experience is meaningless unless there is an objective moral order.

3. The objective moral order is meaningless unless there is a Divine Being.[21]

Trueblood's argument for the first premise consists of a list of the effects the absence of moral realism would yield: there would not be the general agreement on basic moral law, we could not disagree, let alone be wrong, nor could there even be meaningful discussion, since contradictories could both be true.[22] So the price of rejecting moral realism is high. It would certainly violate our common practice and intuitions about morality. Furthermore, without it the atheist lacks any basis for advancing the problem of evil against theism.

The third premise follows from the following subargument. We begin by noting that the moral law is fundamentally different from physical law. There is nothing right or wrong about gravitational pull on me. But we do think this not just of individuals but of society as a whole. How can we then make sense of moral progress in human society?

> The only sense in which progress is possible is the recognition that there is a difference between what the generality of mankind approves and what is really right.
>
> This means that the only locus of the moral law is a superhuman mind. That it must be a mind is clear when we realize that law has no meaning except for minds, and that it must be superhuman is clear when we realize that it cannot be ours. . . .
>
> Only a personal being can appreciate a moral law or be a moral lawgiver. . . . We do not feel shame or pollution when we harm *things* . . . but we do feel these when we violate the rights of *persons*. . . . The practice

---

[21]Trueblood, *Philosophy of Religion*, 114.

[22]Trueblood, *Philosophy of Religion*, 113. Trueblood here refers his readers to G. E. Moore's *Ethics* (New York: Henry Holt, 1912), where Moore argues that the denial of moral realism leads to self-contradiction.

of the honest atheist frequently denies the conscious import of his words, because he is acting in a way which makes no sense *unless his conscious conclusions are untrue.*[23]

We should note here how Trueblood eliminates two options for explaining moral law: It cannot arise from natural law or physical process, nor can it come from us. It must have moral authority over us. These elements have always been part of the argument, but are about to become critical with the dominance of physicalistic naturalism as the metaphysics of much of current philosophy. This also parallels C. S. Lewis's argument, to which we will turn next.

Further Reading

A good study of John Henry Newman is Thomas J. Norris, *Newman and His Theological Method: A Guide for the Theologian Today* (Leiden: Brill, 1977).

A good place to start on the modern history of the argument, and especially Henry Sidgwick, is chapter 1 in David Baggett and Jerry Walls, *Good God: The Theistic Foundations of Morality* (Oxford: Oxford University Press, 2011). This is expanded in their *The Moral Argument: A History* (Oxford: Oxford University Press, 2019).

On Elton Trueblood, see James Newby, *Elton Trueblood: Believer, Teacher and Friend* (San Francisco: Harper & Row, 1990). Trueblood's *Philosophy of Religion* (New York: Harper & Row, 1957) is still a valuable introduction to the subject, and one of only a few from this time period.

4.4 C. S. Lewis and Current Moral Arguments

4.4.1 C. S. Lewis. No doubt the opening five chapters of *Mere Christianity* earn C. S. Lewis (1898–1963) the prize for the best-known and most-read moral argument in the twentieth century and maybe of all time—though perhaps only because no one kept track of Thomas's or Kant's readership back then. These chapters began as a BBC radio broadcast in 1942 with the title "Right and Wrong: A Clue to the

---

[23]Trueblood, *Philosophy of Religion*, 115.

Meaning of the Universe." They were subsequently combined with his talks "What Christians Believe" and published, with a few additions, that same year under the title *Broadcast Talks*.[24] "Right and Wrong," along with "Christian Beliefs," was later combined with two other short broadcast pieces, "Christian Behavior" and "Beyond Personality," to form *Mere Christianity* in 1952.

Lewis's primary field was English literature, and he is widely known for his fiction, especially *The Screwtape Letters*, The Chronicles of Narnia, and The Space Trilogy. After completing his studies, which included philosophy, at Oxford, in 1925 he became a fellow and tutor in English language and literature at Magdalen College, Oxford University, where he stayed until 1954, when he accepted a post at Magdalene College at Cambridge.

"Right and Wrong" was written at a crucial point in British history. The Battle of Britain had ended successfully in October of 1940, but with the cost of over twenty-three thousand lives. The bombing of English cities (the Blitz) continued until mid-1941, and an invasion by Hitler was still greatly feared. Furthermore, initial knowledge of the horrific treatment of Jews and others was beginning to come out. What this had produced was a strong sense of the immorality of Hitler's behavior and something of a recovery of objective moral norms in British life. This served well as the underlying consensus for the starting point of a talk on right and wrong, and especially on how that gives us the meaning of the universe in God.

> Everyone has heard people quarreling. Sometimes it sounds funny and sometimes it sounds merely unpleasant; but however it sounds, I believe we can learn something very important from listening to the kind of things they say. They say things like this: "That's my seat, I was there

---

[24]C. S. Lewis, *Broadcast Talks* (London: Geoffrey Bles, 1942). Unfortunately no original tape of the "Right and Wrong" broadcast appears to have survived. At least none is known to exist, and it has not (yet) shown up on YouTube. We do have four recordings of his voice, including one from another part of what is now *Mere Christianity*.

first"—"Leave him alone, he isn't doing you any harm"—"Why should you shove in first?"—"Give me a bit of your orange, I gave you a bit of mine"—"How'd you like it if anyone did the same to you?"—"Come on, you promised." People say things like that every day, educated people as well as uneducated, and children as well as grown-ups.[25]

This is the simple premise with which Lewis begins the argument. Rather than a subjective experiential base, Lewis's argument begins with a public, empirical, and common observation: a behavior we have frequently engaged in ourselves, and often see and hear in others. The second premise interprets this observation:

> It looks, in fact, very much as if both parties had in mind some kind of Law or Rule of fair play or decent behavior or morality or whatever you like to call it, about which they really agreed. And they have. If they hadn't, they might, of course, fight like animals, but they couldn't *quarrel* in the human sense of the word. Quarreling means trying to show that the other man's in the wrong. And there would be no sense in trying to do that unless you and he had some sort of agreement as to what Right and Wrong are; just as there'd be no sense in saying that a footballer had committed a foul unless there was some agreement about the rules of football.[26]

That "Rule" is what we call the law of nature, which includes the law of *human* nature. It would make no sense to accuse someone of inappropriate action, or encourage or expect an action, and certainly not to offer excuses for our own actions, unless there were some law that exhibited two features: First, it is a *universal* law in that it applies to everyone, including myself. Second, it is a *moral* law, in that it refers to the appropriateness of human behaviors, and we engage each other verbally, not by force.

Animals settle their differences by a show or exercise of force. Human beings, rational agents, use violence only as a last resort, if at all. That demonstrates the moral nature of the law, as well as just how seriously

---

[25]Lewis, *Broadcast Talks*, 9.
[26]Lewis, *Broadcast Talks*, 9-10.

we take it as a *binding* law of nature. When a human being rapes another human being, we do not just treat it as typical animal behavior like our "closest relatives" the primates do. We not only feel the pain, we consider ourselves violated and demand justice, both punishment and restitution. This is a moral issue, not merely a stimulus-response event.

Now the next premise has to counter the most obvious immediate objection. Do not cultures, time periods, religions, peer groups, and so on all have quite different laws? Lewis answers that these differences are superficial and adaptive, and that cultures "have only had *slightly* different moralities."[27] We differ among ourselves as to the precise definition of murder, when it is first degree and when it is merely accidental manslaughter, and all sorts of levels in between. We differ over capital punishment, war—even just war, abortion, assisted suicide, euthanasia, and many other such matters—but we all agree, and have always agreed, that the intentional taking of innocent human life is wrong—morally wrong. And so we construct social means to prevent, enforce, punish, correct, and make restitution for such actions.

This brings Lewis to his initial conclusion: There is a real, objective moral law. This is not subjective feeling or mere opinion. That is why it is irrelevant that we sometimes are mistaken about it, and that none of us perfectly obey it. Lewis here uses the example of arithmetic. The fact that there was that one guy in my first-grade class who kept getting simple addition wrong is irrelevant to the objectivity of mathematical truth. The fact that we would cheat him out of his lunch money by adding incorrectly is just as irrelevant to the objectivity of moral truth. Likewise, the objectivity of the moral law is unaffected by ignorance, mistakes, disagreements, even disobedience. Actually, these factors only serve to underline the objectivity of the law. We cannot disagree about our subjectivities.

---

[27]Lewis, *Broadcast Talks*, 11. I have and will continue sometimes to use my own examples to amplify Lewis's points.

The argument now shifts to a second phase: How do we explain this objective moral law? The answer to this question would then tell us something important about the meaning of our lives, and the universe in general. Two alternatives suggest themselves: human sources and natural sources.

That the law could come from other human beings, in the form of social norms, political agreements, peer influence, even religions and cultural histories, and so on, has already been dismissed. The law is clearly above and beyond us. It decides between us, and it is unaffected by our posture toward it. We all are judged equally by it. If this were not the case we would have no basis for claiming that the moral ideas of the Nazis were "less true."[28] We serve *it*, not the other way around.[29]

There is, then, the materialist option: "People who take that view think that matter and space just happen to exist, and always have existed, nobody knows why; and that the matter, behaving in certain fixed ways, has just happened, by a sort of fluke, to produce creatures like ourselves who are able to think."[30] Today we would refer to this as social evolution, the view that moral norms have evolved, like everything else, by the principles of natural selection. That is, we think, talk, and act as we do because we are caused to.

Lewis responded to this more fully elsewhere. In fact, in his 1947 work *Miracles*, he gave the matter book-length treatment.[31] But here it is very brief. He notes that an observer on another planet would see no difference between our behavior and that of other primates. But we have a different perspective:

> Now the position would be quite hopeless but for this. There is one thing, and only one, in the whole universe, which we know more about than we could learn from external observation. That one thing is Man. We

---

[28]Lewis, *Broadcast Talks*, 17.
[29]This is developed in Lewis, *Broadcast Talks*, 16-18.
[30]Lewis, *Broadcast Talks*, 24.
[31]C. S. Lewis, *Miracles* (London: Geoffrey Bles, 1947).

don't merely observe men, we *are* men. In this one case we have, so to speak, inside information; we're in the know. And because of that, we know that men find themselves under a moral law, which they didn't make, and can't quite forget even when they try and which they know they ought to obey.[32]

We know that we are responding with intentionality to the moral law, that we are not, as human beings, its creator, and that it has authority over us. So, a causal analysis will not suffice. Causality fails to explain morality. And most importantly, we need to conclude to a *moral authority*: some source of moral norms that has the right to hold us to account.

Can we say anything more about the conclusion? In particular, are we justified in calling it "God"? Lewis was careful to point out that this was not, nor was it intended to be, a religious talk. In fact, he noted, the conclusion does not favor any particular religion: It only shows that there is a "Somebody or Something behind the Moral Law."[33] Anything else we would have to learn from the universe itself, but principally from the moral law that holds in the universe. That is pretty meager!

Nevertheless, this source must be capable of authorizing moral law and so must have some mind-type qualities and must be good, at least in the sense that he/she/it is interested in fair play, decency, justice, and the like. Lewis was not interested in taking things further in this talk, but he does conclude by noting that now Christianity does make sense, and that Christianity, in turn, makes sense of all this. But the Christian message about the truth of the source of the moral law is not just comforting. He ends with this caution: "If you're looking for truth, you may find comfort in the end; if you're looking for comfort you will not get either comfort or truth—only soft soap and wishful thinking to begin with and, in the end, despair. Most of us have got over the pre-war

---

[32]Lewis, *Broadcast Talks*, 25-26.
[33]Lewis, *Broadcast Talks*, 30.

wishful thinking about international politics. It is time we did the same about religion."[34]

Now this is a quite different kind of moral argument. It is not only aware of its predecessors but also very much in tune with the times— socially and philosophically. So it is a generally inductive argument, based on observation, not internal subjective experience, and it reaches its conclusion by considering and eliminating relevant alternative explanations until only one is left. Its conclusion is very thin and only has a certain level of probability, and it is certainly plausible that there are overlooked explanations. However, that either moralities are the product of social patterns—other people—or that they are the result of some causal process embedded in evolution certainly seem to be the only real alternatives out there. There may be some fresh variations coming, but they will only be just that, and they will have to face the same objections. It seems likely that the only way to avoid this argument is to somehow sidestep its initial phase that concludes to an objective moral law. That has, in fact, been the subsequent history of this discussion: reduce the strength of the demand for moral values to the point that evolution *will* be the best explanation.

4.4.2 Robert Merrihew Adams. As I noted with the other arguments, the 1960s marked the return, or at least the beginning of one, of the discussion of theism's evidence and reasons in the context of American and European academia. One of the earliest was Robert Adams (b. 1937). After teaching at UCLA, Yale, and Oxford, he became, in 2013, part of the founding faculty of the Rutgers Center for the Philosophy of Religion, along with his late wife, Marilyn McCord Adams (1943–2017), who was also a distinguished philosopher, and who wrote especially on the problem of evil.

In a series of essays between 1973 and 1987, Adams laid out an argument, several times amended and altered, that the proper basis for

---

[34]Lewis, *Broadcast Talks*, 33.

ethical obligation lies in its having been commanded by God. This has come to be known as the divine-command theory (DCT). Put simply, it is the view that "rightness and wrongness consist in agreement and disagreement, respectively, with the will or commands of a loving God."[35] Adams then gives a somewhat Kantian and practical argument from the nature of right and wrong:

(1) It would be demoralizing not to believe there is a moral order of the universe; for then we would have to regard it as very likely that the history of the universe will not be good on the whole, no matter what we do.

(2) Demoralization is morally undesirable.

(3) Therefore, there is moral advantage in believing that there is a moral order of the universe.

(4) Theism provides the most adequate theory of a moral order of the universe.

(5) Therefore, there is a moral advantage in accepting theism.[36]

The outcome of Adams's work on the argument has been to raise two issues that, I would say, have not yet been sufficiently resolved. The first is the matter of whether the DCT is sufficient to ground ethical obligation. Does it even allow for obligation or merely for obedience? I will not look further at the extensive debate that has followed Adams. I have included him in this story because he was really the first to bring the whole argument back to the serious academic discussion in the late twentieth century.

That issue leads inevitably to the broader, second issue of precisely what it is *in* or *about* God that would constitute his authoritative status. This, too, has provoked discussion that is still ongoing, and I will not

---

[35]Robert Merrihew Adams, "Moral Arguments for Theistic Belief," in *Rationality and Religious Belief*, ed. C. F. Delaney (Notre Dame, IN: University of Notre Dame Press, 1979), 117.

[36]Adams, "Moral Arguments," 125.

pursue it in the limiting context of this story, especially since I think it has no real bearing on the soundness of the moral argument itself. The argument merely requires that there is a source of obligation of a particular sort, best exemplified in God. It does not need to spell out how and why that is so.

4.4.3 William Lad Sessions. After his doctoral work at Oxford and Yale University, William Lad Sessions (b. 1943) spent most of his career at Washington and Lee University, where he is now a retired emeritus professor of philosophy. In his 1985 essay "A New Look at Moral Arguments for the Existence of God,"[37] Sessions begins with the observation that after a century of dominating the arguments, between 1930 and 1980 it all but disappeared. While Adams and a few others had begun to take a new look, there were good reasons, he thought, to do so in earnest.

Sessions then lays out a revised form of an argument from the Oxford-educated Alfred E. Taylor (1869–1945) that might serve as an example. Taylor advanced this argument throughout his career but most notably in his posthumously published *Does God Exist?* in 1947.[38] Sessions reconstructs Taylor's argument into more current philosophical idiom, but retains the distinctive feature he finds relevant for contemporary discussion: the metaphor of life as journey or pilgrimage:

(1) The moral life is (or is like) a pilgrimage from the temporal to the eternal.

(2) The goal or end of moral pilgrimage is immortality (or eternal life).

(3) God's existence is a necessary condition for anyone attaining immortality (or eternal life).

(4) Therefore belief in God's existence is rationally justified.[39]

---

[37]William Lad Sessions, "A New Look at Moral Arguments for the Existence of God," *International Journal for Philosophy of Religion* 18 (1985): 51-67.

[38]Alfred Taylor, *Does God Exist?* (New York: Macmillan, 1947). Taylor was the last of the great English idealist philosophers.

[39]Sessions, "New Look," 59.

Now clearly this argument depends on similarities between an ordinary human life and a moral journey, a life lived in search of moral goodness. Perhaps Taylor is a bit idealistic here, but this *is* how most of us live: we want to see progress toward some goal, we want some meaning or purpose out of it, we recognize that there will be setbacks and dangers along the way, and we might even never complete it. Both Taylor and Sessions seem right about this: this is human life. But granted, as Sessions admits, this form of moral reasoning is "non-evidential and person-relative."[40] So we need to modify the conclusion to read that God's existence is rationally justified for those who are seriously committed to the moral life.[41] And this leads Sessions to a further qualification: On what grounds—that is, with what rational justification—is someone seriously committed to a moral life?

So this form of the argument shows only that for someone who sees that life is a moral pilgrimage, theism is rationally justified. One might not think that is much, but Sessions points out that this argument can be helpful to someone seeking an overall consistency in understanding life, and thereby perform a legitimate function in motivating someone to be moral.[42]

4.4.4 Eleonore Stump. A quite different basis for a moral argument is the objective reality of terrifying and horrific evils. Eleonore Stump (b. 1947) holds an MA in biblical studies from Harvard University, and an MA and PhD in medieval philosophy from Cornell University. Her many publications have included the monumental study *Aquinas* (2003); her culminating treatment of the problem of evil, *Wandering in Darkness: Narrative and the Problem of Suffering* (2010); her study of the divine attributes, *The God of the Bible and the God of the Philosophers*

---

[40]Sessions, "New Look," 62.
[41]Sessions, "New Look," 62.
[42]See especially his conclusions in Sessions, "New Look," 64-65.

(2016); and her recent *Atonement* (2018).[43] Certainly one of the leading voices among Christians in philosophy, she has been teaching for many years now at Saint Louis University.

In an earlier, more autobiographical piece titled "The Mirror of Evil,"[44] she lays out an abductive line of reasoning that moves us from the experience of hideous evils committed by human persons to the conclusion that there must be a good God. While this essay does not present us with a formal argument, I would summarize her reasoning as follows:

1. We all recognize certain objective evils in our world.

2. This could not be unless there is an objective moral order.

3. This would all be meaningless unless there is a good God who gives our lives in this world meaning.

4. Therefore, either our lives in this world have no meaning at all, or there is a good God who gives them meaning.

5. Therefore, since there are objective evils, there must be a good God who gives our lives in this world meaning.

The argument begins with the recognition that we all experience certain events as truly evil, even though we cannot say exactly what the epistemic methodology is. It no doubt involves uniquely human reasoning, but includes intuitional and emotive elements as well. Nevertheless, we clearly do perceive some human actions as horrific evils. In fact, referring to the hideous medical experiments on children in the concentration camps, she

---

[43]Eleonore Stump, *Aquinas*, Arguments of the Philosophers (New York: Routledge, 2003); Stump, *The God of the Bible and the God of the Philosophers* (Milwaukee: Marquette University Press, 2016); Stump, *Wandering in Darkness: Narrative and the Problem of Suffering* (Oxford: Oxford University Press, 2010); Stump, *Atonement* (Oxford: Oxford University Press, 2018).

[44]Eleonore Stump, "The Mirror of Evil," in *God and the Philosophers: The Reconciliation of Faith and Reason*, ed. Thomas V. Morris (Oxford: Oxford University Press, 1994). Granted, as the title indicates, her essay is about how our perceptions of evil function as a mirror that allows us to see ourselves as ourselves, but also to see us in our relation to God. There is an epistemic faculty that points us toward God and so allows evil, perhaps surprisingly, to become an argument for the reality of a good God.

claims that if "our ethical theory countenanced those Nazi experiments on children, we'd throw away the theory as something evil itself."[45]

This same capacity to recognize evil also allows us to perceive good. Both can move us to tears. However, it is surely the mirroring force of evil—and the greater the evil, the greater the force—that, almost counterintuitively, points us to God. And what is the logic here?

Here is where we see the abductive nature of Stump's reasoning. We are left with a choice: Either our lives in this world simply have no meaning whatsoever—they are just senseless—or else they do have meaning. But they can only have meaning if there is a good and loving God who mothers this world.[46] What makes the latter the best explanation? Clearly it is the very objectivity of evil that demands it. If evil is only imagined or felt, then it remains subjective. But if our perceptions involve a veridical reasoning faculty, if these horrendous evils *truly* are evil, then there must be a moral order, a moral law, and hence a moral orderer. So in this way "the mirror of evil becomes translucent, and we can see through it to the goodness of God."[47]

We have here an argument for God's reality based on the objective reality of evil, rather than good. In fact, it seems to me that our perceptions of evil can often be even stronger than our perceptions of good. But the two are seen here as reverse sides of a coin. Either way, the facticity of human obligation leads us to God. What is crucial to Stump's reasoning is that it is not just a sovereign God, but one whose loving care for us is exhibited precisely in establishing both good and evil.

4.4.5 James Rachels. Since Darwin, the only real counter to the moral argument has been some sort of evolutionary explanation for our ethical thinking, our perceptions of right and wrong, our social mores and legal structures to enforce them: our conviction that we have

---

[45]Stump, "Mirror of Evil," 238.
[46]This is Stump's phrasing in "Mirror of Evil," 243.
[47]Stump, "Mirror of Evil," 242.

obligations, duties, and objective codes of conduct. By and large, however, evolutionary explanations have tended to just explain away. Naturalism replaced moral realism with theories of sentiment (David Hume), utility (John Stuart Mill), cultural relativism (Ruth Benedict), emotivism (A. J. Ayer), or just simple random gene mutations guided by survival of the fittest (Richard Dawkins, Michael Ruse). But all of these were open to the charge that they do not provide an objective ethics.

James Rachels (1941–2003), in his 1990 book, *Created from Animals: The Moral Implications of Darwinism*, changed all this.[48] He begins here by noting that in the current battle (the 1970s and 1980s), Christian anti-evolutionists were arguing that Darwinism annulled morality, while most evolutionists were simply denying that there were any connections between Darwinism and morality at all. The latter leaves a relativistic morality, while the former ignores science. Neither option will work. Instead, Rachels offered an objective scientific morality that satisfies Darwinist principles. Darwinism, he argued, removes any support for the concept of human dignity, which is what establishes traditional morality: "Darwinism undermines both the idea that man is made in the image of God, and the idea that man is a uniquely rational being. Furthermore, if Darwinism is correct, it is unlikely that any other support for the idea of human dignity will be found. The idea of human dignity turns out to be the moral effluvium of a discredited metaphysics."[49]

The real problem with the old metaphysics of Aristotle and Thomas is its teleology. But Darwin severs any connection between process and purpose, between function and intention. Hence humans have neither some special sort of dignity nor superior rationality. Rachels replaces human dignity with what he calls moral individualism. This amounts

---

[48]James Rachels, *Created from Animals: The Moral Implications of Darwinism* (Oxford: Oxford University Press, 1990).
[49]Rachels, *Created from Animals*, 5.

to saying that every individual being, across all species, is to be treated according to the differences in their individual characteristics. The reverse is also true. Equality in characteristics implies equal treatment. This is the "principle of equality."[50]

What then defines the actual value of a life such that one could develop a morality—in particular a social morality? Rachels proposes that good and evil are defined by what would or would not be a *loss* to some one individual. And clearly the ultimate loss I could suffer would be that of my *biographical life*, the things, events, actions, relationships, interests, and so on that constitute me, even more than just my *biological life*.[51] From this we may then derive specific rules of social morality that are objective because they are based on biologically evolved differences and equalities. What then creates duty or obligation?

> Why should such a rule be accepted? Why, it might be asked, should anyone take the fact that other people value their lives . . . as a compelling reason for accepting inconvenient restrictions on what may be done? Part of the answer is provided by the Darwinian account of the "social instincts." We are social animals, and the capacity for caring about the welfare of others is part of our nature. But at best this only explains why we *do* accept the rule; it does not explain why we *should* accept it. The rest of the explanation is provided by the principle of equality. Each of us—or at least, each normal person among us—is the subject of a life, and each of us would be harmed in the same way by its loss. In this respect we are all in the same boat; there is no relevant difference between us. Therefore, if we think that others should not kill us, we have to acknowledge that we should not kill them.[52]

This now makes it possible to assert an objective morality not based on divine authority, hence not articulated by human superiority either in dignity or rationality. Its seeming objectivity is guaranteed by the

---

[50]Rachels, *Created from Animals*, 176.
[51]Rachels, *Created from Animals*, 199.
[52]Rachels, *Created from Animals*, 200.

relative stability of DNA in the evolutionary process. All human beings everywhere and at every time fall within mostly identical parameters of possible characteristics relevant to how someone is to be treated. But, of course, the same is true for chimpanzees, and since they are substantially identical to humans, their treatment must be similar. Dandelions are very different, but then again, very similar in some basic respects, and so our moral obligations extend to all species, though not equally.

Rachels's explanation of obligation appears entirely circular. Why *should* I accept the rule? Only because the principle of equality that governs rules includes my acknowledging that I *should*. But nothing here actually obligates me. There is no authority invoked here. Evolution itself is just a blind process that determines my actions, though, granted, in some very complex way that I cannot introspect. But this system lacks any moral nuances. There is no responsible, goal-directed, free decision-making.

Despite this obvious circularity, Rachels will seem to many an open door for evolutionary philosophers to assert that they *do* have a realist and objective morality without God, and that theism is not the only ethics game in town.

4.4.6 Sam Harris. Following Rachels's lead, the recent discussion of the argument has been focused on the issue of a physicalistic and naturalistic evolutionary explanation for moral values. There are many proponents of this morality-without-God position, but I will look at just two representative ones. First, at a popular level, is Sam Harris (b. 1967), one of the leading voices of the New Atheism. His training is in neuroscience, with a PhD from UCLA. *The End of Faith* was Harris's public declaration of atheism in 2002. But *The Moral Landscape* in 2010 was his full accounting of morality.[53]

---

[53]Sam Harris, *The Moral Landscape: How Science Can Determine Human Values* (New York: Free Press, 2010).

Harris argues here that there is no human free will, a thesis he went on to discuss more fully in his next book, *Free Will*, in 2012.[54] This becomes the cornerstone of a "scientific" understanding of morality as the evolutionary furthering of human well-being.

The Moral Landscape begins by assuring the reader that morality is objective and scientific, and so there is in fact moral truth. Furthermore, he is quite clear that his claim really is about morality: it is not about what we do, but about what we *should* do.[55] This all seems very reassuring, and rather bold and unexpected from an evolutionary naturalist. But just what is the content of moral truth?

> Once we see that a concern for well-being (defined as deeply and inclusively as possible) is the only intelligible basis for morality and values, we will see that there *must* be a science of morality, whether or not we ever succeed in developing it: because the well-being of conscious creatures depends on how the universe is, altogether. Given that changes in the physical universe and in our experience of it can be understood, science should increasingly enable us to answer specific moral questions. . . . Of course there will be practical impediments to evaluating the consequences of certain actions . . . but I am arguing that there are no obstacles, in principle, to our speaking about *moral truth*.[56]

But now comes the crucial transition. The fact that morality is the science of well-being implies that terms like *ought* are to be jettisoned as "another dismal product of Abrahamic religion."[57] Science is about is, not about ought. So, to say that we ought to do *x* is just to say that everyone will be better off if we do *x*. Now Harris admits that "well-being" cannot be readily defined, but he does offer that we can bounce definitions off of a concept we do understand: the worst possible misery

---

[54]Sam Harris, *Free Will* (New York: Free Press, 2012).
[55]Harris, *Moral Landscape*, 28.
[56]Harris, *Moral Landscape*, 28.
[57]Harris, *Moral Landscape*, 38.

for everyone. That, at least, is the definition of evil, and moving in the opposite direction is good.

Now the final point: In what sense am I responsible for my actions? Harris answers,

> To say that I am responsible for my behavior is simply to say that what I did was sufficiently in keeping with my thoughts, intentions, beliefs, and desires to be considered an extension of them. . . . Judgments of responsibility, therefore, depend upon the overall complexion of one's mind, not on the metaphysics of mental cause and effect.[58]

So here is where we, according to Harris, have to jettison another leftover metaphysical notion: free will. The idea that our thoughts, intentions, and so on are freely chosen and can be freely altered "rests on a cognitive and emotional illusion—and perpetuates a moral one."[59] Morality is a science because human behavior is a science. Free will is nowhere to be found.[60] Hence we need to stop dreaming about what the world *should* be and concern ourselves with what the objective reality of human well-being actually *is*.

4.4.7 Erik Wielenberg. My second example is the philosopher Erik Wielenberg (b. 1972). A PhD from the University of Massachusetts at Amherst, he teaches at DePauw University. He is representative of numerous ethicists currently attempting to construct a naturalist account of human morality without God. I think his has been among the strongest to date, so I will limit my discussion to his 2005 *Value and Virtue in a Godless Universe.*[61]

---

[58]Harris, *Moral Landscape*, 106-7.

[59]Harris, *Moral Landscape*, 111.

[60]In *Free Will*, Harris gives a more extended argument against free will. It ultimately rests on one piece of evidence: the Libet experiments. Curiously, he gives them the older and now discredited interpretation. On this see Steve Taylor, "Benjamin Libet and the Denial of Free Will," *Psychology Today*, September 5, 2017, https://www.psychologytoday.com/us/blog/out-the-darkness/201709/benjamin-libet-and-the-denial-free-will. In any case, these experiments apply only to spontaneous movements and say nothing about our ethical deliberations and decision-making where free will is most obvious and most important.

[61]Erik J. Wielenberg, *Value and Virtue in a Godless Universe* (Cambridge: Cambridge University Press, 2005).

In certain respects Wielenberg might not be considered a full-blown naturalist. He refers to himself as such, and strictly speaking his metaphysics is physicalistic and accepts that causality is confined to material and efficient causes. He refers, however, to his view as Platonic, in that moral values are just intrinsically valuable. In the end, though, this is a broadly naturalist account of morality, as is evident in his final conclusions.[62]

We can summarize his position, as opposed to theism, in five points, in line with his own chapter divisions.

1. We neither need, nor does it add anything, to refer to God as the source of meaning in life. Our lives simply have whatever meaning we give them, given the intrinsic value that relationships, altruism, achievements, and so forth, possess for us.

2. What is the source of moral truth? Wielenberg does not deny that some moral claims could be true in reference to divine or human agency. But in the end, his view is inconsistent with both. "The foundation of morality is a set of axiomatic necessary eternal truths. No being, natural or supernatural, is responsible for the truth of, or has control over, these ethical truths."[63] Thus God cannot impose them on us, or command them for us, because they are just true. God cannot impose on us that $2 + 2 = 4$. It just is so, and there neither is, nor need be, any explanation. So it is not a physical fact, like the sky is blue, but it also is not supernatural. It is how any natural universe must be. No God needed!

3. Why be moral? The answer now is quite obvious. "Grown-ups recognize that the fact that a given action is morally obligatory is itself an overriding reason for performing that action. A morally obligatory action is an action that one *has* to do whether one *wants* to

---

[62]On this point, see the discussion in David Baggett and Jerry Walls, *God and Cosmos: Moral Truth and Human Meaning* (Oxford: Oxford University Press, 2016), 133-44.

[63]Wielenberg, *Value and Virtue*, 66.

do it or not."[64] This, he thinks, actually adds urgency to our obligations, whereas a divine command would lead to complacency.

4. How does this then lead to moral growth and character? It does, Wielenberg argues, precisely because without a God to determine the outcomes, there is genuine hope that we can achieve the growth that is given to us to accomplish in life. And so, "when we know *that* an action is morally obligatory we have at least some inkling of *why* it is morally obligatory."[65]

5. In general, why is an overall naturalistic account preferable to the theistic creed? It is here that Wielenberg clearly opposes the kind of divine morality endorsed in the Old Testament. This is a dangerous and divisive creed that cannot be good for us, he argues, though he accepts that many will choose this creed, and that the naturalism he endorses (here he refers to it as humanism) many will find depressing since there is no afterlife and only internal meaning. So he leaves us with the

> suggestion that we put science to work in the service of the Platonic quest of finding a reliable way of making people virtuous. The track record of science offers some hope in this endeavor. . . . And some of these advances have given at least some of us the ability to live lives that are far healthier and more comfortable than was previously possible. Of course scientific progress has hardly brought moral progress—but it is also true that science has not so far been used explicitly for that purpose.[66]

4.4.8 David Baggett and Jerry Walls. Wielenberg's morality-without-God position has been answered by many, but I think none have done it better than David Baggett (b. 1965) and Jerry Walls (b. 1955) in their *Good God: The Theistic Foundations of Morality*, in 2011, and more

---

[64]Wielenberg, *Value and Virtue*, 80.
[65]Wielenberg, *Value and Virtue*, 96.
[66]Wielenberg, *Value and Virtue*, 155.

extensively in *God and Cosmos: Moral Truth and Human Meaning*, in 2016.[67] Baggett holds a PhD from Wayne State University and previously taught at Liberty University, but now teaches at Houston Baptist University. Walls is scholar in residence and professor of philosophy at Houston Baptist University, and holds a doctorate from Notre Dame.

Their response to Wielenberg is primarily to point out what has not actually happened here. I hasten to add that this response in *God and Cosmos* comes after Wielenberg's even more thorough account in 2014, *Robust Ethics*.[68] I will give their summary list of unjustified and unexplained positions, which follows a specific example: that of deliberate cruelty:

> It is a dubious insistence that says, since explanations have to come to an end, stopping where Wielenberg does is just as good a place as any. It is true that explanations have to come to an end, but the final explanation needs to be adequate to the task. It is not at all clear what explanatory work is done by saying that an act of deliberate cruelty simply makes something wrong. Of course it does, we're inclined to reply, which is part of what is in need of explanation. . . . Similarly, when Wielenberg says deliberate cruelty makes something wrong, what he is saying may well be true, but it doesn't advance the discussion or offer illumination by way of explanation. Why does deliberate cruelty make something wrong? He stops short of getting to the heart of the matter in our estimation.
>
> So, in sum, it's not at all clear that Wielenberg is within his epistemic rights to be sanguine in his affirmation of a human nature or essence on his worldview. Conjoin that concern with these: the distinctive features of morality that produce a significant qualitative chasm between natural and moral facts; the unparsimonious affirmation of non-natural facts instantiated by a world of nonvalue; an unprincipled stopping point of explanation which amounts to more assertion than argument; a

---

[67]David Baggett and Jerry Walls, *Good God: The Theistic Foundations of Morality* (Oxford: Oxford University Press, 2011); Baggett and Walls, *God and Cosmos*.
[68]Erik J. Wielenberg, *Robust Ethics: The Metaphysics and Epistemology of Godless Normative Realism* (Oxford: Oxford University Press, 2014).

historically myopic treatment of the worldview as eliminable that is mainly responsible for the convictions about and grounding for intrinsic human value and dignity. The net effect is that Wielenberg's moral theory seems to contain dim prospects for undergirding something so fundamental and important as intrinsic human dignity and value.

We suspect it is because of the way theism and Christianity, most particularly, have so seeped into the moral consciousness and conscience of so many people within our society that a moral theory could cavalierly treat profound and axiomatic moral truths as sufficiently obvious to need no ontological foundation and be taken seriously. Human beings are indeed valuable creatures, and we live in a world of thick values and virtues and we are cognitively and affectively equipped to apprehend such moral truths.[69]

I conclude that Wielenberg's attempt to prevent the moral argument by offering a better explanation for moral facts fails. It does so not because there is not much the theist can agree with in his overall moral theory, but because it lacks any substantive basis.

Further Reading

We lack a solid collection of current views and discussion on the moral argument. One good place to start on an overview is Mark Linville, "The Moral Argument," in *The Blackwell Companion to Natural Theology*, ed. William Lane Craig and J. P. Moreland (Oxford: Blackwell, 2009), 391-448. This has a helpful bibliography. There is also the excellent, more recent (2018) entry by C. Stephen Evans, "Moral Arguments for the Existence of God," in *Stanford Encyclopedia of Philosophy*, ed. Edward N. Zalta, fall 2018 ed., which also has an extensive bibliography, https://plato.stanford.edu/archives/fall2018/entries/moral-arguments-god/.

A great new history of the moral argument is David Baggett and Jerry Walls's *The Moral Argument: A History* (Oxford: Oxford University Press, 2019).

A critical discussion of Lewis in general, but including his moral argument, is John Beversluis, *C. S. Lewis and the Search for Rational Religion* (Grand Rapids, MI: Eerdmans, 1985).

---

[69]Baggett and Walls, *God and Cosmos*, 142-43.

A positive assessment of Lewis is found in the collection edited by David Baggett, Gary Habermas, and Jerry Walls, *C. S. Lewis as Philosopher: Truth, Goodness and Beauty* (Downers Grove, IL: IVP Academic, 2008). This includes several essays responding to Beversluis, including those by David Horner and David Baggett.

An excellent overview and critique of the attempts at a scientific naturalistic grounding for ethics is James Davison Hunter and Paul Nedelisky, *Science and the Good: The Tragic Quest for the Foundations of Morality* (New Haven, CT: Yale University Press, 2018).

One place to start on a critique of Adams's DCT is Steven Sullivan, "Robert Adams's Theistic Argument from the Nature of Morality," *Journal of Religious Ethics* 21, no. 2 (2001): 303-12.

Among the many issues I have not dealt with here is the Euthyphro dilemma, which goes back to Plato's question in the *Euthyphro*: "Is the pious being loved by the gods because it is pious, or is it pious because it is loved by the gods?" This forms an important part of Wielenberg's antitheistic argument, for example. A good survey of the literature and a theistic response is in Baggett and Walls, *Good God: The Theistic Foundations of Morality* (Oxford: Oxford University Press, 2011), chap. 2.

For more on the issue of God's authority to issue moral obligations, start with Patrick Todd, "Does God Have the Moral Standing to Blame?," *Faith and Philosophy* 35, no. 1 (2018): 33-55.

As mentioned, a more recent statement by Wielenberg is his *Robust Ethics: The Metaphysics and Epistemology of Godless Normative Realism* (Oxford: Oxford University Press, 2014).

Some more defenses and restatements of the moral argument are in Robert Adams, "Moral Arguments for Theism," in *The Virtue of Faith and Other Essays in Philosophical Theology* (New York: Oxford University Press, 1987), 144-63; Donald Burt, "The Problem of Justifying Moral Obligation: An Aspect of the Moral Argument for the Existence of God," *The Proceedings of the ACPA* 49 (1975): 72-91; Douglas Drabkin, "A Moral Argument for Under-taking Theism," *American Philosophical Quarterly* 31, no. 2 (1994): 169-78; C. Stephen Evans, *God and Moral Obligation* (Oxford: Oxford University Press, 2013); John Hare, *God's Command* (New York: Oxford University Press, 2015); C. Stephen Layman, "God and the Moral Order," *Faith and Philosophy* 19 (2002): 304-16; Linville, "The Moral Argument"; Xiusheng Liu, "A Moral Reason to be a Mere Theist: Improving the Practical Argument," *International*

Journal for Philosophy of Religion 79, no. 2 (2016): 113-32; Angus Ritchie, *From Morality to Metaphysics: The Theistic Implications of our Ethical Commitments* (Oxford: Oxford University Press, 2012); and Linda Zagzebski, "Does Ethics Need God?," *Faith and Philosophy* 4 (2004): 294-303.

Another good exchange on the issue of an objective ethics without God is Wes Morriston, "God and the Ontological Foundation of Morality," in *Religious Studies* 48 (2012): 15-34. He is responding here to numerous debates, some published, of William Lane Craig, including with Sinnott-Armstrong in *God? A Debate Between a Christian and an Atheist* (Oxford: Oxford University Press, 2004). Craig responds in a 2018 debate with Morriston that you can view on his website, "Wes Morriston: Problem of Evil and Moral Argument (Part 1)," Reasonable Faith, January 14, 2018, https://www.reasonablefaith .org/media/reasonable-faith-podcast/wes-morriston-problem-of-evil-and -moral-argument-part-1/.

A good collection of objections is the previously mentioned Michael Martin, *Atheism* (Philadelphia: Temple University Press, 1992). Check also the exchange between Martin and Paul Copan in *Philosophia Christi* 2, no. 2 (2000): 75-90.

A good source on naturalism's inability to deliver a solid ethics is Christian Smith, *Atheist Overreach: What Atheism Can't Deliver* (Oxford: Oxford University Press, 2018).

A great recent debate (the actual debate took place in 2018) on the objectivity issue is William Lane Craig and Erik J. Wielenberg, *A Debate on God and Morality: What is the Best Account of Objective Moral Values and Duties?*, edited by Adam Lloyd Johnson (Abingdon, UK: Taylor & Francis, 2020).

4.5 Where We Are Now

No doubt the most recent and exhaustive work on the moral argument has come, as we have just previously seen, from the writing duo of David Baggett and Jerry Walls. Together they have produced three major volumes on the topic: *Good God: The Theistic Foundations of Morality*, published in 2011, is an extended treatment of the argument and its principle objections. *God and Cosmos: Moral Truth and Human Meaning*, which followed in 2016, deals with broader issues of moral realism and the various current attempts to replace theistic accounts.

A history of the argument was added in 2019 with *The Moral Argument: A History*.[70]

What they have argued in both volumes is that current attempts to eliminate the need for God as a basis for morality are dismal failures that wind up denying morality entirely in the process. This is significant because it not only establishes the theistic claim but also undercuts naturalistic atheism by denying it the use of the problem of evil as a defeater for theism.[71] It thus leaves the moral argument standing: that there is a God, the cosmic lawgiver, remains the best explanation for our moral facts.

Here is how they say it in *Good God*:

> The existence of binding moral obligations is harder to square with a naturalistic context than a supernaturalistic one. . . . Wielenberg obviously wants to affirm the existence of moral realism in a strong sense here . . . but without coming to terms with just how deeply naturalism is at odds with such realism. How do such oughts exist in a world where we are causally determined to behave just as we do? How do such binding obligations come to obtain? His naturalist allies have often been the very ones most contributing to the loss of confidence in such moral realism, rendering it more than a little disingenuous for him to treat theism as the bigger culprit undermining such traditional convictions.[72]

So where this leaves us is that any attempt by naturalists to establish an ethic that provides for objective moral obligations that could prevent the moral argument from going forward is doomed from the start. It simply lacks a metaphysics that will allow for human freedom, and therefore responsibility and accountability, nor can it provide for objective value, except in a purely functional or pragmatic sense.

---

[70]Baggett and Walls, *Good God*; Baggett and Walls, *God and Cosmos*; Baggett and Walls, *The Moral Argument: A History* (Oxford: Oxford University Press, 2019).

[71]On this point see Jonathan Smith, "Abductive Moral Arguments and Godless Normative Realism," *Quaerens Deum* 5, no. 1 (2019): https://digitalcommons.liberty.edu/lujpr/.

[72]Baggett and Walls, *Good God*, 16.

It will not do for Wielenberg, Rachels, Harris, and many others to tell us that they really have real value, meaning, and responsibility, when they have no way to sustain these core essentials. Even Houdini cannot pull out of his hat what is not already there. If the metaphysical system only allows for material/efficient causality, then it cannot somehow produce freedom and intrinsic value. No doubt, naturalistic evolution could account for our moral feelings, intuitions, instincts, emotions, sentiments, preferences, predispositions, hard and soft wiring, attractions and repulsions, to some extent even our behaviors. But that does not suffice for an objective morality of obligations.

What is most curious is that Wielenberg and many others style themselves as Aristotelians on the matter of intrinsic value. But at the most critical point they inconsistently abandon him. For Aristotle, final causality is present only because God, the uncaused cause, has structured it so, and he is quite clear in the *Nicomachean Ethics* that this is the grounding for the intrinsicality of moral value.[73] There just is no hope for naturalism—or *in* it either.

---

[73]See Aristotle, *Nicomachean Ethics* 10.8. On this point, see Brian Donohue, "God and Aristotelian Ethics," *Questiones Disputatae* 5, no. 1 (2014): 65-77.

CHAPTER 5

Ontological Arguments

5.1 The Original Meditation

The ontological argument is a unique piece of philosophy in so many ways. For one, it has no prior history before 1077. All of the other arguments are patterns of reasoning perhaps as old as human thought. But this story has a distinct beginning in the mind of St. Anselm of Canterbury.[1] Born in 1033 in Aosta, Italy, Anselm became a Benedictine monk and lived at the Abbey of Bec in Normandy, and served later as archbishop of Canterbury from 1093 till his death in 1109. He was a prolific writer on most of the major theological doctrines and made significant contributions in several areas.

Another rather unique characteristic of this argument is that its story just gets more and more complicated over time. It touches on many of the most basic but also most complex and divisive topics in logic, epistemology, and philosophy of language, beginning with the very definition and application of the word *exist*. With the other three arguments, it seems to me at least that the story has become largely repetitive. There really are no very new objections coming down the road, just old ones retreaded. But the ontological argument has by now become entangled in a virtually impenetrable thicket of arguments.

This is perhaps best seen by the fact that it is not a simple divide between atheist and theist. This has been true from the very beginning. Anselm's argument was immediately countered by an equally

---

[1]An extended argument for this can be found in Yujin Nagasawa, *Maximal God: A New Defence of Perfect Being Theism* (Oxford: Oxford University Press, 2017), 124-31.

God-fearing Benedictine monk, Gaunilo. And just so, there are theists who claim Anselm was correct and some who claim he was wrong and that the argument is just question-begging if not outright silly. But to top it off, there are plenty of theists—even some atheists—who think there is no light at the end of this tunnel, and maybe never will be. I confess up front that I am inclined to think that we are coming to some solid conclusions, though that is not a spoiler alert. We will just have to see how this story unfolds.

Anselm's *Proslogion* was originally titled *Faith Seeking Understanding* (*Fides quaerens intellectum*) and then *An Address on God's Existence* (*Alloquium de Dei existentia*), and completed in 1078. It followed the *Monologion*, an extended meditational discussion of the nature of God. *Proslogion* is a much briefer, cut-to-the-chase argument, though still intended as meditation.

What follows is Anselm's offering of the original argument in the *Proslogion*, then the reply by Gaunilo, and then the response to Gaunilo by Anselm. I have pared these down to the more essential portions.[2]

5.1.1 Anselm's Proslogion.

Truly there is a God, although the fool has said in his heart, There is no God.

AND so, Lord, do you, who do give understanding to faith, give me, so far as you knowest it to be profitable, to understand that you are as we believe; and that you are that which we believe. And indeed, we believe that you are a being than which nothing greater can be conceived. Or is there no such nature, since the fool has said in his heart, there is no God? But, at any rate, this very fool, when he hears of this being of which I speak—a being than which nothing greater can be conceived—understands what he hears, and what he understands is in his understanding; although he does not understand it to exist.

---

[2]For a good structural analysis of these three texts, including a matching of each section of Gaunilo with the related response from Anselm, see Arthur McGill's exegetical section in *The Many-faced Argument*, ed. John Hick and Arthur McGill (New York: Macmillan, 1967).

Hence, even the fool is convinced that something exists in the understanding, at least, than which nothing greater can be conceived. For, when he hears of this, he understands it. And whatever is understood, exists in the understanding. And assuredly that, than which nothing greater can be conceived, cannot exist in the understanding alone. For, suppose it exists in the understanding alone: then it can be conceived to exist in reality; which is greater.

Therefore, if that, than which nothing greater can be conceived, exists in the understanding alone, the very being, than which nothing greater can be conceived, is one, than which a greater can be conceived. But obviously this is impossible. Hence, there is doubt that there exists a being, than which nothing greater can be conceived, and it exists both in the understanding and in reality.

God cannot be conceived not to exist.—God is that, than which nothing greater can be conceived.—That which can be conceived not to exist is not God.

AND it assuredly exists so truly, that it cannot be conceived not to exist. For, it is possible to conceive of a being which cannot be conceived not to exist; and this is greater than one which can be conceived not to exist. Hence, if that, than which nothing greater can be conceived, can be conceived not to exist, it is not that, than which nothing greater can be conceived.

How the fool has said in his heart what cannot be conceived.— A thing may be conceived in two ways: (1) when the word signifying it is conceived; (2) when the thing itself is understood As far as the word goes, God can be conceived not to exist; in reality he cannot.

But, if really, nay, since really, he both conceived, because he said in his heart; and did not say in his heart, because he could not conceive; there is more than one way in which a thing is said in the heart or conceived. For, in one sense, an object is conceived, when the word signifying it is conceived; and in another, when the very entity, which the object is, is understood.

In the former sense, then, God can be conceived not to exist; but in the latter, not at all. For no one who understands what fire and water are can conceive fire to be water, in accordance with the nature of the facts themselves, although this is possible according to the words. So, then, no one who understands what God is can conceive that God does not exist.[3]

I think this argument is best understood as consisting of two parts. There is, first, Anselm's definition (AD), and, second, Anselm's principle (AP). The two work together to produce this unique and rather simple piece of reasoning.

First, a novel definition. Anselm was a real innovator: today we would say he was not afraid to think outside the box. In this case, he provided an enormous improvement over Augustine's definition of God. Now, *definition* is not exactly the right word. The question early Christian philosophers were attempting to answer is how we know when something can properly be attributed to God. What is the decision procedure that allows us to say that God has some property X? Augustine's answer was "that than which there is nothing better."[4] God is the perfection of goodness. He just *is* the Good. So X may be attributed to God if it is as maximal as X can be.

Anselm here corrected a weakness in Augustine's definition. God could be that than which nothing is better in X-ness, without being infinitely X. He might be best but still finite. We might even think that God could have evil properties. Now Augustine could avoid the matter of evil properties by arguing that, following Plato, evil is privation. It is not a degree of goodness at all but the absence of goodness. But how do we strengthen this decision procedure and avoid God's having finite properties? Anselm's conclusion was that God must be understood as a "being greater than which cannot be conceived" (*aliquid quo maius nihil cogitari potest*). We can shorten this to "greatest conceivable being," or GCB.[5] This seems to avoid at least the obvious problems with Augustine's definition.

---

[3] Anselm, *Proslogium* 2-4, trans. Sidney Deane (Chicago: Open Court, 1903).
[4] See Augustine, *De doctrina Christiana* 1.7.
[5] See the discussion in Stephen T. Davis, *God, Reason and Theistic Proofs* (Grand Rapids, MI: Eerdmans, 1997), 17-19, as to whether this equates to greatest-*possible*-being.

Now this definition itself is much older. It was used by the Stoics. Seneca, in his *On Providence*, said that God is *qua nihil maius cogitari potest*: "that which nothing greater can be thought."[6] We do not know if this is where Anselm first learned it, though it differs of course in referring generally to "greater" rather than "better." Anselm actually used both Augustine's "better" (*melius*) and Seneca's "greater" (*maius*).[7] But what is new here is Anselm's recognition that the definition by itself enables an argument.

What is interesting about Anselm's actual argument, however, is that he does not simply begin by stipulating this as God's definition. It has rightly, I think, been argued that that would be viciously circular. To begin with the premise "God is . . ." and then conclude that "God is" is to beg the question. Anselm no doubt had his bad days, but this argument was carefully thought through, written out, and then published, and Anselm was not that foolish.

What he said is that the atheist "understands what he hears, and what he understands is in his understanding; although he does not understand it to exist."[8] So this is merely a possible definition of something, which the atheist understands quite well, though it is not attached to an existing object, including God. The words allow us to form a concept. This meaning of AD is made quite clear both in Gaunilo's reply as well as in Anselm's response to him, as we will see below. And most obviously: the word "God" does not appear in the argument in the final three paragraphs of *Proslogion* 2 at all.

Think of it this way. Suppose I program my computer to list every possible sequence of eight English words. Most of these will be

---

[6]Seneca, *On Providence* 1.13.

[7]A good discussion of Stoic arguments and definitions that have some similarity to Anselm's argument can be found in Nagasawa, *Maximal God*, 126-31. He argues here that while there were similar definitions, the resulting arguments were not a priori arguments like Anselm's. So he really is the inventor of the ontological argument. And, for what it is worth, it was Kant who came up with the name.

[8]Anselm, *Proslogium* 2.

meaningless, including, for example: *a-a-a-a-a-a-a*. There will be many more that are meaningful in some sense, but clearly have no possible referent, like: *big-small-thick-thin-blue-red-dog-cat*. There will, however, be many sequences of eight that are understandable: they make sense to us. We can conceive of something possible that this defines. And that is what I think Anselm means here by the definition: "a being greater than which cannot be conceived." It is just an understandable sequence of eight words (at least in English!). It can be thought, or, as Anselm puts it rather Platonically, it can "exist in the understanding."

Now to make this into an argument we need AP: To exist in the understanding and in reality is greater than to exist in the understanding alone. What does that mean? In what sense is real existence greater than mental existence? This is especially difficult when we recognize that in Anselm's ontology both have existence. Thoughts, concepts, ideas—all are actual. Whether one thinks of them as physical brain states, or with Anselm as nonphysical mental constructs, they are part of our ontology.

There has been much discussion here, but ever since Aristotle, and especially with the medievals, there had been a common understanding that existence is to be defined as causal connectedness. The properties of an object or event specify its powers or capacities, as well as its limitations or liabilities. To be, to have properties, is to have causal import or power. So then, to be greater in existence is to have more, better, larger, or higher quality causal connectivity. As Stephen Davis concludes here, "If we define greatness . . . as *power, ability,* or *freedom of action,* comparisons clearly can be made, even among beings of widely different kinds."[9]

AP, then, merely specifies the obvious: that, whatever causal power a concept does have, that concept *plus* its real-world counterpart has

---

[9]Davis, *God, Reason and Theistic Proofs*, 20. Davis teaches at Claremont McKenna College and holds the PhD from Claremont Graduate University.

more. So Anselm's argument is just that AD, given AP, demands that GCB exists in reality. That somehow seems too easy a move. It still does for most people when they first hear the ontological argument, and it certainly did to a now famous but hitherto unknown contemporary of Anselm: Gaunilo.

5.1.2 *Gaunilo's Reply on Behalf of the Fool:* Pro Insipiente. We know very little of Gaunilo of Marmoutiers (994–1083) beyond his reply to Anselm: A one-hit wonder if there ever was one. He was a fellow Benedictine monk, but at the Abbey of Marmoutiers in Lyon, France. What we can say is that he quite ably located the major objections to Anselm's argument. Here are the crucial excerpts.

> The fool might make this reply:

> This being is said to be in my understanding already, only because I understand what is said. Now could it not with equal justice be said that I have in my understanding all manner of unreal objects, having absolutely no existence in themselves, because I understand these things if one speaks of them, whatever they may be?

> Unless indeed it is shown that this being is of such a character that it cannot be held in concept like all unreal objects, or objects whose existence is uncertain: and hence I am not able to conceive of it when I hear of it, or to hold it in concept; but I must understand it and have it in my understanding; because, it seems, I cannot conceive of it in any other way than by understanding it, that is, by comprehending in my knowledge its existence in reality.

> Moreover, the following assertion can hardly be accepted: that this being, when it is spoken of and heard of, cannot be conceived not to exist in the way in which even God can be conceived not to exist. For if this is impossible, what was the object of this argument against one who doubts or denies the existence of such a being?

> Hence, I am not able, in the way in which I should have this unreal being in concept or in understanding, to have that being of which you speak in concept or in understanding, when I hear the word *God* or the

words, *a being greater than all other beings*. For I can conceive of the man according to a fact that is real and familiar to me: but of God, or a being greater than all others, I could not conceive at all, except merely according to the word. And an object can hardly or never be conceived according to the word alone.

For when it is so conceived, it is not so much the word itself (which is, indeed, a real thing—that is, the sound of the letters and syllables) as the signification of the word, when heard, that is conceived. But it is not conceived as by one who knows what is generally signified by the word; by whom, that is, it is conceived according to a reality and in true conception alone. It is conceived as by a man who does not know the object, and conceives of it only in accordance with the movement of his mind produced by hearing the word, the mind attempting to image for itself the signification of the word that is heard. And it would be surprising if in the reality of fact it could ever attain to this.

Thus, it appears, and in no other way, this being is also in my understanding, when I hear and understand a person who says that there is a being greater than all conceivable beings. So much for the assertion that this supreme nature already is in my understanding.

For example: it is said that somewhere in the ocean is an island, which, because of the difficulty, or rather the impossibility, of discovering what does not exist, is called the lost island. And they say that this island has an inestimable wealth of all manner of riches and delicacies in greater abundance than is told of the Islands of the Blest; and that having no owner or inhabitant, it is more excellent than all other countries, which are inhabited by mankind, in the abundance with which it is stored.

Now if some one should tell me that there is such an island, I should easily understand his words, in which there is no difficulty. But suppose that he went on to say, as if by a logical inference: "You can no longer doubt that this island which is more excellent than all lands exists somewhere, since you have no doubt that it is in your understanding. And since it is more excellent not to be in the understanding alone, but to exist both in the understanding and in reality, for this reason it must exist. For if it does not exist, any land which really exists will be more excellent than it; and so the island already understood by you to be more excellent will not be more excellent."

If a man should try to prove to me by such reasoning that this island truly exists, and that its existence should no longer be doubted, either I should believe that he was jesting, or I know not which I ought to regard as the greater fool: myself, supposing that I should allow this proof; or him, if he should suppose that he had established with any certainty the existence of this island. For he ought to show first that the hypothetical excellence of this island exists as a real and indubitable fact, and in no wise as any unreal object, or one whose existence is uncertain, in my understanding.[10]

Now it is clear from the first several paragraphs that Gaunilo read Anselm correctly to mean by understanding "knowing the meaning of the words." So the fool, whom Gaunilo wanted to defend, does understand GCB, but does not get the connection to real existence.

There are essentially two objections here, though they are connected. The first is that, in general, we cannot move from contents of the mind, a word, to real things. You can describe something to me in sufficient detail that I understand what you are talking about—that is, I form a concept of it. But that is where the epistemic process stops: there is no further inference to existence in the real world.

Note that neither Gaunilo here, nor Anselm in his response below, is talking about mental image or picturing in the mind. Later empiricists will read that into this debate because they had no other way of conceptualizing mental operations. Hence we will get Descartes's argument and Kant's objection to that argument. Gaunilo and Anselm, however, are speaking of the mental capacity to form concepts—ideas, thoughts—from which we may, in turn, form arguments. Gaunilo's point, and he was surely right, is that, in general, these concepts have no implications for real-world existence, even if AP is correct.

---

[10]Gaunilo, *In Behalf Of The Fool* 2, 4, 6, trans. Sidney Deane (Chicago: Open Court, 1903).

Suffice it to say, most of the subsequent objections to Anselm are some version of Gaunilo's: You cannot move from logic to the real world. This will become more and more detailed and sophisticated over the centuries, but somehow always the same. Every few years, it seems, along comes a new version of this objection. Someone finds a new way of specifying precisely where the logic goes wrong in Anselm. I will argue that Anselm would always respond exactly as he does to Gaunilo: This is a perfectly valid principle, but there is just this one exception—the GCB, that is, AD. But again, I am getting ahead of the story.

Gaunilo's second objection, the one for which he lives forever in philosophical lore, is the most-excellent-lost-island objection. Here the move in logic is not from the merely conceivable in general, but from *greatest* conceivable. Does "greatest" justify an exception to the logical barrier? Gaunilo argued that no qualifications to the concept of an island, not even "inestimable value," will warrant a move to real existence. There are no exceptions to the rule!

Note that Gaunilo has no quarrel with either AD or with AP. The components of the argument are not the problem. We will note some later issues raised here, but they are relatively easily handled. Both he and Anselm also clearly agree that this is an argument about AD, not God. The only real issue with this argument is this connection problem. On to Anselm's response.

5.1.3 Anselm's response to Gaunilo. It appears that Anselm knew nothing of Gaunilo prior to this reply, nor does he think much of the contents of the reply. Gaunilo simply missed the whole point of the argument, he thought. In the first chapter he basically restates the argument in a way that shows Gaunilo's whole argument to be irrelevant. In chapter two he argues that the GCB is in fact a perfectly conceivable idea, and in three responds to the lost-island objection.

CHAPTER I.

A general refutation of Gaunilo's argument. It is shown that a being than which a greater cannot be conceived exists in reality.

You say—whosoever you may be, who say that a fool is capable of making these statements—that a being than which a greater cannot be conceived is not in the understanding in any other sense than that in which a being that is altogether inconceivable in terms of reality, is in the understanding. You say that the inference that this being exists in reality, from the fact that it is in the understanding, is no more just than the inference that a lost island most certainly exists, from the fact that when it is described the hearer does not doubt that it is in his understanding.

But I say: if a being than which a greater is inconceivable is not understood or conceived, and is not in the understanding or in concept, certainly either God is not a being than which a greater is inconceivable, or else he is not understood or conceived, and is not in the understanding or in concept. But I call on your faith and conscience to attest that this is most false. Hence, that than which a greater cannot be conceived is truly understood and conceived, and is in the understanding and in concept. Therefore either the grounds on which you try to controvert me are not true, or else the inference which you think to base logically on those grounds is not justified.

But you hold, moreover, that supposing that a being than which a greater cannot be conceived is understood, it does not follow that this being is in the understanding; nor, if it is in the understanding, does it therefore exist in reality.

In answer to this, I maintain positively: if that being can be even conceived to be, it must exist in reality. For that than which a greater is inconceivable cannot be conceived except as without beginning. But whatever can be conceived to exist, and does not exist, can be conceived to exist through a beginning. Hence what can be conceived to exist, but does not exist, is not the being than which a greater cannot be conceived. Therefore, if such a being can be conceived to exist, necessarily it does exist.

Furthermore: if it can be conceived at all, it must exist. For no one who denies or doubts the existence of a being than which a greater is inconceivable, denies or doubts that if it did exist, its non-existence, either in reality or in the understanding, would be impossible. For otherwise it would not be a being than which a greater cannot be conceived. But as to whatever can be conceived, but does not exist—if there were such a being, its non-existence, either in reality or in the understanding, would be possible. Therefore if a being than which a greater is inconceivable can be even conceived, it cannot be nonexistent.

Do you believe that this being can in some way be conceived or understood, or that the being with regard to which these things are understood can be in concept or in the understanding? For if it cannot, these things cannot be understood with reference to it. But if you say that it is not understood and that it is not in the understanding, because it is not thoroughly understood; you should say that a man who cannot face the direct rays of the sun does not see the light of day, which is none other than the sunlight. Assuredly a being than which a greater cannot be conceived exists, and is in the understanding, at least to this extent—that these statements regarding it are understood.

CHAPTER II.

The argument is continued. It is shown that a being than which a greater is inconceivable can be conceived, and also, in so far, exists.

I HAVE said, then, in the argument which you dispute, that when the fool hears mentioned a being than which a greater is inconceivable, he understands what he hears. Certainly a man who does not understand when a familiar language is spoken, has no understanding at all, or a very dull one. Moreover, I have said that if this being is understood, it is in the understanding. Is that in no understanding which has been proved necessarily to exist in the reality of fact?

But you will say that although it is in the understanding, it does not follow that it is understood. But observe that the fact of its being understood does necessitate its being in the understanding. For as what is conceived, is conceived by conception, and what is conceived by conception, as it is conceived, so is in conception; so what is understood, is understood by understanding, and what is understood by understanding, as it is understood, so is in the understanding. What can be more clear than this?

After this, I have said that if it is even in the understanding alone, it can be conceived also to exist in reality, which is greater. If, then, it is in the understanding alone, obviously the very being than which greater cannot be conceived is one than which a greater can be conceived. What is more logical?

CHAPTER III.

A criticism of Gaunilo's example, in which he tries to show that in this way the real existence of a lost island might be inferred from the fact of its being conceived.

BUT, you say, it is as if one should suppose an island in the ocean, which surpasses all lands in its fertility, and which, because of the difficulty, or the impossibility, of discovering what does not exist, is called a lost island; and should say that the be no doubt that this island truly exists in reality, for this reason, that one who hears it described easily understands what he hears.

Now I promise confidently that if any man shall devise anything existing either in reality or in concept alone (except that than which a greater be conceived) to which he can adapt the sequence of my reasoning, I will discover that thing, and will give him his lost island, not to be lost again.

But it now appears that this being than which a greater is inconceivable cannot be conceived not to be, because it exists on so assured a ground of truth; for otherwise it would not exist at all.

He, then, who conceives of this being conceives of a being which cannot be even conceived not to exist; but he who conceives of this being does not conceive that it does not exist; else he conceives what is inconceivable. The non-existence, then, of that than which a greater cannot be conceived is inconceivable.[11]

---

[11] Anselm, *Reply to Gaunilo*, trans. Sidney Deane (Chicago: Open Court, 1903).

In many ways Anselm's response simply restates the original argument. He saw no need for a really detailed refutation since, he concluded, Gaunilo had misunderstood the concept of a GCB. There is something uniquely empowering about AD. It, and only it, overrides all versions of the connection objection. In fact, he jokingly offered to give someone whatever object it is for which this works, other than, of course, GCB.

Take the island example. The only way it could be the greatest conceivable island would be to take each of its properties to the max. So, how many grains of sand make up its beach? How many palm trees, luscious fruits, great seafood restaurants, and so on are there here? To meet AD there would have to be infinite of each. But then it would, in fact, be an infinite being and not just a perfect island. Islands are inherently incapable of being "greatest conceivables," *as islands*. Maxed out, there is an infinite being, and there can only be one of them, and so we have arrived at God—and a really existing one at that.

So Anselm's argument leaves us with two options, it seems. We either reject AP, or we conclude that a GCB exists. As long as AP holds, and it is hard to see what could be wrong here, and as long as AD is coherent, and that, too, is difficult to dispute, then the conclusion follows. Again, the critical point is that "greater cannot be conceived" demands a single exception to the rule about crossing from logic to reality. As we will see, these same objections will be made again and again as we continue the story of this argument.

Further Reading

For the full text of Anselm and Gaunilo, as well as Anselm's other important works, see *Anselm of Canterbury: The Major Works*, ed. Brian Davies and G. R. Evans (Oxford: Oxford University Press, 1998).

There is no end of literature on Anselm's argument. While somewhat dated, I think the best place to start is still John Hick and Arthur McGill, eds., *The*

Many-faced Argument (New York: Macmillan, 1967). It provides excellent exegesis and interpretation, plus a good selection of secondary literature, and a very good, though of course pre-1967, bibliography.

An older research bibliography on Anselm and subsequent discussion is Terry Miethe, "The Ontological Argument: A Research Bibliography," *Modern Schoolman* 53 (1976): 148-66.

An older anthology of Anselm and subsequent forms of the argument, along with brief introductions, is Alvin Plantinga, ed., *The Ontological Argument* (Garden City, NY: Anchor, 1965). For a newer collection of essays, see Graham Oppy, ed., *Ontological Arguments* (Cambridge: Cambridge University Press, 2018).

A new discussion is Yujin Nagasawa, *Maximal God: A New Defense of Perfect Being Theism* (Oxford: Oxford University Press, 2017), in which he argues at length that the argument remains unrefuted. This also has an excellent bibliography and would be good place for advanced students to start.

Stephen Davis has published widely on this and the other arguments. See his bibliography at PhilPeople.org, https://philpeople.org/profiles/stephen -t-davis/publications.

5.2 Later Medieval and Modern Discussion

5.2.1 *Thomas Aquinas.* One of the earliest after Gaunilo to discuss Anselm was someone we have already come to know well: Thomas Aquinas (1225–1274). Here are his comments on the Anselmian argument.

Chapter 10

[2] Those propositions are said to be self-evident that are known immediately upon the knowledge of their terms. Thus, as soon as you know the nature of a whole and the nature of a part, you know immediately that every whole is greater than its part. The proposition God exists is of this sort.

[5] What is naturally known is known through itself, for we do not come to such propositions through an effort of inquiry. But the proposition that God exists is naturally known since, as will be shown later on, the desire of man naturally tends towards God as towards the ultimate end. The proposition that God exists is, therefore, self-evident.

Chapter 11

[2] In part, however, the above opinion comes about because of a failure to distinguish between that which is self-evident in an absolute sense and that which is self-evident in relation to us. For assuredly that God exists is, absolutely speaking, self-evident, since what God is, is His own being. Yet, because we are not able to conceive in our minds that which God is, that God exists remains unknown in relation to us. So, too, that every whole is greater than its part is, absolutely speaking, self-evident; but it would perforce be unknown to one who could not conceive the nature of a whole.

[3] . . . What is more, granted that everyone should understand by the name God something than which a greater cannot be thought, it will still not be necessary that there exist in reality something than which a greater cannot be thought. For a thing and the definition of a name are posited in the same way. Now, from the fact that that which is indicated by the name God is conceived by the mind, it does not follow that God exists save only in the intellect.[12]

Thomas's point seems to be that the argument is sound, but only God knows it to be so, since only God himself truly understands—"sees"— his essence sufficiently to know that it includes existence.[13] We can know God's nature through analogy by knowing the creation. For us, then, the argument simply begs the question.

Thomas's points are, I think, correct in general. But I also think that he misses Anselm's key first premise, and construes it as a conception of God, rather than an open definition.[14] Nevertheless, following Thomas, no one of note really advocates Anselm's argument until it is picked up by Descartes.

---

[12]Thomas Aquinas, *Summa contra Gentiles* 1.10-11, excerpts, trans. Anton Pegis (New York: Hanover House, 1955–1957).

[13]For more on Thomas's objection see Brian Leftow, "Aquinas" in *Ontological Arguments*, ed. Graham Oppy, Classical Philosophical Arguments (Cambridge: Cambridge University Press, 2018), 44-52.

[14]On this, see Norman Geisler's chapter on ontological arguments in his *Philosophy of Religion* (Grand Rapids, MI: Zondervan, 1974). One needs to appreciate that Geisler is a strong defender (as am I!) of Thomas's metaphysics.

5.2.2 René Descartes. When René Descartes (1596–1650) took up Anselm's argument again, it would look quite different. Descartes, born and educated in France, was a brilliant mathematician, scientist, and philosopher. He served in the Dutch army and spent most of his adult life in the Netherlands, where he is still considered part of that country's Golden Age that included Grotius and Huygens, Rembrandt and Vermeer, and witnessed the height of the Netherlands' political and economic power that extended around the globe. This included, of course, a bustling new trading post on the southern tip of Manhattan Island, christened New Amsterdam.

Descartes's *Meditations* signals a fresh start in philosophy: a subjective turn but with a mathematical methodology. Descartes wanted to start at the beginning and, after ruthlessly applying the internal methodology of the skeptic, ask what is left that cannot be doubted and on which we can safely construct the house of knowledge. This is an enterprise of introspective deductive reasoning that reaches and then builds on his famous *cogito ergo sum*—"I think, therefore I am." What I further discover are innate, built-in ideas, which I neither learned nor created. This, he concluded, is where the ontological argument can begin. In a private letter he famously remarked that "I dare well to boast of having found a proof of God's existence which I find entirely satisfactory, and by which I know God exists, more certainly than I know the truth of any geometric proposition."[15]

> The most important point is that I find in myself countless ideas of things that can't be called *nothing*, even if they don't exist anywhere outside me. For although I am free to think of these ideas or not, as I choose, *I didn't invent them*: they have their own true and immutable natures, which are not under my control. Even if there are not and never were any triangles outside my thought, still, when I imagine a triangle I am constrained in

---

[15]René Descartes, "Letter to Mersenne," November 25, 1630, in *Descartes Selections*, ed. R. M. Eaton (New York: Charles Scribner & Sons, 1927).

how I do this, because there is a determinate nature or essence or form of *triangle* that is eternal, unchanging, and independent of my mind. . . .

It does not help to point out that I have sometimes seen triangular bodies, so that the idea of the triangle might have come to me from them through my sense organs. I can prove truths about the properties not only of triangles but of countless other shapes that I know I have never encountered through the senses. These properties must be something, not pure nothing: whatever is true is something; and these properties are true because I am clearly aware of them. . . .

The preceding two paragraphs lead to this conclusion: The mere fact that I find in my thought an idea of something x, and clearly and distinctly perceive x to have a certain property, it follows that x really does have that property. Can I not turn this to account . . . to prove the existence of God? The idea of God (that is, of a supremely perfect being) is certainly one that I find within me, just as I find the ideas of shapes and numbers; and I understand from this idea that it belongs to God's nature that *he always exists*. This understanding is just as clear and distinct as what is involved in mathematical proofs of the properties of shapes and numbers.[16]

What to make of this? Two matters to note before we look at objections to Descartes. This is clearly not Anselm's argument, since it begins with an actual definition of *God*, not simply a possible definition per se—that is, a random and meaningful string of words. And second, his comparison is to geometric and mathematical "ideas," not actual objects in the real world. Both of these differences play a key role in the refutations by Kant, Frege, and Russell yet to come. They will focus on the questions about properties of God, including "existence," and whether it follows from God's *nature* that God must exist. That is a very different argument!

Much lively conversation and debate followed the publication of Descartes's argument. The most important is the correspondence with Marin Mersenne over the very possibility of God's existence (taken up

---

[16]René Descartes, *Meditations on First Philosophy* 5, trans. John Cottingham, rev. ed. (New York: Cambridge University Press, 1988), 73.

later by Leibniz), and with Pierre Gassendi over the issue of whether existence is a perfection (taken up later by Kant).[17] Another version of this argument is developed by Descartes's young contemporary in Amsterdam Baruch Spinoza (1632–1677), with whom Descartes also had correspondence. This argument, however, began with a causal premise and is likely best seen as dependent on the cosmological argument.[18]

5.2.3 Gottfried Wilhelm Leibniz. The German mathematician and philosopher G. W. Leibniz (1646–1716) continued the Cartesian tradition of a rationalist reconstruction of knowledge. He actually took it to an extreme of thinking that we could assign a letter to every object, put all of the laws of nature into formulas, and then be able to derive the Big Formula of the world.[19] In his *Monadology* he actually worked out the basic metaphysics of such a system, following this kind of mathematical model.

We looked at his cosmological argument, but Leibniz also considered and accepted Descartes's ontological argument. This, he argued, can be reduced to a simple modal form something like this:[20]

(1) If God is possible, then God exists.

(2) God is possible.

(3) Therefore, God exists.

Premise (2) certainly presents a problem. Can we show that God's existence is at least not impossible? And so he adds an important consideration that will counter what remains still today a frequent

---

[17]This is all included in Descartes's correspondence and can be found in *The Philosophical Writings of Descartes*, trans. John Cottingham, Robert Stoothoff, and Dugald Murdoch (New York: Cambridge University Press, 1984–1991).

[18]See the discussion in Geisler, *Philosophy of Religion*, 144-45.

[19]See his early (he was only nineteen!) paper "Of the Art of Combination," in *Leibniz: Logical Papers*, trans. and ed. G. H. R. Parkinson (Oxford: Clarendon, 1966).

[20]By "modal" I mean that Leibniz, following his mathematical modeling, uses the syntax of "possible," "impossible," and "necessary" to indicate the logical standing of terms. We will see this developed by Alvin Plantinga in section 2.5.1.

objection, and one perhaps already raised by Gaunilo. How can we be sure that the properties of a perfect being, who has all properties—or, better, perfections—do not conflict or even contradict? These sorts of contradictions are often alleged by atheists, such as between his justice and his mercy, or between his omnipotence and omniscience. That sub-argument is our only interest here:[21]

> Indeed, if there is to be any reality in the essences or possibles, that is, in the necessary truths, this reality must be founded on the existence of the necessary being whose essence implies its existence, that is, to which it suffices to be possible in order to be actual.
>
> Thus God alone (or the necessary being) has the privilege of existing necessarily, provided only he be possible. Now, since nothing can hinder the possibility of the substance which contains no limits, no negation, and hence no contradiction, this provides a sufficient reason for the knowledge a priori of God's existence. Besides, we have proved it by the reality of the eternal truths. In addition, we also have proved this existence a posteriori by the existence of contingent beings. For the sufficient and ultimate reason of these can lie only in the necessary being which has in itself the reason of its existence.[22]

This seems a simple and obvious point. If two properties, or even objects or events, are infinite, then they cannot overlap, conflict, or contradict precisely because they are unlimited. So they must in fact be one and the same, and our different designators are picking up only different connotations or applications, or maybe points of view. This is just what all theisms have always held—namely, that God's numerous attributes are simply our finite ways of trying to label his unlimited being from our limited perspectives.

We should note that this defense is quite unattached to merely Descartes's argument. It can be viewed as an independent argument and

---

[21]For a good discussion of both his ontological argument and this subargument see Maria Rosa Antognazza's, "Leibniz" in Oppy, *Ontological Arguments*, 75-98.

[22]Leibniz, *Monadology* 44-45, trans. Paul Schrecker and Anne Martin Schrecker (Indianapolis: Bobbs-Merrill, 1965), 154-55.

applies to any consideration of God's definition, or list of properties or attributes. That would include not only Anselm's argument, but many others to come along as we continue this account.

5.2.4 *Immanuel Kant.* Probably the most famous critique of the ontological argument came from Immanuel Kant (1724–1804). He is writing specifically against Descartes, but this critique has been held by many to apply equally for Anselm, and has become pretty much the standard refutation:

> It is absurd to introduce—under whatever term disguised—into the conception of a thing, which is to be cogitated solely in reference to its possibility, the conception of its existence. If this is admitted, you will have apparently gained the day, but in reality have enounced nothing but a mere tautology. I ask, is the proposition, this or that thing (which I am admitting to be possible) exists, an analytical or a synthetical proposition? If the former, there is no addition made to the subject of your thought by the affirmation of its existence; but then the conception in your minds is identical with the thing itself, or you have supposed the existence of a thing to be possible, and then inferred its existence from its internal possibility—which is but a miserable tautology. The word reality in the conception of the thing, and the word existence in the conception of the predicate, will not help you out of the difficulty. For, supposing you were to term all positing of a thing reality, you have thereby posited the thing with all its predicates in the conception of the subject and assumed its actual existence, and this you merely repeat in the predicate. But if you confess, as every reasonable person must, that every existential proposition is synthetical, how can it be maintained that the predicate of existence cannot be denied without contradiction?— a property which is the characteristic of analytical propositions, alone.
>
> I should have a reasonable hope of putting an end for ever to this sophistical mode of argumentation, by a strict definition of the conception of existence, did not my own experience teach me that the illusion arising from our confounding a logical with a real predicate (a predicate which aids in the determination of a thing) resists almost all

the endeavours of explanation and illustration. A logical predicate may be what you please, even the subject may be predicated of itself; for logic pays no regard to the content of a judgement. But the determination of a conception is a predicate, which adds to and enlarges the conception. It must not, therefore, be contained in the conception.

Being is evidently not a real predicate, that is, a conception of something which is added to the conception of some other thing. It is merely the positing of a thing, or of certain determinations in it. Logically, it is merely the copula of a judgement. The proposition, God is omnipotent, contains two conceptions, which have a certain object or content; the word is, is no additional predicate—it merely indicates the relation of the predicate to the subject. Now, if I take the subject (God) with all its predicates (omnipotence being one), and say: God is, or, There is a God, I add no new predicate to the conception of God, I merely posit or affirm the existence of the subject with all its predicates—I posit the object in relation to my conception. The content of both is the same; and there is no addition made to the conception, which expresses merely the possibility of the object, by my cogitating the object—in the expression, it is—as absolutely given or existing. Thus the real contains no more than the possible. A hundred real dollars contain no more than a hundred possible dollars. For, as the latter indicate the conception, and the former the object, on the supposition that the content of the former was greater than that of the latter, my conception would not be an expression of the whole object, and would consequently be an inadequate conception of it. But in reckoning my wealth there may be said to be more in a hundred real dollars than in a hundred possible dollars—that is, in the mere conception of them. For the real object—the dollars—is not analytically contained in my conception, but forms a synthetical addition to my conception (which is merely a determination of my mental state), although this objective reality—this existence—apart from my conceptions, does not in the least degree increase the aforesaid hundred dollars.

By whatever and by whatever number of predicates—even to the complete determination of it—I may cogitate a thing, I do not in the least augment the object of my conception by the addition of the statement: This thing exists. Otherwise, not exactly the same, but something more than what was cogitated in my conception, would exist, and I could not affirm that the exact object of my conception had real existence.[23]

At first glance, this objection seems pretty straightforward and obviously true.[24] If I come to the checkout line and try to pay the cashier the $100 I owe by saying that I am picturing in my mind a $100 bill with all of the appropriate properties—rectangular, green print on white paper, number 100 in each corner, and so on—the cashier is not going to be satisfied and rather likely to demand a real one: one that exists, not one that is just in my mind. Suppose I quickly apologize and say that I had forgotten to add existence to the list of properties and have now done so. I have in my mind an actually existing $100 bill. Does that now satisfy the cashier? More specifically, have I actually added anything to my imagined bill?

Kant's point, of course, is that nothing at all has been added. Adding green, for example, did make a real change in my mental picture, but existence did not. So predicates like green and rectangular express real properties, but existence is not a property at all. It is just a stand-in for "has properties." To say that A exists is shorthand for the claim that something has certain defining properties that characterize it as A.

This is why one cannot simply define something into existence by saying that its definition includes existence. It is not a property that could somehow be included in a definition in such a way that it would somehow instantiate the corresponding object, say an ideal island. There is no magic here!

But on closer investigation something seems wrong with this point. Surely there is an obvious difference between my real mental image or

---

[23]Immanuel Kant, *The Critique of Pure Reason*, trans. F. Max Muller (New York: Doubleday, 1896), 1, part 2, div. 2, book 2, chap. 3, sec. 4.

[24]I should quickly add that some have seen as many as four different objections here. See, for example, Lawrence Pasternack, "Kant," in Oppy, *Ontological Arguments*, 99-120, esp. 103-15. For our purposes I simplify this and only discuss the standard existence-is-not-a-predicate objection.

picture of A, and a real A—a really real A. That difference seems to consist precisely in the actual existing of A. The actual object A has some kind of property of "real existence" that mental object A lacks. Besides, there is a big difference between a mental image (picture in my mind) and a concept—that is, a mental construct.

Nevertheless, Kant's critique was to become standard. For now, we will have to be content to follow it as it repeatedly appears throughout the nineteenth and into the twentieth centuries. We should note that Kant did not, of course, hold that God does not exist, nor that necessary existence is somehow contradictory or logically incoherent. He only held that this specific argument, Descartes's argument, does not work.[25]

5.2.5 Gottlob Frege. Friedrich Ludwig Gottlob Frege (1848–1925) was a highly influential German logician, mathematician, and philosopher of language. In his consideration of the ontological argument, Frege put it this way:

> Neither in "*A is identical with itself*" nor in "*A exists*" does one learn anything new about *A*. Neither statement can be denied. In either you can put anything for *A*, and it still remains true. They do not assign *A* to one of two classes in order to mark it off from some *B* which does not belong to that class. . . . The judgments "This table exists" and "This table is identical with itself" are completely self-evident, and . . . consequently in these judgments no real content is being predicated of this table.[26]

Frege was here more precise. This has to do with judgments not concepts. But the import is the same: existence as a predicate adds no content. So in reference to the ontological argument, an argument that adds existence to a judgment about God adds nothing. It certainly cannot instantiate God.

---

[25]See the discussion in Nicholas Everitt, "Kant's Discussion of the Ontological Argument," *Kant Studien* 86, no. 4 (1995): 385-405.

[26]From Frege's posthumous writings, quoted in Pavel Tichy, *The Foundations of Frege's Logic* (Berlin: de Gruyter, 1988), 182.

5.2.6 *Bertrand Russell.* Another familiar character in this story is Bertrand Russell. He was strongly influenced by, among others, Frege, and, with his friend Alfred North Whitehead, wrote *Principia Mathematica*, a philosophical study of the relationship between logic and mathematics, which extended Frege's work and established Russell as one of the leading logicians and mathematicians of the twentieth century.

It is not surprising that Russell would find the ontological argument, along with Frege's objection, highly intriguing. Russell himself says in his autobiography that in his early years when he first studied the argument he was convinced by it and shouted "Great God in Boots!—the ontological argument is sound!" His study of Frege, however, led him in a different direction. This formulation of the objection will become the most widely known and used version of the "existence-is-not-a-predicate" objection in the last century.

He states this objection first in his 1900 study *The Philosophy of Leibniz*. Here it is the simple point that there is no difference in properties between "a hundred thalers which I merely imagine" and "a hundred thalers which really exist."[27] This is then developed more extensively in 1918 in "The Philosophy of Logical Atomism" as follows:

> It is of propositional functions that you can assert or deny existence. You must not run away with the idea that this entails consequences that it does not entail. If I say "The things that there are in the world exist," that is a perfectly correct statement, because I am there saying something about a certain class of things; I say it in the same sense in which I say "Men exist." But I must not go on to "This is a thing in the world, and therefore, this exists." It is there that the fallacy comes in, and it is simply, as you see, a fallacy of transferring to the individual that satisfies a propositional function, a predicate which only applies to a propositional function. You can see this in various ways. For instance, you sometimes know the truth of an existence-proposition without knowing any instance of it. You know that there are people in Timbuctoo, but I doubt if

---

[27]See Bertrand Russell, *Philosophy of Leibniz* (London: George Allen & Unwin, 1900), 176.

any of you could give me an instance of one. Therefore, you clearly can know existence-propositions without knowing any individual that makes them true. Existence-propositions do not say anything about the actual individual but only about the class or function.[28]

This is essentially Kant's criticism again. Russell here distinguishes between existence predicates of propositions and those of things. In short, while existence may meaningfully be predicated of propositions or concepts, it cannot be meaningfully predicated of individual objects in reality. And so, Russell argues, the ontological argument fails because it predicates existence of God. However, both Frege's and Russell's objections suffer the same fate as Kant's.

5.2.7 Norman Malcolm and Charles Hartshorne.

The 1960s saw a renewed interest in the argument and, most importantly, a return to Anselm. It had remained a mere philosophical curiosity, relegated to history's dustbin by the Kant-Frege-Russell objection. But in the early years of that decade two philosophers from very different vantage points both published articles claiming that Anselm was right after all. Not, however, in *Proslogion* 2: that had fallen prey to Kant. But *Proslogion* 3 is a whole different story. *Proslogion* 2 is an argument about existence, but "exists" is not a property or perfection and cannot therefore be predicated in the real sense of the term. But in chapter three, Anselm proposes a new second argument that rests on "necessary existence." That, it can be argued, *is* a perfection.

Norman Malcolm (1911–1990), a Harvard graduate from Nebraska, taught most of his career at Cornell University. He spent a number of years at Cambridge, where he became friends with Ludwig Wittgenstein and honed his craft as an analytic philosopher and one of the founders of ordinary language philosophy.

---

[28]Bertrand Russell, "The Philosophy of Logical Atomism," originally published in the journal *The Monist* in 1918, is included in the collection of Russell's papers *Logic and Knowledge* (London: George Allen & Unwin, 1956), 234, and other collections as well.

Now Malcolm admits that Anselm does not appear to think of *Proslogion* 3 as a separate argument from *Proslogion* 2. We can and should, however, regard it as such, especially since it can be reconstructed as having a very different first premise, one that will give it a different relation to the Kantian dogma.

In this argument the perfection being ascribed to God is not "existence" but "the logical impossibility of nonexistence."[29] That, he says, is just "necessary existence." And now we have a very different argument. AP now becomes AP[1]: A thing is greater if it necessarily exists than if it does not necessarily exist.

Malcolm, the ordinary-language philosopher, then clarifies necessary existence as nondependence. God, he says, "cannot be thought of as being brought into existence by anything or as depending for his continued existence on anything. To conceive of anything as dependent on something else for its existence is to conceive of it as a lesser being than God":[30]

> Let me summarize the proof. If God, a being greater than which cannot be conceived, does not exist, then he cannot *come* into existence. For if he did, he would either have been *caused* to come into existence or have *happened* to come into existence, and in either case he would be a limited being, which by our conception of him he is not. Since he cannot come into existence, if he does not exist, his existence is impossible. If he does exist, he cannot have come into existence (for the reasons giving), nor can he cease to exist, for nothing could cause him to cease to exist nor could it just happen that he ceased to exist. So if God exists, his existence is necessary. Thus, God's existence is either impossible or necessary. It can be the former only if the concept of such a being is self-contradictory or in some way logically absurd. Assuming that this is not so, it follows that he necessarily exists.
>
> . . . *Necessary existence* is a property of God in the same sense that *necessary omnipotence* and *necessary omniscience* are his properties. And

---

[29]Norman Malcolm, "Anselm's Ontological Arguments," *The Philosophical Review* 69, no. 1 (January 1960): 47. This paper is found also in numerous anthologies.
[30]Malcolm, "Anselm's Ontological Arguments," 48.

we are not to think that "God necessarily exists" means that it follows necessarily from something that God exists *contingently*. The a priori proposition "God necessarily exists" entails the proposition "God exists," if and only if the latter also is understood as an a priori proposition: in which case the two propositions are equivalent. In this sense Anselm's proof is a proof of God's existence.[31]

The key to this argument, of course, is Malcolm's position that Kant's dictum does not apply to "necessary existence." That is because the dictum applies only to contingent existence, and with contingent things there is no connection between concept and thing. I have a concept of purple elephant, but nothing about that concept entails anything at all as to its instantiation. "But once one has grasped Anselm's proof of the necessary existence of a being greater than which cannot be conceived, no question remains as to whether it exists or not, just as Euclid's demonstration of the existence of an infinity of prime numbers leaves no question on that issue."[32] It seems to me that at this point it is clear that Malcolm has missed the simple point of the first premise of the *Proslogion* 2 argument, that his understanding of the first premise of the *Proslogion* 3 argument just is AD, and so what he gives us just is Anselm's original argument in *Proslogion* 2. And for exactly the reasons he gives, Kant's dictum does not apply.

Like Malcolm, Charles Hartshorne (1897–2000) was also a Harvard PhD and also spent some of his career in Europe, including some time working with Alfred North Whitehead, whose process metaphysics strongly influenced him, and which he did much to develop in original directions, including panentheism. He taught at the University of Chicago, Emory University, and for many years until his retirement at the University of Texas. He delivered his last lecture at age ninety-eight.

---

[31]Malcolm, "Anselm's Ontological Arguments," 50-51.
[32]Malcolm, "Anselm's Ontological Arguments," 53.

Again, Hartshorne thinks that Kant's objection applies to *Proslogion* 2, but that *Proslogion* 3 contains a quite different argument based on necessary existence. He published this in several formats. His 1962 book, *The Logic of Perfection*,[33] advanced this argument in highly complex and symbolic form. That same year, however, he published it in more simplified language with the title "What Did Anselm Discover?"[34] Here is his summary:

> To exist necessarily is better than to exist contingently; hence the greatest conceivable being can exist only necessarily. Moreover, whatever could be necessary is necessary ("reduction principle" of modal logic); hence to say that God does not exist necessarily is to say that he could not do so, and since he also could not exist contingently, it is to say that he could not exist at all. . . . The only logically admissible way to reject theism is to reject the very idea of God as either contradictory or empty of significance.[35]

So the atheist must show either that the concept of God is contradictory, but Leibniz has shown that to be impossible, or else show that the concept—that is, AD—is without meaning, but surely that would not be an option either. Even for the fool!

Now Hartshorne is well aware of the primary difficulty with this argument: it seems to magically move things from concept to reality. That is just bad logic, even for God, is it not?

> Let us now consider Gaunilo's undeservedly famous attempt to achieve a *reductio ad absurdum* against Anselm, an attempt which the saint rightly refused to take seriously. If greatest conceivable being must exist, why not greatest conceivable island? Of course the answer is obvious: "greatest conceivable island" has no clear meaning; moreover, an island

---

[33]Charles Hartshorne, *The Logic of Perfection* (LaSalle, IL: Open Court, 1962). Advanced readers will want to go to this source.

[34]Charles Hartshorne, "What Did Anselm Discover?," *Union Seminary Quarterly Review* 17 (1962): 213-22. I will here use Hartshorne's slightly revised version with the same title in *The Many-faced Argument*, ed. John Hick and Arthur McGill (New York: Macmillan, 1967).

[35]Hartshorne, "What Did Anselm Discover?," 322.

could not exist necessarily, for it is competitive with other possibilities, such as the surrounding water's being at a high enough level to submerge the island. "Unsurpassable, necessary island" is nonsense. If "unsurpassable and necessary being" is also nonsense, then positivism is correct. But the nonsense could not be *for the same reason*, since "island" limits perfection while "being" does not. So the refutation is a failure. Could an "island" be the creator of all things?[36]

We have seen this point before. Gaunilo's objection fails for "necessary existence" just as it fails for "existence" when applied to the greatest conceivable being. No finite being or collection of finite beings could be a necessary being.

5.2.8 *John Hick and Arthur McGill.* In 1967, Hick and McGill published an anthology of recent work on Anselm's ontological argument.[37] This highlighted Malcolm and Hartshorne, but others as well, including a section from Karl Barth's *Anselm: Fides Quaerens Intellectum*, which had appeared in English in 1960.[38] Most importantly, it included a lengthy introductory chapter by McGill and a concluding one by Hick, both of which focus particularly on the two-argument thesis of Malcolm and Hartshorne.

John Hick (1922–2012) held a DPhil from Oxford and a DLitt from Edinburgh, and taught at Birmingham University, Claremont Graduate University, Princeton Theological Seminary, and Cambridge University, and for one memorable—for me at least—semester at Boston University. Among his many scholarly writings, he will likely best be remembered for his classic *Evil and the God of Love* (1966).

Hick's argument in "A Critique of the 'Second Argument'" is that both Malcolm and Hartshorne fail to distinguish logical necessity from factual necessity. Clearly, he argues, neither the biblical authors, nor

---

[36]Hartshorne, "What Did Anselm Discover?," 332.
[37]Hick and McGill, *Many-faced Argument*.
[38]Karl Barth, *Anselm: Fides Quaerens Intellectum*, trans. Ian Robertson (London: SCM, 1960).

Anselm, nor Thomas, nor even Kant, intended to claim that there is a *logical* contradiction involved in asserting God's nonexistence. They all claimed that God, as creator of all things, the eternal one, does not merely exist as ordinary contingent things do, nor did he come into existence at some point, but rather he could not fail to exist: his existence is ontologically necessary.

This distinction, Hick argues, invalidates both arguments. Hartshorne clearly states that he means logical necessity throughout.[39] Malcolm, though he begins by identifying AD as referring to ontological necessity, reverts to logical necessity in order to make the argument proceed. Hick quotes him here: "God's existence is either impossible or necessary. It can be the former only if the concept of such a being is self-contradictory or in some way logically absurd. Assuming that it is not so, it follows that he necessarily exists."[40] Therefore, neither argument proves that God exists, only that God either exists or his existence is impossible.[41]

Hick does think that there is only one argument here, as a good exegesis shows. But he argues that Anselm's original argument succumbs to the objection that "one is never entitled to deduce from a concept that anything exists which corresponds to that concept."[42]

Arthur McGill (1926–1980) was a prolific writer, best known for his treatments of the theology of suffering and death. With a Harvard BA and Yale PhD, he taught primarily at Princeton and Harvard University.

McGill's chapter in this anthology, "Recent Discussions of Anselm's Argument," argues two critical points. The first is that modern and contemporary philosophy, especially Kant, misunderstands AD

---

[39]John Hick, "A Critique of the 'Second Argument,'" in Hick and McGill, *Many-faced Argument*, 348-51.
[40]Hick, "Critique of the 'Second Argument,'" 354.
[41]Hick, "Critique of the 'Second Argument,'" 356.
[42]John Hick, *The Existence of God* (New York: Macmillan, 1964), 3.

because it misses the notion of "concept" for Anselm. Why is Anselm so sure that by merely hearing the words, we will know that the object of the definition, the referent of the concept, has "a secure basis in reality"?[43] This connection between thought and reality has often been blamed on Anselm's so-called Platonism. But it is not that at all.

Our problem, and Kant's, is that we live on the other side of the subjective turn in philosophy. Hume forever has split mind and reality. The mind is now just the brain receiving sense data, which remain as impressions. "Modern science arose out of the conviction that, in order to understand the truth about nature, men must disregard everything that has been said and rely only on direct experience. That is, they must conduct experiments."[44] Language cannot form concepts, and reasoning from concepts cannot give us knowledge. So imagining in the mind, for Kant and his subsequent and contemporary followers, means constructing a mental (brain) image or picture. Given that understanding, of course one cannot move from definition to reality. To know what someone's words mean is only to "penetrate their subjectivity."[45] McGill saw hope for philosophy in Martin Heidegger, for whom language opens us to reality, but little has changed since then.

This view of knowledge cannot be completely correct, however. Let me illustrate what is wrong here with an anecdote of my own. A few years ago, watching the celebration in Edinburgh, Scotland, of Peter Higgs's Nobel Prize in physics, I was struck by his answer to a reporter's question. The reporter was puzzled by the fact that Higgs had discovered the boson some fifty years before an accelerator experiment in 2013 could verify it. Higgs's answer was that to do physics today is a matter of paper and pencil. It's just thinking about formulas. Now

---

[43] Arthur McGill, "Recent Discussions of Anselm's Argument," in Hick and McGill, *The Many-faced Argument*, 103.

[44] McGill, "Recent Discussions of Anselm's Argument," 110.

[45] McGill, "Recent Discussions of Anselm's Argument," 109.

this is, of course, not always or even mostly true of our knowledge, but it often is.

The obvious fact, reflected in McGill's understanding of Anselm's argument, is that we are quite capable of knowing reality by words: "conceiving," as he calls it. This is different from knowing by experience, or understanding.[46]

We now can see clearly who Anselm's fool is: it is not the village idiot, but someone who does not know how to hear and grasp the meaning of words. This is why this is such a different kind of argument. It is, McGill says, "autonomous." One does not need to conduct any experiments, observations, or surveys. "In the proof itself . . . he goes out of his way to emphasize that men have only to hear and understand the words of the key phrase for the argument to convince them."[47] If we see this exegetical point, then all of the Kantian-type objections evaporate.[48] In this he seems to me to be quite right.

McGill's second key point follows closely from Hick's idea that both Malcolm and Hartshorne mistakenly use logical necessity rather than factual. There are not two arguments here. There is just one extended thought experiment beginning with the establishment of God's existence in chapter two, moving on then to show how different aspects of his nature follow from this initial understanding. In 3a it is God's necessity, in 3b it is God as Creator, and this continues until the final summary in 9.[49]

So, McGill argues, Anselm is quite well aware of what he is doing here, and of the logic of each of his steps. That by itself does not mean that there are no other problems with the argument, but, for McGill, no one had identified them yet.

---

[46]McGill, "Recent Discussions of Anselm's Argument," 108.

[47]McGill, "Recent Discussions of Anselm's Argument," 104.

[48]See the discussion in McGill, "Recent Discussions of Anselm's Argument," 33-38.

[49]See the details in McGill, "Recent Discussions of Anselm's Argument," 39-50. This is an excellent historical (especially using Karl Barth and Eric Stolz) and exegetical study. However, it is far beyond our concerns here.

5.2.9 *Kurt Gödel.* We will look at one more example of a modal argument. Kurt Gödel (1906–1978), one of the greatest logicians of all time, was an Austrian who immigrated to America and began teaching at Princeton in 1940. He was a great innovator in logic and mathematics, best known for his incompleteness theorem, published in 1931—at age twenty-five! He first wrote this modal ontological argument, in symbolic notation in the form of a mathematical proof, in about 1941. He kept it private for most of his career, but in 1970 he indicated to friends that he was finally satisfied with the proof. It was not published until 1987, and has had something of a life of its own in the philosophical literature ever since. What follows is Graham Oppy's "translation" into ordinary English. It remains a highly daunting technical proof.

> **Definition 1**: x is God-like if and only if x has as essential properties those and only those properties which are positive
>
> **Definition 2**: A is an essence of x if and only if for every property B, x has B necessarily if and only if A entails B
>
> **Definition 3**: x necessarily exists if and only if every essence of x is necessarily exemplified
>
> **Axiom 1**: If a property is positive, then its negation is not positive
>
> **Axiom 2**: Any property entailed by—i.e., strictly implied by—a positive property is positive
>
> **Axiom 3**: The property of being God-like is positive
>
> **Axiom 4**: If a property is positive, then it is necessarily positive
>
> **Axiom 5**: Necessary existence is positive
>
> **Axiom 6**: For any property P, if P is positive, then being necessarily P is positive
>
> **Theorem 1**: If a property is positive, then it is consistent, i.e., possibly exemplified
>
> **Corollary 1**: The property of being God-like is consistent

Theorem 2: If something is God-like, then the property of being God-like is an essence of that thing

Theorem 3: Necessarily, the property of being God-like is exemplified[50]

The key term that needs careful definition here is "positive." This is actually quite unclear in Gödel, and this vagueness is the basis for most of the objections to his proof. It seems to simply mean any property that can be attributed without any negation. And so for every property P, either P or -P is a positive property. So the standard divine attributes like good, powerful, wise, loving, and so on seem to be such positive properties. The objections arise because of definition one, which seems to imply that God has all properties. That is difficult since some positive properties, "colorful" for example, do not seem attributable to God. And worse yet, if they are attributable to God, then they are necessary, and then all positive properties are necessary. Now both of these objections have been answered, the answers have been responded to, and so on. The conversation is highly technical and still ongoing. Since it only has application to Gödel's argument, I will leave it to the reader to pursue it further.

This proof also depends on a standard rule of modal logic, that whatever is strictly necessary in *any* possible world must be necessary in *every* possible world, so that what is possibly necessary is just necessary. This is really the basis for any truly modal argument. So all that is needed is to show that God as necessary being, however defined, is possible. This rule is generally accepted by logicians. This is important because it is foundational for *all* modal ontological arguments, including Plantinga's, to which we turn next.

Further Reading

On the view that *Proslogion* 2 and 3 present different arguments see, in addition to Hick and McGill, Jonathan Barnes, *The Ontological Argument* (London:

---

[50]See Graham Oppy, *Ontological Arguments and Belief in God* (Cambridge: Cambridge University Press, 1996), 224-25.

Macmillan; St. Martin's, 1972), 18-25. This is, in general, a good study with a
good bibliography.

A good study, but very advanced, of Descartes, Spinoza, Leibniz, and Kant is
Jordan Howard Sobel, *Logic and Theism: Arguments For and Against Beliefs
in God* (Cambridge: Cambridge University Press, 2004), chap. 2. There are
also excellent secondary studies of each of the key figures, along with good
bibliographies, in Graham Oppy, ed., *Ontological Arguments* (Cambridge:
Cambridge University Press, 2018).

Another good source on the modern discussion is Lloyd Strickland, *Proofs of God
in Early Modern Europe: An Anthology* (Waco, TX: Baylor University Press, 2018).

For a discussion on the Kant-Frege-Russell objection, including their differences
see Graham Oppy, *Ontological Arguments and Belief in God* (Cambridge:
Cambridge University Press, 1995), chap. 1, sec. 6. This is also a good source
on the modal arguments. See chap. 4.

A good resource on the recent discussion of the ontological argument is
"Selected Bibliography on the History of the Ontological Argument from
Barth to the Present Time (1931–2010)," Bibliographia.co, https://www
.bibliographia.co/ontological-proof-contemporary-biblio.htm. This gives an
especially good listing of the debate over Gödel's proof up to 2010. If you want
to continue the study of Gödel's proof, this is a good place to start.

For an exchange on Gödel's proof see Alexander R. Pruss, "A Gödelian Ontological
Argument Improved," *Religious Studies* 45, no. 3 (2009): 347-53, and Graham
Oppy, "Pruss's Ontological Arguments," *Religious Studies* 45, no. 3 (2009): 355-63.

5.3 Alvin Plantinga's Modal Form

5.3.1 Alvin Plantinga. Alvin Plantinga (b. 1932) has certainly been a
force to reckon with. A Yale PhD, he taught for twenty years at Calvin
College, then for almost thirty at the University of Notre Dame, and is
now back at Calvin. He has been a debate-ender on several crucial
issues. His early work in epistemology, including the three-volume
Warrant, put a stop to the idea still current in the 1960s that belief in
God was not reasonable. *God, Freedom, and Evil* seems to have finally
defeated the *logical* problem of evil. And it may well be that his *The
Nature of Necessity* has produced a sound modal ontological argument.
It certainly eliminates several key objections.

In his 1965 *The Ontological Argument* and his 1970 *God and Other Minds* Plantinga argued that all forms of the argument fail, and specifically Malcolm's is defeated by his use of logical necessity.[51] At the same time, Plantinga also demonstrated that none of the standard objections succeed either. There is here an extensive treatment both of Kant's objection, as well as of William Alston's refutation of AP.[52] But then in *God, Freedom, and Evil* and *The Nature of Necessity*, both in 1974, he advances a modal logic form of the argument that goes beyond previous versions.[53]

In what follows, I will stick to the simpler version in *God, Freedom, and Evil*. The version in *The Nature of Necessity* is lengthy and presumes a good knowledge of modal logic in symbolic form, as well as possible-world semantics. Advanced readers will certainly want to look there. *God, Freedom, and Evil* is a fairly popular-level treatment of a number of core problems in Christian theism, though there are applications to any religious theology: the existence of God, human free will, and the problem of evil.

Plantinga begins by dismissing Anselm's argument itself on grounds that it begs the question. It assumes that God is a being in the beginning premise. Interestingly, Plantinga dismisses the usual criticisms, including Kant's. Then he proceeds to reject the Malcolm-Hartshorne argument since it does not show that God has maximal greatness in every world, hence perhaps not in this world. And again he dismisses

---

[51] Alvin Plantinga, ed., *The Ontological Argument: From St. Anselm to Contemporary Philosophers* (Garden City: Anchor, 1965); Plantinga, *God and Other Minds: A Study of the Rational Justification of Belief in God* (Ithaca, NY: Cornell University Press, 1970).

[52] This discussion of the argument takes up almost seventy pages, whereas the cosmological and teleological argument each only get about twenty, and the moral argument just a few sentences. For Alston's article, see William Alston, "The Ontological Argument Revisited," *Philosophical Review* 69 (1960): 432-74. At this point, Alston was an atheist. Ten years later he became a theist and a Christian, and, with Plantinga, one of the founders of the Society of Christian Philosophers.

[53] Alvin Plantinga, *God, Freedom, and Evil* (New York: Harper & Row, 1974); Plantinga, *The Nature of Necessity* (Oxford: Clarendon, 1974).

the typical logical points made against necessary existence, including, again, Kant's.[54]

Now he is ready to restate a modal-logic argument.[55]

(25) It is possible that there be a being that has maximal greatness.

(26) So there is a possible being that in some world W has maximal greatness.

(27) A being has maximal greatness in a given world only if it has maximal excellence in every world.

(28) A being has maximal excellence in a given world only if it has omniscience, omnipotence, and moral perfection in that world.[56]

This argument, however, is still questionable because of (26). It is possible, after all, that there are possible beings that do not in fact exist. But the argument can be restated again in language that replaces "possible beings" with "properties" (we no longer fear Kant) that are "instantiated."[57] Now we get the following "triumphant" argument:

(29) There is a possible world in which maximal greatness is instantiated.

(30) Necessarily, a being is maximally great only if it has maximal excellence in every world.

(31) Necessarily, a being has maximal excellence in every world only if it has omniscience, omnipotence, and moral perfection in every world.[58]

If this being exists in every world, then it must exist in the actual world. What should we then conclude about this argument?

It is certainly valid, given its premise, the conclusion follows. The only question of interest, it seems to me, is whether its main premise—that

---

[54]See the discussion in Alvin Plantinga, *God, Freedom, and Evil* (1974; repr., Grand Rapids, MI: Eerdmans, 1977), part 2, sec. c. 1-8.

[55]I stick here and throughout with Plantinga's numbering of the premises.

[56]Plantinga, *God, Freedom, and Evil*, 108.

[57]Plantinga, *God, Freedom, and Evil*, 110.

[58]Plantinga, *God, Freedom, and Evil*, 111.

maximal greatness *is* possibly instantiated—is *true*. I think it *is* true; hence I think this version of the ontological argument is sound.

But here we must be careful, we must ask whether this argument is a successful piece of natural theology, whether it *proves* the existence of God. And the answer must be, I think, that it does not. An argument for God's existence may be *sound*, after all, without in any useful sense proving God's existence. . . .

It must be conceded that not everyone who understands and reflects on its central premise—that the existence of a maximally great being is *possible*—will accept it. Still, it is evident, I think, that there is nothing *contrary to reason* or *irrational* in accepting this premise. What I claim for this argument, therefore, is that it establishes, not the *truth* of theism, but its rational acceptability. And hence it accomplishes at least one of the aims of the tradition of natural theology.[59]

To summarize the flow of the logic of the argument, it is simply this: If a maximally great being is possible, then it is necessary, and therefore it is actual. The atheist can have no objection to the logic. It is certainly valid. This is really an elegant and simple argument. The only possibility open here for the atheist is to somehow show that the existence of God is *not* possible. As Yujin Nagasawa assesses it, it shows that "the existence of God is either 0 per cent or 100 per cent probable."[60]

Still, Plantinga concludes that the argument can only show rational acceptability. That is due to the lack of any solid argument for the possibility premise. For that we will have to wait for Nagasawa's work, which we will come to at the end of this chapter. Nevertheless, Plantinga has made an enormous contribution to the argument. Beginning with *God and Other Minds*, and *God, Freedom, and Evil*, and then, ultimately, *The Nature of Necessity*, he demonstrates, first, that none of the standard objections are successful, and, second, that the argument is itself sound and acceptable. And further, he is quite clear that his

---

[59]Plantinga, *God, Freedom, and Evil*, 112.
[60]Nagasawa, *Maximal God*, 185.

modal argument is just a restatement of Anselm's argument into a clearer contemporary semantics.[61]

5.4 The Current Discussion

The Hartshorne-Malcolm resurrection of the *Proslogion* 3 argument certainly initiated a whole new phase of interest and discussion. Much of this tended to bypass Descartes and Kant (as well as Frege and Russell) and refocus on Anselm. Plantinga added another whole chapter to this revival narrative. The result in the late twentieth and on into the twenty-first centuries has been an explosion of publications, as well as many doctoral dissertations, on the ontological argument, both those allegedly locating the *real* fatal flaw and those refuting them and endorsing the argument.

The present result is highly complex at best, even for those following the discussion closely. On top of that, much of this discussion has become extremely technical, as a result of Gödel and especially Plantinga's *Nature of Necessity*. For our purposes here, I will attempt to simplify all this and stick to the essential issues. A good place to start is Peter Millican's paper in 2004. It is especially helpful because he summarizes the discussion under nine objections.

5.4.1 Peter Millican. Peter Millican (b. 1958) teaches at Hertford College, Oxford. He holds a master's in computer science, and his doctoral dissertation was on Hume, induction, and probability. To top it off, he is a chess grandmaster. In his essay "The One Fatal Flaw in Anselm's Argument," which appeared in *Mind* in 2004, he lists the following nine objections to the argument:

(a) *The neo-Platonic presupposition*

Anselm's notion of "greatness" and also his specific judgments of relative greatness, presuppose a neo-Platonic background of "degrees of

---

[61]See Plantinga, *Nature of Necessity*, 198-202.

existence" and metaphysical "perfections" which would now be generally rejected. Without it, his key phrase "something-than-which-nothing-greater-can-be-thought," and hence his entire argument, cannot make sense.

(b) *The mental entity confusion*

Anselm treats the mental existence of something-than-which-nothing-greater-can-be-thought as involving mere understanding of the phrase, whereas in moving on . . . he treats this mental "existent" as an entity in its own right. This is a confusion. . . .

(c) *The intentional object fallacy*

Even if the notion of mental entities that genuinely "exist in the mind" can be made sense of in some way, it still seems questionable to infer from (1) *"The Fool understands the phrase 'something-than-which-nothing-greater-can-be-thought'"* the apparently far more significant existential claim (2) *"Something-than-which-nothing-greater-can-be-thought exists in the Fool's mind."*

(d) *The comparison difficulty*

There seems to be something logically odd about purporting to compare something that exists only "in the mind" with something existing in reality.

(e) *The unique referent problem*

Anselm seems to equivocate between the indefinite "*something*-than-which-nothing-greater-can-be-thought" and the apparently more specific "*that*-than-which-nothing-greater-can-be-thought." . . . His introduction of the phrase "*that*-than-which-nothing-greater-can-be-thought" . . . , moreover, is presumably illegitimate unless he has already established that there is one and only one thing to which this phrase can refer, and he can do this only by *antecedently* proving the existence of God.

(f) *The Kantian dogma ("existence is not a predicate")*

As Kant famously argued . . . it seems dubious to consider something's existence as a property that characterizes it, and hence as a factor than can contribute to the assessment of its greatness. Rather, its existence seems to be something presupposed if it is to have any properties at all.

(g) *The separate realms principle*

Kant rounds off his discussion of the Ontological Argument by stating the principle "Whatever, therefore, and however much, our concept of an object man contain, we must go outside it, if we are to ascribe existence to the object." . . . This implies a gulf between the realm of concepts and the realms of real things: no matter what concepts we devise, it is always a further question n whether or not they are realized or instantiated in reality.

(h) *The Aquinas rebuttal*

Aquinas seems to suggest, in his *Summa Contra Gentiles*, that there is no contradiction as claimed . . . , because unless the real existence of that-than-which-nothing-greater-can-be-thought is already presupposed, there cannot be a contradiction in our thinking of "something greater . . . than anything given in reality or in the intellect."

(i) *Gaunilo reductios*

If Anselm's argument were indeed sound, then it would be hard to see why equivalent arguments could not be constructed to prove the existence of a supremely excellent island, a perfect Pegasus, an Antigod whose evil is unsurpassably effective, and so on; but it is grossly implausible to suggest that these things do exist, or even if they did, that their existence could be proved in this *a priori* manner.[62]

This catalog of objections is extremely helpful for our discussion. Most of them we have already considered. For now, however, I want to pursue Millican's actual argument, because he thinks that Anselm can avoid all of these objections by using a consistent concept of "natures" that will allow distinctions in greatness and show how "instantiated" *is* a predicate.

---

[62]Peter Millican, "The One Fatal Flaw in Anselm's Argument," *Mind* 113 (July 2004): 442-45. I have shortened each of these objections.

Natures are "constituted purely by the descriptive properties that characterize them."[63] What is important is that they have no per se connection to any specific individuals, real or imagined, and are wholly independent of instantiation considerations. Millican's use of "nature" is, I think, much the same as what Anselm accomplishes in AD: a conceivable description. We can now list criteria by which we wish to judge the "greatness" of natures, properties like power, wisdom, goodness, and so on. It will then give us a hierarchy of greatness among natures. So far, this is surely innocent enough, and it seems quite Anselmian, as well.

All that remains, in order to get Anselm's argument, is some way to represent AP. To do that, Millican argues, we need only include among the characteristics of natures something like "instantiated." We can then restate AP as follows: "A nature which is instantiated in reality is greater than one which is not."[64] Now we can clearly see how it would make sense that a nature designated "God" has a level of greatness unsurpassed by anything else even if uninstantiated, but unsurpass*able* if instantiated.

But now comes the kicker: adding "exists" to a nature changes nothing. We are still talking about a nature, even if we say it exists, or even *necessarily* exists. In any case, while we can say that an instantiated nature is greater than a corresponding uninstantiated one, we are still only talking about natures. No doubt Anselm is right that instantiation contributes greatly to greatness, so much so that he thinks the argument is complete. But the problem is that Millican's version of AP leaves us with no reason to think that it is God who has the greatest nature that can be thought. It might just as well be the human being who has had the most power, the most wisdom, and the highest degree of goodness. If instantiated, that nature would be the greatest, just because *any*

---

[63]Millican, "One Fatal Flaw," 451.
[64]Millican, "One Fatal Flaw," 458. Millican calls this restatement PSE, the principle of the superiority of existence.

instantiated nature is greater than *any* uninstantiated nature. Millican suggests that might well be the Roman emperor Marcus Aurelius. In any case, on any understanding of AP, as interpreted by Millican, the atheist is not obliged to think that the nature "God" must be instantiated. The argument fails.

We should note that Millican can now show that Kant is wrong to argue that existence is not a property. It is just an empty one that does not add anything to a nature. So Millican concludes that what is going on here is not some misguided deep philosophical theory but just a simple, shallow category mistake.[65]

5.4.2 Yujin Nagasawa. Yujin Nagasawa (b. 1975) teaches at the University of Birmingham. He has already published extensively in philosophy of religion, including his recent book on Anselm's argument, *Maximal God: A New Defense of Perfect Being Theism*.[66] In 2007, he responded to Millican in the same auspicious journal, *Mind*. He argues that Millican is right that Anselm can avoid the nine "deep" philosophical objections, but wrong to argue that he succumbs to a "shallow" category mistake. Nagasawa's argument here, and much more extensively in his book a decade later, leaves the argument still standing. At least, if the argument does fail, it does not fail in any way Millican has discovered. Nagasawa concludes the paper by noting that after "more than nine hundred years, the ontological argument is still powerful enough to torment its opponents."[67]

After summarizing Millican's theory of natures, and his subsequent defeater, Nagasawa goes on to show that Millican misconstrues AP. Millican understands AP as "A nature which is instantiated in reality is greater than one which is not." But this is a much stronger—bigger—claim

---

[65]See Millican, "One Fatal Flaw," 473-74. I have greatly simplified and shortened Millican's argument. Hopefully I have done it sufficient justice. I encourage advanced readers to work through this articulate and detailed forty-page article in *Mind* for themselves.

[66]Nagasawa, *Maximal God*.

[67]Yujin Nagasawa, "Millican on the Ontological Argument," *Mind* 116 (October 2007): 1038.

than AP as Anselm himself proposes. In this sense: Millican's AP, as we saw, says that *any* instantiated nature is greater than any uninstantiated one. Nagasawa argues that Anselm's AP applies only to one nature—namely, AD. He has no need of, nor does he ever advance, Millican's strong principle.[68] Rather, he holds the much weaker principle: The nature "God" that is instantiated in reality is greater than the nature "God" that is conceived only in the mind because existence is a great-making property.[69] If we look at *Proslogion* 2, Nagasawa is correct; Anselm clearly applies AP only to AD.

That being established, Nagasawa can then conclude that while Millican is right about the other nine deep objections, he is wrong about his own shallow one. Given Nagasawa's interpretation of AP,

> it is indeed *im*possible for atheists to think of a nature that is greater than a-nature-than-which-no-greater-nature-can-be-thought. Therefore, the argument goes through and successfully yields the conclusion that a-nature-than-which-no-greater-can-be-thought must be instantiated in reality. While there is no textual evidence that this is the correct interpretation of Anselm's argument, it is at least as consistent with relevant passages in Anselm's texts as is Millican's. . . .
>
> Whether or not the ontological argument on the above interpretation ultimately succeeds is, of course, a matter for further debate. Nevertheless, it is perfectly clear by now that the argument does not fail in the way Millican thinks it does; if it does fail, the failure is not due to its shallow logical details.[70]

This debate between Millican and Nagasawa has continued, and is summarized and extended again in Nagasawa's recent *Maximal God*.[71] We will return to Nagasawa's 2017 conclusions about Anselm's argument at the end of this section.

---

[68]Nagasawa, "Millican on the Ontological Argument," 1034. Again, I have not, and cannot here do justice to Nagasawa's careful exegesis of both Anselm and Millican.

[69]I am paraphrasing Nagasawa, "Millican on the Ontological Argument," 1035.

[70]Nagasawa, "Millican on the Ontological Argument," 1036-37.

[71]See Nagasawa, *Maximal God*, secs. 5.3-9.

And so the argument stills haunts us. It seems too easy to be true, but we cannot pinpoint where it fails. We do want to look at other recent discussions, including, next, attempts to revive the Kant-Frege-Russell objection. While in some ways the Millican-Nagasawa exchange might seem to end the debate, the Kantian objection is perhaps more subtle and also comes in a variety of forms.

5.4.3 Elliott Sober. Elliott Sober (b. 1948), a Harvard PhD in philosophy, is a professor at the University of Wisconsin, Madison, specializing in philosophy of science, especially biology. He has, as we have seen, played an important role in the argument over intelligent design, but has also contributed to the discussion of the ontological argument. Here is a simplified version of what he argues defeats the argument: a form of Kant's "existence-is-not-a-predicate" objection:

> Let's simply build the property of existence into the definition of a being and see what happens.
>
> Unicorns don't exist. The concept of unicornhood isn't exemplified in the actual world. Consider, however, a new concept, which I call E-unicornhood. An E-unicorn is by definition something that is an existing unicorn. Does it follow from the definition of an E-unicorn that there are E-unicorns? Not at all. The concept includes the property of existence, but that doesn't imply that the concept is actually exemplified. The definition simply describes what a thing must be like if it is to count as an E-unicorn. The definition tells us that if something is an E-unicorn, then that thing will have the property of existing. Now let's define the concept of an E-God. An E-God is a being who is all-powerful, all-knowing, all-good, and who actually exists. Does it follow from the definition of an E-God that there is an E-God? Not at all. The definition simply describes what a thing must be like if it is to count as an E-God. The definition tells us that if something is an E-God then that thing will have the property of existing. . . .
>
> Anselm argued that our concept of God has built into it the idea that God necessarily exists. Just as God is by definition omnipotent, it also

is true that God, by definition, necessarily exists. My criticism of the Ontological Argument comes to this: let's grant that God is by definition the greatest possible being. And let us grant that necessary existence is a perfection. What follows from this is that necessary existence is part of the concept of God. Necessary existence is built into the concept of God, just as omnipotence is. But the fact that existence is built into a concept doesn't imply there are things to which the concept applies.

If we concede that God is defined as an omnipotent being, all this means is that if God exists, then that being must be omnipotent. Likewise, if we concede that God is defined as a necessarily existent being we are merely saying that if there is a God, then that being necessarily exists. The definitions don't entail the existence of anything that is omnipotent nor do they entail the existence of anything that necessarily exists. It is for this reason that the Ontological Argument is invalid.[72]

This objection holds that existence is a property but not one that could somehow bridge the gap from concept to real thing. A concept of something really existing is different from that something really existing. Sober's point, again like Kant's, seems at one level obviously right. Adding existence to the definition or concept of anything, including God, does not and cannot just *make* it exist. Granted! But nowhere does Anselm say this. AD is something quite different. Many others have made this point. Just a few examples: Alvin Plantinga says,

> But is it relevant to the ontological argument? Couldn't Anselm thank Kant for this interesting point and proceed merrily on his way? Where did he try to define God into being by adding existence to a list of properties that defined some concept? . . . If this were Anselm's procedure—if he had simply added existence to a concept that has application contingently if at all—then indeed his argument would be subject to the Kantian criticism. But he didn't, and it isn't.[73]

---

[72]Elliott Sober, "The Ontological Argument," in *Core Questions in Philosophy: A Text with Readings*, 6th ed. (London: Pearson Education, 2013), 98-99.
[73]Plantinga, *God, Freedom, and Evil*, 97.

The noted medievalist Brian Davies simply says that in "the *Proslogion* . . . Anselm does not seem to be arguing that '—exists' is or is not a first-level predicate."[74] E. J. Lowe says that Kant's objection "is just a red herring with no real bearing on the ontological argument."[75]

In fact Kant is quite clear himself that he is critiquing Descartes, not Anselm.[76] I will leave standing the question of how and if the objection applies to Descartes, Spinoza, or Leibniz. In any case, I conclude that Anselm *does not* fall prey to the Kantian dictum.

5.4.4 Peter van Inwagen. Here is a good example of the objection that the argument begs the question—that is, that it is in some way circular by assuming the conclusion in the premises. Peter van Inwagen (b. 1942), who holds a PhD from the University of Rochester, taught for many years at Syracuse University, and is now at Duke University and the University of Notre Dame. He was president of the Society of Christian Philosophers from 2010 to 2013.

In his essay "Begging the Question," van Inwagen argues that virtually all modal ontological arguments, in any version, include a "possibility premise," something like "It is possible for there to be a necessarily existent being that has all perfections essentially."[77] And this is precisely where the defect in the argument is located:

> There seems to be no *a priori* reason, or none accessible to the human
> intellect (perhaps none accessible to any finite intellect) to think that it
> is possible for there to be a necessarily existent being that has all perfec-
> tions essentially. I myself think that this premise is true—but only

---

[74]Brian Davies, "Anselm and the Ontological Argument," in *The Cambridge Companion to Anselm*, ed. Brian Davies and Brian Leftow (Cambridge: Cambridge University Press, 2004), 171.

[75]E. J. Lowe, "The Ontological Argument," in *The Routledge Companion to Philosophy of Religion*, ed. Chad Meister and Paul Copan (London: Routledge, 2007), 337.

[76]See the discussion in Jordan Howard Sobel, *Logic and Theism: Arguments for and Against Beliefs in God* (Cambridge: Cambridge University Press, 2004), 68-69.

[77]Peter van Inwagen, "Begging the Question," in Oppy, *Ontological Arguments*, 242. The argument in this essay goes back to his essay "Three Versions of the Ontological Argument," in *Ontological Proofs Today*, ed. Mirosław Szatkowski (Frankfurt: Ontos, 2012). Thus it is really earlier than Nagasawa's book in 2017.

because I think that there in fact *is* a necessarily existent being who has all perfections essentially. And my reasons for thinking that are by no means *a priori*; they depend (so *I* suppose) on what that being has revealed about himself to humanity. And I do not mean simply that no *conclusive* reason for thinking that such a being is possible can be supplied by *a priori* human reasoning. I mean that human reason is impotent to discover by *a priori* reasoning any consideration whatever that should cause a human reasoner to raise whatever prior probability he or she may assign to the possibility of such a being.

And I would go further. I would say that, divine revelation apart, a human being should either assign a prior probability of 0.5 to the proposition that it is possible for there to be a necessarily existent being who possesses all perfections essentially, or else refuse to assign it any probability at all.[78]

So, the possibility premise is unsupported. Van Inwagen thus concludes that Plantinga is wrong to think that the argument still does have epistemic value, because it can be used to show that it is not irrational to believe its conclusion. But that cannot be so, if accepting the conclusion of this, or any argument for that matter, involves accepting the conclusion of a *circular* argument. There might, of course, be other reasons for believing that God exists—and van Inwagen thinks there are—but this one will not do.

So how might we resolve these differing positions on the possibility premise? Nagasawa has had the last word on this, at least so far.

5.4.5 *Yujin Nagasawa—again.* After numerous journal articles on the ontological argument, Nagasawa in 2017 published his magnum opus on the subject. This includes a review and extension of his debate with Millican. Most importantly, however, this concludes with a rejoinder to the begging-the-question objection by way of examining the possibility premise. I will let this be the end of the story to date.

---

[78]Van Inwagen, "Begging the Question," 242-43.

Nagasawa thinks that this argument is superior to the other three classical arguments because none of them establishes the full perfect-being theism that is alone suitable for worship. Anselm's argument in *Proslogion* 2, set in its best current form as a modal argument (he thinks Plantinga's is the most elegant), will give us the complete concept in one simple move. All we need is the possibility premise, call it PP, that "it is possible that a maximally great being exists." The rest is uncontroversial, standard logic. From the possible existence of maximal greatness follows its necessary existence, from which follows its existence in the actual world. And a being of maximal greatness must include omniscience, omnipotence, and omnibenevolence.[79]

What remains, however, is a real defense of PP. Plantinga thinks it is rational to accept it and that the full argument is thus reasonable. Van Inwagen argues that the argument then remains question-begging and thus not rationally acceptable. In light of the fact that atheists have contended that PP is *not* possible, how should we mount a plausible defense? Nagasawa looks at five ways to argue for PP, all of which have some weakness or defect.

The first is the argument that conceivability shows possibility. But this is highly contentious for a number of reasons, but at least because the atheist argues that the nonexistence of God is conceivable.[80] The second involves deriving possibility from "experientiability" or imaginability. However, it is at least questionable that this could work for God's "omni-" properties. Can we really experience or imagine omnipotence? Third, PP has been supported as necessary for a flourishing life or as a condition that meets our natural desires. This, Nagasawa argues, may well be true, but these observations would at best support the probability of PP. The fourth is a deontic argument, something like

---

[79]See the discussion in Nagasawa, *Maximal God*, 180-86.

[80]I am briefly summarizing these five arguments. To do them and their defenders justice, see Nagasawa's detailed treatment in *Maximal God*, 187-202.

"God can exist because he ought to exist." But this seems only to amount to saying that it is desirable that God exist, and certainly the atheist could, and would want to, argue the opposite. We might be better off if God non-exists.

The final argument for PP is that of Leibniz, which we discussed earlier. Leibniz argues that "positive properties" are necessarily mutually consistent because they are defined as unanalyzable and hence without limits. Since God is a "most perfect being" his properties cannot contradict, and so the aggregate must be possible. Nagasawa thinks this is problematic, since one would have to show that all inconsistency claims fail. This is so, he argues, because Leibniz developed his concept of God from a "bottom-up perspective."[81] That is, it is constructed incrementally by adding components—properties—and then having to argue that they must be consistent.

Nagasawa suggests we do this top-down instead. We do this by appealing to the maximal-God thesis to begin with. If we do so, then the PP will follow by itself. As he puts it,

> The maximal God thesis explicates the perfect being thesis by saying that God is the being that has the maximal consistent set of knowledge, power, and benevolence. According to the maximal God approach, this is what the perfect being thesis means when it says that God is the being than which no greater is metaphysically positive. This suggests that once we accept the maximal God thesis and the perfect being thesis, we can automatically derive that it is possible that God exists because here God is understood as the being that has the maximal *consistent* set of knowledge, power, and benevolence. In other words, the maximal concept of God is *by definition* internally coherent because its components are mutually consistent (and internally coherent). This guarantees the possibility of the existence of God. That is, the possibility of God's existence comes with perfect being theism for free given the maximal God thesis. It is important to remind ourselves that . . . necessary

---

[81]Nagasawa, *Maximal God*, 203.

existence is included in the notion of the being than which no greater is metaphysically possible. For God to be greater than all other meta-physically possible beings, He has to be ontologically superior to all other metaphysically possible beings. No being can be ontologically superior to all other metaphysically possible beings if it is a merely contingent being.[82]

This way there is no need for any special or separate argument for PP. Nagasawa notes that it might still appear as if this argument is question-begging. But that is only because in any deductive argument the conclusion is *always* entailed by its premises. Furthermore, in this case, the modal ontological argument, there really only is one informative premise—namely, PP. So Nagasawa concludes that this is a perfectly sound argument.

Now what? I will make just one observation at this point. And that is that we are right back to Anselm's original argument. After redoing the language semantics and reconstructing the logic, we are back to a simple definition, Anselm's definition, which, once we meditate on it—that is, understand its meaning implications—we have to conclude that this maximally great being exists in reality. It is just that profoundly simple.

Further Reading

For a good introduction to modal logic as it pertains to matters related to God, see Brian Leftow, *God and Necessity* (Oxford: Oxford University Press, 2012), chap. 1.

Another good discussion of logical necessity and the ontological argument can be found in Stephen Parrish, *God and Necessity* (Lanham, MD: University Press of America, 1997).

The bibliography in Yujin Nagasawa's *Maximal God* is a good place to start. It includes many important names that I have simply had to leave out here. There is hardly anyone in philosophy of religion, atheist and theist, in the last sixty years who has not written on this argument.

---

[82]Nagasawa, *Maximal God*, 204.

An excellent bibliography, but limited to 1995, is in Graham Oppy, *Ontological Arguments and Belief in God* (Cambridge: Cambridge University Press, 1995).

For another exchange on the begs-the-question objection, see William Rowe, "The Ontological Argument," in *Philosophy of Religion: An Introduction* (Belmont, CA: Thompson Higher Education, 2007), chap. 3, and the detailed response from Keith Burgess-Jackson, "Does Anselm Beg the Question?," *International Journal for Philosophy of Religion* 76, no. 1 (2014): 5-18.

A good follow-up on Plantinga's argument is Joshua Rasmussen, "Plantinga," in Oppy, *Ontological Arguments*, 176-95.

5.5 Where We Are Now

5.5.1 Graham Oppy.
We will let Graham Oppy have the last word. It appears that all of the objections to Anselm's argument fail. That of course does not mean that Descartes's argument still stands. My own view is that it does succumb to some versions of Kant's objection, since it begins by affirming that God, the really existing God, has certain perfections, and that is either circular, or it treats "exists" as just another property like "green" or "rectangular." But there is no doubt that this discussion will go on, especially in regard to Plantinga's modal-logic version, though I think that Nagasawa is right.

Oppy's 2018 collection, *Ontological Arguments*, brings together an excellent array of both historical commentary and current discussion, written by some of the best minds in philosophy of religion, both theists and atheists. In his introductory essay, "Ontological Arguments in Focus," he makes several valuable points for our assessment of the argument at this point in history as well as looking ahead.[83]

Let me begin with his closing point: The current state of the argument is so confusing, he thinks, that we need to give careful thought as to what exactly constitutes a successful argument in general. This is especially obvious here, since even theists are divided, somewhere near

---

[83]Graham Oppy, "Introduction: Ontological Arguments in Focus," in Oppy, *Ontological Arguments*, 1.

evenly, on the issue. And atheists are also divided among themselves as to precisely what goes wrong in the logic. So he ends with this assignment: "One gap in our understanding of ontological arguments—and arguments more generally—that might be filled in the next fifty years concerns the standards of assessment that successful arguments must meet. This gap gives us much to ponder."[84]

Now, I think it is safe to say that Oppy greatly overstates the general case about standards of assessment. There are, of course, areas of science where the situation is unclear. Exactly how to verify multiverse and string theory may not be entirely obvious yet. And no doubt there are all sorts of details in ethical decision-making that remain murky. But the standards that govern normal deductive and inductive arguments, even related to God, have long been established, and so the other three arguments are not faced with the sorts of problems we have here.

Might Oppy perhaps be right about this one? Anselm's original argument seemed simple enough at first glance. But even his contemporaries were baffled and confused. Nine hundred years later it remains a bit unclear to some as to exactly what the argument is about, let alone what a good solution would be. Is it about God, the concept of God, a possible God, the definition of God, just a random possible definition, or something else? I grant Oppy that there is some confusion here, but it is not about the standards for a successful argument. I think he is just wrong on that.

I think the real problem is that we have here a curiously simple argument that appears on first hearing to be perfectly sound. And yet history is replete with those who have tried to give the argument in terms that would make clearer sense, or else to find some deeper-level deficiency in it. Why? I think it is our natural response that something as big as God could not be found at the end of a simple little piece of reasoning. Especially we philosophers cannot handle that.

---

[84]Oppy, "Introduction," 18.

But on the other hand, why is it such a bad thing for the existence of a necessary being to be so readily demonstrated? If there is a necessary being, a being greater than which cannot be conceived to exist, would that not just be obvious? Even if the actual presence of God is hidden from us, and even if we are dependent on revelation and ordinary effect-to-cause reasoning for insight into his actual nature, it seems that his reality as such would just be evident to our meditative thinking.

Now to Oppy's first point. He begins with the claim, "If you have good all-things-considered reason to suppose that God does not exist, then you have all the reason you need to suppose that there are no successful ontological arguments."[85] That surely does not follow. Suppose the problem of evil gives someone a good and strong reason to think there is no God. What follows from that in relation to any of the arguments *for* God's existence? We have seen some examples of this, and the conclusion is just that nothing really follows.

It is frequently the case that we have some strong initial reasons for some conclusion, only to be surprised later to find strong reasons for the opposite conclusion that also help us understand how we misunderstood that initial reasoning. We will simply have to look at each of the arguments, including each of the extant ontological arguments, on its own merits.

How to conclude the story of this strange and many-faced argument? After all of the debate, especially in the last sixty years, it appears that none of the objections raised against Anselm's original argument still stand. This is especially true of its current modal version. That is, if we take AD as exactly that—a possible definition—then it follows that for this definition alone, there must be a corresponding being in reality. If it is possible, and it is, then it is necessary, and hence it is actual. If it exists in every possible world, then it exists in the actual world. And so, I conclude there is here a sound argument for God's existence.

---

[85]Oppy, "Introduction," 14.

I have been working on this argument since the first year in my doctoral program in 1972. I almost wrote my dissertation on it but found I could not come to a final conclusion back then. Much has happened since then, and I have followed the discussion closely. I now find Nagasawa's conclusions rather convincing.

I do admit, though, that this argument, at least by itself, has had little if any success in persuading atheists to change their position. Now I do know of atheists who have abandoned their view as a result of each of the other three arguments. But they are a very different type of argument. They are ordinary evidence-to-conclusion, effect-to-cause arguments, and the only question is whether the argument has sufficient strength to require the conclusion. This is just a unique argument: truly unique. There really is just *one* single case in which a definition itself requires existence. And that is so odd that most of us are reluctant to change beliefs as a result.

CHAPTER 6

The End of the Story—For Now

6.1 Are There Bigger Issues?

There are, I think, some considerations to think about at the conclusion of our narrative. Two, in particular, have a summary bearing on the entire discussion. The first is the matter of how and if these arguments hang together. Do they reinforce or add to each other, and what about other arguments and evidences for God's reality? The second is the matter of what role faith or belief has to play in relation to rational considerations.

6.1.1 Cumulative-case arguments. So, first, exactly how do these four, along with other arguments relate? I want to begin this discussion by considering what is perhaps the most potent objection to adding these arguments together into some larger case: what has come to be called a cumulative case. This came most notably from Antony Flew. Then, we will look at the best response to this objection from Basil Mitchell.

6.1.1.1 Antony Flew. It has been alleged, for example by Antony Flew (1923–2010), that the case for God's existence suffers from the "leaky-bucket problem." After discussing many of the arguments for God's existence, and finding some fault or faults in all of them, Flew says this:

> It will not do at all—notwithstanding that it is quite often done—having
> found that one sort of argument is unsound, first to shift ground to another,
> and then, when that in turn is shown to be broken-backed, to suggest that
> this demonstration is not after all to the point since the second argument
> should really be so construed as to be implicitly dependent upon the first.
> Nor, incidentally, will it do to recognize that of a whole series of arguments
> each individually is defective, but then to urge that nevertheless in sum they

comprise an impressive case: perhaps adding as a sop to the Cerberus of criticism that this case is addressed to the whole personality and not merely to the philosophical intellect. We have here to insist upon a sometimes tricky distinction: between, on the one hand, the valid principle of the accumulation of evidence, where every item has at least some weight in its own right: and, on the other hand, the Ten-leaky-buckets-Tactic, applied to arguments none of which hold water at all. The scholarly and the businesslike procedure is to examine arguments one by one, without pretending—for no better reason than that they have been shown to be mistaken—that clearly and respectably stated contentions must be other than they are.[1]

Flew, who later, as a result of carefully examining these arguments, but especially the fine-tuning argument, became a theist, is certainly right about this in general.[2] Multiple weak arguments, regardless of how many, do not add up to one strong one.

Imagine John is on trial for murder. The district attorney's case consists of a ballistics test with a 70 percent likelihood of being a match; eyewitnesses who unfortunately did not have a clear line of vision were drunk at the time and are not really sure it was John; and, at best, a weak motive: John was known not to like the victim much. In this case surely a series of moderately probable arguments add up to an even less moderately probable conclusion. This *is* a series of leaky buckets. That is, none of the elements of the case are highly probable, and so the total case is not strengthened by there being multiple elements.

But suppose that each element is strong or highly probable. Now a 99.999 percent likely ballistics test by itself does not prove John guilty. Someone else may have stolen his gun and used it. But, in conjunction with other strong pieces of evidence and reliable witness reports, we do have a very strong case. And that is the situation here. Each of the

---

[1]Antony Flew, *God and Philosophy* (New York: Dell, 1966), 141.
[2]See his own statement in Antony Flew with Roy Abraham Varghese, *There Is a God: How the World's Most Notorious Atheist Changed His Mind* (San Francisco: HarperOne, 2008). See also his interview with Gary Habermas in "My Pilgrimage from Atheism to Theism: A Discussion Between Antony Flew and Gary Habermas," *Philosophia Christi* 6, no. 2 (2004): 197-211.

arguments only demonstrates a part of the conclusion—part of a larger definition of God—but together they make a very good case for an infinite, perfectly good, intelligent, and personal source of the universe.

6.1.1.2 Basil Mitchell. Our actual situation, however, is very different. Basil Mitchell (1917–2011), after noting that there are of course *possible* objections to each of the arguments, but that they all have satisfactory rejoinders, argues that the right approach here is analogous to a legal case:

> The debate between theists and atheists is unlikely to make progress, so long as it is confined to a single argument, such as the cosmological argument, or, indeed, to whole series of arguments, if these are to be taken piecemeal without at any stage being brought into relation to one another. Here, at least, the Cartesian strategy of "dividing the question" must be resisted. The debate, to be useful, must take the form of a dialogue in which, as John Wisdom observes (in relation to a legal judgment), "The process of argument is not a chain of demonstrative reasoning. It is a presenting and representing of those features of a case which severally co-operate in favor of the conclusion."[3]

Thus there is a larger strategy here, in which these and other arguments work together, though we must carefully observe Mitchell's (and Wisdom's) three guidelines for a case. First, each argument must stand on its own—that is, be independently sound. Second, they must cooperate or reinforce each other. Something must tie them together. Third, it must be clear that they are directed to the same conclusion.

Now I would submit that, as Mitchell argues, the case for the existence of God clearly meets all three requirements. Kant's frequently repeated claim that the arguments are all dependent on the ontological argument's conclusion to a necessary being is clearly false. Each argument defines its own conclusion. They are reinforcing in that they all

---

[3]Basil Mitchell, *The Justification of Religious Belief* (London: Macmillan, 1973), 45. This quote from John Wisdom (1904–1993) is found in his *Philosophy and Psycho-analysis* (London: Blackwell, 1953).

conclude to the source of contingent things, but in different ways. And what unites them ultimately is the cosmological argument's conclusion to the source of existence, and hence of all aspects of contingency. There can be only one uncaused cause of all things. There is one God.

We also need to add here that there are many other arguments and evidences that form part of this case. I have in fact restricted this journey through history to the four primary *philosophical* arguments. There is much more to be said. I will here mention, but only briefly, four categories of argument left to be explored.[4]

6.1.1.3 Arguments from religious experience. William James collected a great variety of accounts of people who had some form of contact with the transcendent.[5] They occur in every religion. There seems to be a strong basis for an argument here, as long as one keeps to the normal criteria for experience in general. William Alston in his *Perceiving God* and William Wainwright in *Mysticism* have established sound rules here.[6] This allows for religious experience to stand, yet within the context of solid epistemological parameters.

Cautions here result from James's conclusion that religious experiences have no common denominators, either in terms of a definition of the object of experience, or of the modality of the experience itself.

6.1.1.4 Arguments from miracles. A recent study by Craig Keener, titled *Miracles*, establishes that there are thousands of well-documented events in human history that (1) require an intelligent agent or person causation and (2) require some sort of supernatural causation—that is, they cannot occur as a result of natural or even human causes.[7]

---

[4]A broader discussion of the different arguments available can be found in Jerry Walls and Trent Dougherty, eds., *Two Dozen (or So) Arguments for God: The Plantinga Project* (Oxford: Oxford University Press, 2018). Many of these are specialized forms of the four major arguments discussed above.

[5]William James, *The Varieties of Religious Experience* (New York: Longmans, Green, 1902).

[6]William Alston, *Perceiving God: The Epistemology of Religious Experience* (Ithaca, NY: Cornell University Press, 1991); William Wainwright, *Mysticism* (Hempstead, UK: Harvester Press, 1981).

[7]Craig Keener, *Miracles: The Credibility of the New Testament Accounts*, 2 vols. (Grand Rapids, MI: Baker Academic, 2011).

Here, too, we need to abide by normal historiographical standards (Hume and his current followers are just wrong that we need impossibly more) in verifying such events, but given sufficient evidence, and if they meet the two above criteria, we can form good arguments, not just for their own historicity, but also for the reality of an intentional personal agent beyond the confines of the natural universe.

One of the best-attested events in ancient history is the resurrection of Jesus. N. T. Wright ranks it as well-attested as Caesar Augustus's death in AD 14, and the fall of Jerusalem in 70.[8] And Richard Swinburne gives it a probability of 97 percent.[9] This can then be used as the basis of a best-explanation inductive argument against naturalism and in favor of God's existence and theism in general.

6.1.1.4.1 Gary Habermas. Gary Habermas (b. 1950), who earned his PhD from Michigan State University and teaches at Liberty University, states the argument this way:

> It would seem, then, that the Christian theistic framework both accounts better for the known data [regarding the resurrection of Jesus], as well as being more internally consistent. On the Christian thesis, Jesus was raised from the dead and was thereby shown to be correct concerning his theistic perspective. The God of the universe raised Jesus, approving both Jesus' personal claims to deity and the central thrust of his mission— to offer the opportunity for eternal life. This appears to be Jesus' view and also best represents the repeated emphasis of the earliest apostolic witness that we find in the New Testament.[10]

So, given the overwhelming evidence for the resurrection of Jesus, we can move inductively directly to the conclusion that God exists and

---

[8]N. T. Wright, *The Resurrection of the Son of God* (London: SPCK, 2003), 710.

[9]See Richard Swinburne, "The Probability of the Resurrection of Jesus," *Philosophia Christi* 15 (2013): 251, http://users.ox.ac.uk/~orie0087/pdf_files/Papers%20from%20Philosophical%20Journals/Swinburne_2013-resurrection.pdf. It is also in his *The Resurrection of God Incarnate* (Oxford: Clarendon, 2003), 217.

[10]Gary Habermas, "Evidential Apologetics," in *Five Views on Apologetics*, ed. Steven Cowan (Grand Rapids, MI: Zondervan, 2000), 119-20. See also Habermas, *The Risen Jesus and Future Hope* (Lanham, MD: Rowman and Littlefield, 2003), chap. 2.

that naturalism is false. This, it seems to me, is a powerful argument, dependent simply on overwhelming historical evidence.

6.1.1.5 Consensus Gentium *arguments.* Frequently maligned, arguments based on universal agreement are nevertheless obviously valuable. It is hard to imagine how an idea could be prevalent in every people group throughout known history and yet be entirely fallacious. Just how strong such an argument might be is of course certainly open to debate. It does have a formidable history, however. It can be found, for example, in such diverse and illustrious company as Plato, John Locke, David Hume, Jonathan Edwards, and John Stuart Mill.

A good place to start, especially since it includes a good bibliography, is Thomas Kelly's "*Consensus Gentium*: Reflections on the 'Common Consent' Argument for the Existence of God."[11]

6.1.1.6 Transcendental arguments. Theologians and philosophers in the Reformed tradition of Christianity have held to coherence criteria for truth, as well as severe restrictions on the human capacity to know and specifically to do philosophy. As a Christian epistemology, this is often referred to as presuppositionalism. This has led to a quite different format of argumentation, a kind of reverse procedure that begins with some feature of our reality, knowledge, truth, value, for example, and proceeds by showing that God is a necessary presupposition for it. So the logic of the argument itself dictates that we *always* begin with God, not our observations and reflections.

6.1.1.6.1 Cornelius Van Til. Such an apologetic can be found foremost in the work of Cornelius Van Til (1895–1987), who argues that we must begin with the trinitarian God:

---

[11]Thomas Kelly, "*Consensus Gentium*: Reflections on the 'Common Consent' Argument for the Existence of God," in *Evidence and Religious Belief*, ed. Kelly James Clark and Raymond J. VanArragon (Oxford: Oxford University Press, 2011), 135-56, https://www.princeton.edu/~tkelly/cg.pdf. Thomas Kelly writes extensively on this topic.

The ontological Trinity will be our interpretative concept everywhere. God is our concrete universal; in Him thought and being are coterminous, in Him the problem of knowledge is solved. If we begin thus with the ontological Trinity as our concrete universal, we frankly differ from every school of philosophy and from every school of science not merely in our conclusions, but in our starting-point and in our method as well. For us the facts are what they are, and the universals are what they are, because of their common dependence upon the ontological Trinity.[12]

So the truth of God's existence is not a conclusion at all, but rather the necessary starting point of every argument, in Van Til's thinking.[13] God, or specifically the Trinity, is thus the presupposition of all knowledge, and any apologetic is based on a successful coherence of the resulting worldview. Apologetics could not launch from some neutral territory— there is none.

6.1.1.6.2 Lydia Jaeger. A good current example of this type of argument comes from the French philosopher of science Lydia Jaeger (b. 1965). She is the Academic Dean at the Institut Biblique de Nogent-sur-Marne near Paris. She holds the PhD in philosophy from the Sorbonne and did postgraduate work in physics and mathematics at the University of Cologne. She is the author of five books in philosophy of science, most notably perhaps, *Einstein, Polanyi and the Laws of Nature*.[14]

She accepts a blended Cosmo-Teleological Argument, but only in the context of a presuppositional epistemic framework. That means, she argues, that there is no neutral worldview territory. Arguments for God's existence work only within the context of theism. We must *start* with God. And so, what was an evidential argument becomes a transcendental one. Hence, without beginning with God there is no truth,

---

[12]Cornelius Van Til, *Common Grace and the Gospel* (Phillipsburg, NJ: P&R, 1972), 64.
[13]For a good discussion of Cornelius Van Til see John Frame, *Cornelius Van Til: An Analysis of His Thought* (Phillipsburg, NJ: P&R, 1995).
[14]Lydia Jaeger, *Einstein, Polanyi and the Laws of Nature* (West Conshohocken, PA: Templeton Press, 2010).

no science, no facts. And thus, in reverse, that we can do science and find truth *presumes* an intelligently ordering and causing God. As Jaeger puts it, "Creationism obliges us to denounce the claim to neutral rationality, which has often accompanied the use of theistic proofs."[15]

> By neglecting the radical way in which knowledge is rooted in God, the way the physico-theological proof has traditionally been used has left it vulnerable to the Kantian critique: the transcendent Being is not found at the end of any immanent causal chain. God is not the first (or last) element that lies within the world. Even if such an argument were to succeed, it would not prove God's existence, but only that of an immanent god—which, incidentally, would be nowhere near sufficient to halt the regression induced by the repeated request for explanation.[16]

The basic logic of the cosmological argument remains intact,[17] but it can be valid as an argument for the true God only if it begins with theistic/creationist presuppositions. If we begin with God, then human reason does not overstep its bounds when it speaks of God.[18]

I would only note that one does not have to accept the initial epistemic move of the transcendental argument—and I do not—in order to see its value, not only by itself, but also within a larger case for God's existence. It certainly demonstrates the overall coherence of a theistic worldview with the way the universe actually is. If you begin with God, it certainly makes sense that there is the causal, intelligent, and moral ordering of things. On the other hand, if you begin with a "nothing," that somehow becomes a deterministic-material-universe-generating-process, such an ordered universe seems far less compellingly coherent.

If we then take all these arguments, together with the classic four, there is an exceedingly strong case for God's existence. And I certainly

---

[15]Lydia Jaeger, *What the Heavens Declare: Science in the Light of Creation*, trans. Jonathan Vaughan (Eugene, OR: Wipf and Stock, 2012), 126.

[16]Jaeger, *What the Heavens Declare*, 127.

[17]See the discussion on Jaeger, *What the Heavens Declare*, 124.

[18]See Jaeger, *What the Heavens Declare*, 128.

grant that the ontological argument is not highly persuasive these days. Many of these component arguments are strong inductive and abductive arguments. They have exceptionally high probability, even if we sometimes cannot give them some precise numerical probability calculation. Furthermore, these are only the positive arguments. A total case would have to also include an array of arguments *against* physicalism, materialism, or, in general, naturalism.[19]

It would, of course, also include a response to what is perhaps the only actual positive argument for atheism: the problem of evil. However, given a strong case for the existence of God, the problem of evil can only modify our theology in relation to God; it cannot disprove his existence. As we have seen before with this objection to each of the classic arguments, the evidence is the evidence.

6.1.2 Where does faith fit in? Second, there is this matter of faith. Is not belief in God a matter of personal faith and not a matter of knowledge? In fact, does not human reasoning eliminate faith? Does not God himself demand that we approach him trusting and believing, not questioning and reasoning?

No doubt there is a sense in which this is true. A relationship with God is like any other relationship in which there is accountability or confidence: there has to be a level of faith that underlies it and makes it work. Basil Mitchell, who we met before, illustrates this well with his famous story of "the Stranger":

> In time of war in an occupied country, a member of the resistance meets one night a stranger who deeply impresses him. They spend that night together in conversation. The Stranger tells the partisan that he himself is on the side of the resistance—indeed that he is in command of it, and

---

[19]The best recent collection of such arguments—from an atheist—can be found in Thomas Nagel's *Mind and Cosmos: Why the Materialist Neo-Darwinian Conception of Nature Is Almost Certainly False* (Oxford: Oxford University Press, 2012). See, too, Gary Habermas, *The Risen Jesus and Future Hope* (Lanham, MD: Rowman & Littlefield, 2003), chap. 3.

urges the partisan to have faith in him no matter what happens. The partisan is utterly convinced at that meeting of the Stranger's sincerity and constancy and undertakes to trust him.

They never meet in conditions of intimacy again. But sometimes the Stranger is seen helping members of the resistance, and the partisan is grateful and says to his friends, "He is on our side."

Sometimes he is seen in the uniform of the police handing over patriots to the occupying power. On these occasions his friends murmur against him: but the partisan still says, "He is on our side." He still believes that, in spite of appearances, the Stranger did not deceive him. Sometimes he asks the Stranger for help and receives it. He is then thankful. Sometimes he asks and does not receive it. Then he says, "The Stranger knows best." Sometimes his friends, in exasperation, say "Well, what *would* he have to do for you to admit that you were wrong and that he is not on our side?" But the partisan refuses to answer. He will not consent to put the Stranger to the test. And sometimes his friends complain, "Well if *that's* what you mean by his being on our side, the sooner he goes over to the other side the better."[20]

This story illustrates two things about belief in God. First, there is bound to be much in life that does not make sense to *us* if God is really in charge. All too often the good guys do not come out on top—at least not in the short term, and sometimes never. Many people's lives are full of what seems to be pointless suffering, tragedy, and evil. Why do bad things—and really horrific things—happen to good and innocent people? It certainly does not always appear that there is a sovereign God who is in control. Here there certainly is a proper place for trust in a God who often seems as hidden as the Stranger, and whose purposes we cannot understand. We need to exercise faith properly, but we will still often feel "the full force of the conflict."[21] And, as Mitchell's story illustrates so well, we must remember that the war is not over yet.

---

[20]Basil Mitchell, "Theology and Falsification," in *New Essays in Philosophical Theology*, ed. Antony Flew and Alasdair MacIntyre (New York: Macmillan, 1955), 103-4.

[21]Mitchell, "Theology and Falsification," 105.

Second, this kind of faith has to be based on some solid footing if it is, itself, to make sense. What is critical in Mitchell's story is that we have, in fact, met the Stranger in person *before* we placed our trust in him. I cannot trust my wife until I get to know her—her character, her strengths and weaknesses. As my children grew older, they wanted me to trust them, but that was only possible if they first demonstrated that they could be trusted.

Just so, I cannot trust or believe in God unless and until he evidences his reality. Apart from God's showing himself, faith in him would not be rational. Now there are, of course, other ways in which God has demonstrated his reality.[22] Foremost here would be the historical appearance of God in Jesus of Nazareth.

However, my point in this book has been to show that a critical piece of this revelatory demonstration are those conclusions that human reason, simply observing the world around us, can draw about his very existence. Without this, at some point, our trust in the Stranger becomes just silly.[23] That is the proper role of reason in relation to faith.

What I have concluded is that theism—that is, the belief that there is a single, infinite God, the cause of all things—is a well-justified, true belief. It is perfectly reasonable and rational to claim to know that such a God exists. There are, of course, possible objections available, but they all have been given solid and reasonable responses. Atheism is not the most reasonable conclusion, though certainly rational in the standard philosophical sense. There is, no doubt, the possibility of serious future defeaters, but, given the long history of this discussion, the answers are most likely already there.

---

[22]For treatments of this as "getting-to-know-you" evidence of the Stranger, see the following discussions by notable philosophers: Richard Swinburne, *Resurrection of God Incarnate*; Swinburne, *Was Jesus God?* (Oxford: Oxford University Press, 2010); Gary Habermas, *The Historical Jesus* (Joplin, MO: College Press, 1996); William Lane Craig, *The Son Rises* (Chicago: Moody, 1981).

[23]Mitchell, "Theology and Falsification," 104.

Therefore, it is only sensible that someone place their trust in God. In fact, it *is* the only sensible option.

Further Reading

A broader discussion of different arguments available can be found in Jerry Walls and Trent Dougherty, eds., *Two Dozen (or So) Arguments for God: The Plantinga Project* (Oxford: Oxford University Press, 2018).

In addition to the sources mentioned in the text and notes, an excellent discussion of the arguments from religious experience and miracles can be found in Richard Swinburne, *The Existence of God*, 3rd ed. (Oxford: Oxford University Press, 2004). The book also concludes with a good treatment of cumulative-case argumentation titled "The Balance of Probability."

For more on miracles see David Basinger, *Miracles* (Cambridge: Cambridge University Press, 2018).

There is a large body of literature available on the transcendental argument. Begin with Michael Butler, "The Transcendental Argument for God's Existence," http://www.butler-harris.org/tag/. This has extensive bibliographical information, including on Cornelius Van Til.

An excellent and affirming discussion of the transcendental argument can be found in Stephen Parrish, *God and Necessity* (Lanham, MD: University Press of America, 1997), 175-95.

A quite different sort of argument, one based on our common human needs, is Clifford Williams, *Existential Reasons for Belief in God: A Defense of Desires and Emotions for Faith* (Downers Grove, IL: IVP Academic, 2011).

Another good discussion of cumulative-case issues, and Hume's objection to them, is R. Douglas Geivett, "David Hume and a Cumulative Case Argument," in *In Defense of Natural Theology: A Post-Humean Assessment*, ed. James F. Sennett and Douglas Groothuis (Downers Grove, IL: InterVarsity Press, 2005), 297-329.

For introductory material on the matter of reason and faith see John Piper, *Think: The Life of the Mind and the Love of God* (Wheaton, IL: Crossway, 2010), also available free full-text online at https://document.desiringgod.org /think-en.pdf?ts=1439242077; J. P. Moreland, *Love Your God with All Your Mind: The Role of Reason in the Life of the Soul* (Colorado Springs: NavPress, 1997); and Josh McDowell, *Beyond Belief to Convictions* (Wheaton, IL: Tyndale House, 2002).

A very technical study of "belief" for advanced students, including the distinction between *belief in* and *belief that*, is Donald Evans, *Faith, Authenticity, and Morality* (Toronto: University of Toronto Press, 1980).

6.2 What Will the Sequels Be Like?

So where does the narrative go from here? I am neither a prophet, nor the son of a prophet—though my father did teach seminary courses on the Old Testament prophets—but I do get a sense that things may be changing. The secularistic naturalism that has dominated the academic world for half a century, and has increasingly come to define the global culture, is beginning to show signs of wear. To what extent, and exactly when there will be another paradigm shift in our culture's worldview, God only knows (really!).

I will simply list a few signs of possible change on the horizon. We have actually talked about both of the examples I want to mention, but now a bit more detail on their changes. Antony Flew and Thomas Nagel have both been at the top of their field. Both have been able defenders of atheism, and Nagel still is. Both had a lengthy publishing history defending a form of physicalistic naturalism. And both have renounced it, Flew in *There Is a God: How the World's Most Notorious Atheist Changed His Mind*, in 2008,[24] shortly before he died, and Nagel in *Mind and Cosmos* in 2012. The subtitle of Nagel's book says it clearly: *Why the Materialist Neo-Darwinian Conception of Nature Is Almost Certainly False.*

6.2.1 Antony Flew. Antony Flew makes it quite clear that he was finally persuaded by the evidence, and specifically by the fine-tuning form of the argument to design. In chapter five of *There Is a God*, he concludes that "when correctly formulated, this argument constitutes

---

[24]Antony Flew with Roy Abraham Varghese, *There Is a God: How the World's Most Notorious Atheist Changed His Mind* (San Francisco: HarperOne, 2008). Some have doubted that this is really Flew and not Varghese, but Flew clearly affirms the content of the book. He also says these same things in his interview with Gary Habermas in "My Pilgrimage from Atheism to Theism: A Discussion Between Antony Flew and Gary Habermas," *Philosophia Christi* 6, no. 2 (2004): 197-211.

a persuasive case for the existence of God."[25] After three more chapters discussing the flow of current science, including multiverse solutions, Flew concurs with many of the leading scientists of the twentieth and twenty-first centuries, Albert Einstein, Werner Heisenberg, Max Planck, Erwin Schrodinger, Paul Dirac, Paul Davies, John Barrow, John Polkinghorne, Freeman Dyson, Francis Collins, Owen Gingerich, Martin Rees, John Leslie, and Roger Penrose, that science reveals an intelligent source of the universe: "Those scientists who point to the Mind of God do not merely advance a series of arguments or a process of syllogistic reasoning. Rather, they propound a vision of reality that emerges from the conceptual heart of modern science and imposes itself on the rational mind. It is a vision that I personally find compelling and irrefutable."[26]

It is true that Flew's God is not personal. He has described his view as more like Spinoza's or Aristotle's God. It is also true that, as best we know, he never converted to his father's Christianity. He found that he just could not stomach the doctrine of hell. Nevertheless, he clearly saw how insufficient naturalism is to handle the evident design of the universe. Only a Mind will do.

6.2.2 Thomas Nagel. Thomas Nagel mentions that, in part, he was influenced by the evidence for intelligent design and states that, while its defenders have been scorned, the position "does not appear to me to have been destroyed."[27] He cites three types of evidence for which materialist evolutionary naturalism cannot provide a sufficient explanation and so must be false. They can be summarized by the point that evolutionary naturalism cannot explain the evident teleology in nature. Specifically, it fails to explain (1) consciousness, (2) cognition, and (3) value.

---

[25]Flew with Varghese, *There Is a God*, 95.
[26]Flew with Varghese, *There Is a God*, 112.
[27]Nagel, *Mind and Cosmos*, 11.

We have already considered the general point about teleology at the end of the chapter on the teleological argument. Here I want to look briefly at his culminating argument about *value*. His primary question is about our nature, given that we recognize and respond to values. And now it is clear that materialist naturalism will not provide an answer, since it cannot give us the two things needed in order to act in response to perceived values. First is a "conscious control of action that cannot be analyzed as physical causation," which includes some form of free will.[28] And this, he insists, is not compatible with a Darwinian account of how motivations work.[29]

Second, there is the matter of intentionality. "Human action . . . is explained not only by physiology, or by desires, but by judgments."[30] Being motivated by values involves "the recognition of reasons in an argument" that allows for the formation of a factual belief.[31] This requires teleology—that is, "a cosmic predisposition to the formation of life, consciousness, and the value that is inseparable from them."[32]

This is as far as Nagel has come. But it is far enough to conclude that "materialist neo-Darwinianism" will not—in fact, cannot—provide the metaphysical resources necessary to make sense of *our* lives in *our* world.

Conclusion

It should be clear by now that theism can and does make sense, and make sense of our lives. Further, what we learned from the cosmological argument is that Nagel is wrong about God. There is, of course, a transcendence to God's nature that places him outside of the physical universe. But, of course, our finite human intentionality also transcends

---

[28]Nagel, *Mind and Cosmos*, 113.
[29]Nagel, *Mind and Cosmos*, 114.
[30]Nagel, *Mind and Cosmos*, 114.
[31]Nagel, *Mind and Cosmos*, 113.
[32]Nagel, *Mind and Cosmos*, 123.

physico-chemical limitations while remaining closely connected to them. So too the infinite God is intimately connected by way of both his creative and his continuing providential activity.

Flew took both steps—out of naturalism and into theism—while Nagel has only taken the first. Will these and many similar moves become enough of a groundswell that our culture's worldview will abandon its current naturalistic obsession: what Nagel calls a "triumph of ideological theory over common sense"?[33] And will our society return to the recognition that only God provides a full and meaningful explanation of us, our lives, our understandings, our values, and our future?

I do not know the answer to either of these questions. But I do hope that this story about our story will provide some helpful insights as to why we can and should, both as individuals and as a global society, come back to the real God who created us so that we can truly understand ourselves and him.

---

[33]Nagel, *Mind and Cosmos*, 128.

Finding the Textbook You Need

The IVP Academic Textbook Selector
is an online tool for instantly finding the IVP books
suitable for over 250 courses across 24 disciplines.

ivpacademic.com